Beyond Information

The Natural History of Intelligence

Also by the same author

Information and the Internal Structure of the Universe:
An Exploration into Information Physics

Tom Stonier

Beyond Information

The Natural History of Intelligence

Springer-Verlag
London Berlin Heidelberg New York
Paris Tokyo Hong Kong
Barcelona Budapest

Professor Tom Stonier, BA, MSc, PhD, FRSA
838 East Street
Lenox
Massachusetts 01240
USA

ISBN 3-540-19654-4 Springer-Verlag Berlin Heidelberg New York
ISBN 0-387-19654-4 Springer-Verlag New York Berlin Heidelberg

British Library Cataloguing in Publication Data
Stonier, Tom
  Beyond Information: Natural History of Intelligence
  1. Title
  003
  ISBN 3-540-19654-4

Library of Congress Cataloging-in-Publication Data
Stonier, Tom
  Beyond information: the natural history of intelligence/Tom Stonier
     p.   cm.
  Includes bibliographical references and index.
  ISBN 0-387-19654-4
  1. Artificial intelligence – History.   I. Title.
Q335.S86   1992   91-45658
006.3'3'09–dc20   CIP

Composition by Genesis Typesetting, Laser Quay, Rochester, Kent
Printed and bound by Page Bros (Norwich) Ltd, Mile Cross Lane, Norwich
34/3830-543210 Printed on acid-free paper

To Chris Evans
Fallen comrade in the struggle to understand the future

Acknowledgements

The writing of this book was begun while the author was a Fellow at the Institute for Advanced Studies in the Humanities at the University of Edinburgh. The author wishes to thank the Institute and its Director, Professor Peter Jones for providing this opportunity, and to my colleagues at the time, for helpful discussions.

The same is true for my colleagues at Bradford University, in particular Drs John Sharp and Stanley Houghton. In a similar vein, Derek Kozikowski, Jefferson Stonier, Peter Stonier and Marcus Topham took time out for some in-depth explorations – for which I thank them.

All, or parts of the manuscript were examined on a professional basis by Dr Philip Barker (Teesside), Dr Nick Beard (London), Dr Nigel Franks (Bath), and Dr Andrew Sysons (Coventry), and I thank them for their critical commentary.

After most of the manuscript had been completed, it was a great pleasure to spend a long weekend walking and discussing various aspects of the phenomenon of information, including this manuscript, with Professor Klaus Haefner (Bremen) who made many useful suggestions and helped crystallise a number of thoughts.

Marlene Ellison, as with previous tomes, bore the brunt of an author who is forever changing his mind. Her patience, good cheer and competence were invaluable in the preparation of the manuscript.

Almost all my writing is done at home. Writing is not an easy matter for me – as a result, I don't do many things I should, and do some things I shouldn't – all of which puts a lot of strain on personal relations. I thank my wife Judith for sharing my life.

Lastly, I would like to thank John Watson, for editorial encouragement and support, as well as the rest of the Springer-Verlag UK team – in particular, Jane Forbes, Rosie Kemp, Lindsey Roper and Linda Schofield.

Tom Stonier
December 1991

Contents

· 1 ·

Introduction

Preamble

The emergence of machine intelligence during the second half of the twentieth century is the most important development in the evolution of this planet since the origin of life two to three thousand million years ago. The emergence of machine intelligence within the matrix of human society is analogous to the emergence, three billion years ago, of complex, self-replicating molecules within the matrix of an energy-rich molecular soup – the first step in the evolution of life. The emergence of machine intelligence within a human social context has set into motion irreversible processes which will lead to an evolutionary discontinuity. Just as the emergence of "Life" represented a qualitatively different form of organisation of matter and energy, so will pure "Intelligence" represent a qualitatively different form of organisation of matter, energy and life.

The emergence of machine intelligence presages the progression of the human species as we know it, into a form which, at present, we would not recognise as "human". As Forsyth and Naylor (1985) have pointed out: "Humanity has opened two Pandora's boxes at the same time, one labelled genetic engineering, the other labelled knowledge engineering. What we have let out is not entirely clear, but it is reasonable to hazard a guess that it contains the seeds of our successors". The question is not whether intelligence will supersede life, but how fast?

This book therefore concerns itself with the long-term future of the human species. As such, it aims to alert the general public to the implications of this extraordinary technology emerging in our midst – a technological development unparalleled in human history.

This book does not view *machine intelligence* as a technology which threatens the *physical destruction* of humanity. Machine intelligence is not like nuclear missile technology, a sword of Damocles over our heads waiting for some hysterical human reaction or computer malfunction to trigger a nuclear disaster.* Nor does machine intelligence presage some environmental disaster such as the destruction of the ozone layer, or warming the earth to some intolerable level. Quite to the contrary, the proper development of machine intelligence will allow us to test out various scenarios and simulate various options, thereby providing us with powerful tools to augment informed judgement. The appropriate development of machine intelligence can, in fact, improve the quality of life in a myriad of other ways. Nor does the author fear the long-term implications – that within a very few generations, humanity will evolve beyond what we currently consider (though do not understand) to be human. What the author does fear is that we will do so blindly.

The Need for a Science of Machine Intelligence

There is a second reason for writing this book. It is already hidden in the above considerations: If machine intelligence is designed to augment human judgement, we had better make it work well! This is particularly crucial when we are dealing with military technology. Not only are electronic battlefields becoming the norm in military planning, but the Strategic Defense Initiative, better known as Star Wars, is designed to rely largely on artificial intelligence systems.

The shift to computer-based command decision systems is necessitated by the increasing speed with which decisions need to be made. The pressure of time can lead to serious human errors. A tragic example is the shooting down of a civilian Iranian airliner by an American warship in the Persian Gulf in July 1988. The nervous commander, responsible for the safety of a ship and its crew, ordered launch at an incoming blip on his radar screen before it could reach striking range. Given more time, he could have ascertained that it was an airbus – not a fighter – flying on course in a civilian air-lane.

---

* The immediate and long-term consequence of a nuclear war have been analysed in detail previously: T Stonier (1964), *Nuclear Disaster*, Penguin, Harmondsworth.

Would an expert system controlling launch have behaved differently? As more and more military systems become computerised, and as more and more countries manage to introduce advanced technologies to their armed forces, the matter can no longer be considered academic. It is true that elaborate safety back-ups frequently have been built into such systems, particularly those involving strategic nuclear strike forces. However, there are two dilemmas which should give cause for alarm. The first is that a system to negate launch in response to false alarms must be balanced by systems to activate launch before it is too late. The second relates to systems complexity and is more subtle: Not only do the chances of a malfunction increase exponentially as systems grow more complex, but after a point, complex systems acquire properties which cannot be anticipated.

The mid-1980s saw three high technology failures – the Space Shuttle Challenger mid-air explosion, the poisonous fumes of Bhopal descending on a sleeping and unsuspecting city, and the Chernobyl meltdown. In all three cases one can identify human errors. The temptation to reduce these by the use of computer-based expert systems is great. In the author's view it would be justified if we knew what we were doing. But we don't. At least, not yet.

The second reason for this book, therefore, is to help clarify some of the problems and concepts in a fledgling new scientific discipline – *knowledge engineering*. This is in line with a number of authorities such as Gordon Scarrott (1986), who for a number of years has championed the need for a "science" of information. Similarly, Alan Bundy (1988), professor of artificial intelligence at Edinburgh University, has argued that "We need to make AI into an engineering science: we need scientific knowledge about AI so that we can design large, usable and reliable expert systems".

Knowledge Engineering

A steam engine, no matter how well designed, is useless if it is not supplied with water for its boilers, and fuel to heat the water. Similarly, a computer, no matter how sophisticated, is useless if you have no data to feed into its memory and no rules to drive the inference machinery designed to process such data. Knowledge engineering attempts to codify and distil information so that it can fuel the increasingly powerful logic machines processing the data stored in their memories. Intelligent knowledge-based systems (IKBSs) and expert systems are computer-based systems which take information and process it in an "intelligent" manner. Doing this effectively is the task of the knowledge engineer.

The irony is that whereas the mechanical engineer working with water and steam understands both the nature of the inputs, and the thermodynamic processes going on inside the steam engine, the knowledge engineer (and, for that matter, anyone else) has virtually no understanding of the phenomenon which we call "intelligence". To make matters worse, there does not even exist as yet a genuine theory of information. What generally passes for a theory of information, is, in fact, a theory of communication – able to analyse the statistical probability of certain symbols appearing, but unable to analyse the meaning of such symbols.* Thus the software engineer struggling to become a knowledge engineer is in the embarrassing situation of understanding neither the input (information) nor the processes going on inside a computer (intelligence operations).

To achieve a good theoretical grasp of the concepts of information and intelligence requires an interdisciplinary approach. This leads to a problem with a book such as the present one. The problem was stated succinctly over forty years ago by physics Nobel Laureate Erwin Schrödinger (1944) in the preface to his classic little book *What is Life?*: "A scientist is supposed to have a complete and thorough knowledge, at first hand, of some subjects, and, therefore, is usually expected not to write on any topic of which he is not a master". Schrödinger, however, argues that: "The spread, both in width and depth, of the multifarious branches of knowledge . . . has confronted us with a queer dilemma. We . . . are only now beginning to acquire reliable material for welding together the sum-total of all that is known into a whole; but, on the other hand, it has become next to impossible for a single mind fully to command more than a small specialised portion of it". He concludes: "I can see no escape from this dilemma . . . than that some of us should

---

* This theory – credited to Shannon and Weaver, derived from the work of Hartley, and modified by Brillouin and other telecommunications experts – has been discussed in detail in a previous work: *Information and the Internal Structure of the Universe*, Springer-Verlag, London, 1990.

venture to embark on a synthesis of facts and theories . . . at the risk of making fools of ourselves" [p. vii].

Writing a book such as this is made more difficult for another, related reason. In some of the fields covered, progress is so rapid that even the experts can hardly keep up with the flows of new information. For the present author it proved maddening that every time the manuscript appeared to be finished, there would appear another relevant article, or the author's attention would be called to yet another book of great significance. This means that the present work will become dated with respect to certain of its details. Hopefully, however, the main themes will prove to withstand the test of time.

The present work is meant to be one of a trilogy: The first book, entitled *Information and the Internal Structure of the Universe* (Stonier 1990b), examines some of the implications of the proposition that information has *physical* reality. The present examines the evolution of intelligence from proto-intelligent systems to the most intelligent systems conceivable. The third book, entitled *Beyond Chaos*, will attempt to outline the requirements of a general theory of information. It will expand on the explorations begun in the first two books, then merge the insights obtained by studying physical systems on the one hand and advanced intelligence on the other. It is hoped that the trilogy will contribute towards the development of a general theory of information.

A Brief Overview of the Book

The book is divided up into nine chapters beginning with the present one, the Introduction, which provides the rationale for the book, places it in the context of the trilogy and considers: What is information? What is intelligence? *Information* is considered to be a basic property of the universe, and *intelligence* an inevitable evolutionary product of advanced information systems. As such, intelligence comprises a spectrum of phenomena.

This concept, that intelligence involves a *spectrum*, is considered in greater detail in the second chapter, with a still greater amplification in the next three chapters: Chapter 3 looks at the evolution of proto-intelligence into intelligence; Chapter 4 examines the evolution of collective intelligence in animal societies; while Chapter 5 traces the evolution of human culture and technology, and its concomitant increase in human collective intelligence. Chapter 6 looks at the evolution of humanly created machine intelligence, while Chapter 7 compares and contrasts computers and the human brain. Chapter 8 examines the future of machine intelligence, with special emphasis on the "neural network" type of computer as well as other technological possibilities. The chapter concludes that computers will rapidly become more intelligent than humans and considers the probability of a merging of machine intelligence with human collective and individual intelligence. The final chapter summarises the preceding and reaches the conclusion that the merging of machine and human intelligence will create an evolutionary discontinuity which will propel humanity beyond itself.

Problems with Definitions

There are serious problems with trying to define the terms relevant to this book – information, organisation, intelligence, self-consciousness, knowledge, insight, wisdom, etc. The major problem is that nearly everybody believes they know and understand these terms very well. This belief reflects the fact that the definitions are deeply entrenched in our *human* language, *human* perceptions, *human* arrogance – in short, in terms of a purely *human* context. In addition, there has been created an enormous literature beginning with the philosophers of ancient times, both East and West, resulting in a sub-branch of philosophy – epistemology.

To a large extent, the epistemological literature may be ignored for the same reasons physicists tend to ignore the literature of natural philosophers prior to Galileo: Although of interest to the history of thought, such physics literature lacked sufficient experience with physical *experiments*. Similarly, any epistemological work written before the advent of computers can only be of limited value. The same may be said for literature not conversant with the constellation of modern cognitive sciences, neurophysiology and ethology. It is not that these philosophical analyses have no value, but given the depth and the scope of this literature, it is simply not cost effective for the present author to try to cover it. Suffice it to state that the present author applauds the increasing number of technically minded philosophers who are becoming professionally involved with artificial intelligence (see the preface to Pollock 1989).

What Is Information?

Gordon Scarrott (personal communication, 1988), one of the most thoughtful of contemporary knowledge engineers, defines "organisation" and "information" recursively: "An organised system (OS) is an interdependent assembly of elements and/or organised systems. Information is that which is exchanged between the components of an organised system to effect their interdependence". The trouble with this definition of information is that it fails to assess the information content of organised systems in which there is no direct exchange of information between components. For example, the English alphabet represents an organised system: The "q" is always followed by a "u", yet there is no feedback loop between the two letters – no information is exchanged between them. Instead, it is their *information environment* (in this case, the English language) which supplies the rules of their association. Scarrott's concept, however, may be applied fruitfully when analysing biological, social, and other systems engaged in *information processing*.

It is crucial, if we are going to develop a general theory of information and intelligence, that we do not confuse the *processing* of information with *information* itself. For the purpose of this book, information is an abstract concept (like energy) which manifests itself by organising systems. "Information" is no more, or no less, an abstract concept than "energy". A system is considered to contain energy if it contains the potential to perform work. Similarly, *a system contains information if it causes the system itself or some other system to become organised*. That is, what mass is to matter, and heat to energy, organisation is to information. Mass, heat and organisation reflect the amount of matter, energy and information a system contains. The more intrinsic information a system contains, the greater and more complex will be its organisation. The term "intrinsic" is inserted here to differentiate it from "stored", or other information which may have been added to the system without causing a basic reorganisation of the system. A computer storing information is still a computer irrespective of whether it is engaged in storing a lot of information or none.

The problem is that whereas we have the technology to measure quantitatively the amount of mass contained by a system – for example, by weighing it – we are still having problems quantifying organisation. However, changes in entropy, which can be measured

quantitatively in physical systems, can be used to measure changes
in the organisation of such systems. Obviously the matter becomes
increasingly difficult to analyse as we move from physical to
biological and social systems. By the time we reach human systems,
the matter becomes very knotty indeed. For one thing, we tend to
confuse "information" with "meaning". The information contained
in a book is there irrespective of whether anyone reads the book, or
is unable to decipher the meaning because it is written in a foreign
language. Similarly, a radio wave carrying a message is carrying the
information irrespective of whether anyone turns on the radio or
not, or if they do, are unable to understand the foreign language
broadcast.

The idea that "information" has physical reality (and is not
related merely to human information activities), is axiomatic to
creating a general theory of information. It is also a prerequisite for
analysing the phenomenon of intelligence. If this basic insight about
information is not accepted, much of the rest of this book will make
no sense.

The reader is referred to earlier works by the author (Stonier
1986a,b; 1989; 1990a,b) for a more detailed discussion of the role of
information in physical systems and the proof that information is not
dependent on human mental activity. However, it may be
worthwhile to summarise briefly the arguments presented in
Information and the Internal Structure of the Universe.

DNA, the chemical which codes genetic information, has been
around for perhaps a thousand million years, human beings for only
a few million. Therefore, we must conclude that "information" has
been around for a very long time – a lot longer than humanity.

The DNA of a cell comprises the most advanced biological
information system at the cellular level. It possesses a clearly
identified code which is deciphered by the metabolic machinery of
the cell to produce both another cell and a duplication of the DNA.
In contrast, viral DNA does not produce another cell – only more
virus.

Closely related to DNA is RNA. RNA viruses such as the AIDS
virus, like their DNA counterparts, are able to reproduce
themselves by activating the host's metabolic machinery. Normal
(non-viral) RNA in cells consists of several distinct categories which
act not only as messengers – that is, as the transmitters of
information – but also as the transformers of that information into
its practical application, the manufacture of proteins. Both DNA
and RNA act as templates. So do membranes. Membranes

compartmentalise the metabolic activities of cells. They are crucial to the organisation of the cell: Without membranes there can exist no cells. The origin of life must have involved the organisation of pre-existing membrane structures into cellular structures. Membranes defined the boundary between the cell and its environment.

Membranes act by letting certain chemicals pass through, and denying passage to others. As such, they are engaged in an information processing activity. Thus membranes may act not only as templates controlling their own duplication but, as with RNA, their cellular function may involve information processing. *filter*

If we admit to DNA containing information, we must also admit the same property to RNA and to membranes. But it is unreasonable to stop there: Proteins are an intrinsic part of complex membranes and participate intimately in the information processing involved in the selective passage of molecules. Other cellular proteins, the enzymes, catalyse chemical reactions by providing templates to allow reactants to combine. Conversely, enzymes may split larger molecules into smaller ones, again by organising the cleavage site so as to allow the dissociation to proceed at relatively low energy levels. Enzyme catalysis must be understood not merely in terms of altered activation energies, but in terms of an input of information which lowers the requirement for energy.

The same argument can be made for inorganic catalysts. The classic classroom demonstration of dropping a crystal of manganese dioxide into a solution of potassium permanganate exemplifies an autocatalytic process in which an inorganic crystal duplicates itself from a substratum whose chemical composition is different. Again, it is insufficient to analyse such a process purely in terms of traditional molecular and energy changes. Instead, one should consider that the seed crystal provided the information necessary for the initiation of the reaction, and that the whole process also involves information processing. Such processing results in changes in the molecular organisation of the system. These changes in the organisational state of the system show up as changes in entropy.

Once again, one cannot draw the line at manganese dioxide: Any seed crystal dropped into a saturated solution of itself results in the formation of more crystal, causing the system to become more organised. The seed crystal provided the information for initiating the process, and acted as a template for organising diffusing molecules into a crystalline structure. It is perfectly reasonable to consider that the seed crystal supplied information to the system. Even if the amount of information contained by an inorganic seed crystal, when compared to that contained by DNA, proves to be rather small, one must accept that the difference is quantitative, not qualitative.

If something as simple as an inorganic crystal may possess information (albeit only relatively small amounts), is it unreasonable to postulate that all organised structures contain information? In the author's view, the answer is inescapable. In this book, therefore, the matter has been treated as axiomatic: *Any system exhibiting organisation contains information.*

To understand the relationship between information and organisation, one may compare these two entities to energy and heat. A few centuries ago, the concept of "energy" did not exist. An object was hot or cold the way objects may be hard or soft. It was known, of course, that the same object might be hot under one circumstance and cold under another. Furthermore, you could heat up an object, for example, a stone, by exposing it to a fire or to the sun. This could be nicely explained by the theory of the four elements derived from the ancient Greeks: If everything was made up of a combination of earth, water, air and fire, then, when you heat up an object, you are adding the element "fire". Hence the object now contained fire.

It is important to differentiate between the concepts "a stone contains heat", and "a stone contains energy". The first implies that you can't do much with it – at best, you can transfer heat to another object. In contrast, "energy" is defined as the capacity to do work, and work may involve other forms of energy such as mechanical energy. That is, water heated to become steam, contains not only heat, but also possesses the energy with which to drive a steam engine.

In a similar manner, contrast the difference between the concepts "a system exhibits organisation", and "a system contains information". As with "heat" and "energy", the first is an almost wholly static concept. Organisation is achieved by applying work to a system, causing it to become organised. Once the system is organised – that's it: Organisation is the end product.

In contrast, if one adds information to a system one has a common coin, like energy, which may be extracted to perform work, to organise another system, or in some other manner, be transformed or transferred.

One simple example should suffice: "A steam engine converts heat energy into mechanical energy". That sentence, read out loud to another person in the room, illustrates the difference between organisation and information: As far as the printed words on a page are concerned, the various lines and dots are organised into letters, the letters into words, the words into a sentence. By reading it to another person, the *information* is transferred, not the *pattern* of dye molecules on the sheet of paper. The information in the recipient's head is now also stored as a pattern, but of a very different kind – a pattern of neural connections. If the sentence were typed into a computer, the information would be stored as a pattern of on/off switches. If the spoken sentence were recorded on a tape player, the information would be stored as patterns of magnetised regions on the tape. In each case, *information* is the common coin, *patterns of organisation* are its product; the nature of these patterns is determined by the properties of the system acted upon by the information.

What Is Intelligence?

A pocket calculator can extract the square root of a number in a twinkling of an eye – much faster than we can. Does that mean that a pocket calculator is more intelligent than a human being? What does it mean to be intelligent?

Dictionaries tend to define intelligence in terms of the ability to understand, the capacity to comprehend, the perception of the significance of an act or a communication. Someone who is intelligent is someone who possesses intelligence. In these terms, a pocket calculator could not be considered as intelligent. A calculator does not perceive the significance of either the problem, or the solution. In fact, it does not comprehend its own processes – it merely performs them in accordance with the program engineered into it.

Dictionary definitions are a good place to start. They help define a common perception. However, if we are to understand the phenomenon of intelligence, we will need to go beyond the ordinary usage of the term – we need to explore much further.

Intelligence: A Spectrum of Phenomena

Intuitively, even the most anthropocentric of us feels that higher animals possess some form of intelligence. No dog lover really can believe that dogs are devoid of intelligence. Even the owners of pet fish recognise personalities in the various fish in their tank – some are more aggressive, others placid, some are keen to school, some are solitary and defend their territories vigorously, all learn quickly the signals that they are about to be fed. It is this ability to learn, whether by fish or fowl, dog or human, that we recognise the glimmering of intelligence.

It is true that fish are not "intelligent" the way we are. We are, after all, by far the most intelligent creature on earth – at least so we are led to believe. However, if we concede some sort of intelligence to animals – fish, parrots, dogs and monkeys – then we recognise that intelligence may exist as a spectrum of phenomena, that it is not an all or nothing affair. It is this intuition which becomes crucial for developing an understanding of the phenomena of intelligence. It is also this intuition which was formalised by that most profound of observers of biological phenomena, Charles Darwin, – when he proposed the doctrine of "mental continuity", stating that the differences in mental activity between various species of animals were differences of degree, not of kind (see review by Menzel 1986).

If intelligence must be viewed as involving a *spectrum* of phenomena, such a spectrum is not a simple, single dimensional one. It is not like, let us say, the light spectrum. In the case of light, we know that it is a part of the electromagnetic spectrum with "red" at the long wavelength end and "violet" at the other. In between, the wavelength of light decreases while the frequency increases in a simple linear fashion. The spectrum of intelligence does not work that way because the more advanced the intelligence, the more complex it becomes. Advanced forms of intelligence must be judged by an increasing number of *independent* parameters. The matter may be exemplified by using *colour* rather than *light* as an analogy. Colour comprises part of our perception of that portion of the electromagnetic spectrum which we "see". (We may also "feel" part of that spectrum if it is sufficiently intense, as when we bask in the sun.) In the case of light intensity, if we illuminate an object with one light source, then illuminate it more by adding a second light source, the object will appear brighter. The two sources together add up quantitatively, and there is no qualitative change in our perception of the object (unless the first source was so dim that we couldn't see the object in the first place). Not so, if we add various wavelengths of light which engender in us the perception of colour. When we look at a mixture of wavelengths we see neither the sum nor the average of the wavelengths. If we were to mix equal portions of bluish and reddish wavelengths (400 nm and 700 nm, respectively), the sum should be 1,100 and the average 550 nm. The former is in the infrared region beyond our visual perception; the latter should appear as green. Instead we see the colour "magenta". If we mix all the wavelengths together, we see white. The nature of our human photoreceptors coupled to the neural networks which interpret the stimulation of those receptors is such that it becomes possible to mix relatively narrow bands of electromagnetic radiation (for example, those diametrically opposed on the Munsell colour chart) to achieve the impression of white light.

Our impression of colour, in fact, appears to involve the perception and interpretation of at least three independent parameters. These parameters have been defined and quantified by Munsell (1946) as *hue* (the family name for a specific *colour* – red, yellow, purple, etc. – which relates to specific wavelengths, or mixtures of them), *value* (which describes the *intensity* of the light and distinguishes whether a colour is light or dark) and *chroma* (the saturation of a distinctive hue, or the degree of departure from a colour sensation of white or grey).

Using other definitions, it is clear that we are able to distinguish at least three independent parameters, each of which may vary quantitatively, but whose combinations gives us a sense of qualitative differences: First, we can discriminate between various wavelengths or frequencies of light; second, we perceive the intensity of light, that is, the levels of energy emitted by the source of light; and third, we are able to detect how pure the frequency is, or whether it is a mix of several wavelengths. The human perception of colour is, in fact, so complex that it is still not fully understood. As Chamberlin and Chamberlin (1980) have pointed out [p. 7]: "No one theory at present satisfactorily explains all the observed facts and theoretical considerations".

Mammalian "intelligence" – the ability to perceive and analyse an organism's environment – is heavily dependent on eyes in order to see and interpret various aspects of the environment (blind species such as moles are obviously excepted). One could consider, therefore, our (human) perception of colour to be more sophisticated and superior to that of an animal, such as a cat, which is red blind. We, like other higher primates, have no difficulty in picking out red cherries on a green cherry tree. Cats do: Cats would see the leaves and fruits as various shades of grey. So obviously human vision is superior. Or is it? Cats are not particularly interested in cherries. Instead a cat's eye is designed for night vision and allows cats to move rapidly and stealthily in the dark where we would stumble around. So which visual system is superior?

The visual perception of objects, movement and changes in our environment is only a small part of our human intelligence which helps us to analyse and respond intelligently to our surroundings. Cognitive scientists, in the past, have tried to measure the "intelligence quotient" (IQ), or some other single parameter of intelligence in human individuals, or across species. Their results have been given a weight of authority that is wholly unjustified. The manifestations of human individual intelligence is determined by a variety of cultural and environmental forces, as well as genetic ones. All of these inputs are multidimensional. Even "identical" twins will have differences in their brain structures at birth (Edelman, as reviewed by Rosenfield 1988, p. 186).

Measurements across species become increasingly tenuous. By the time we deal with brains – even insect brains – we are dealing with advanced forms of complexity. We should compare intelligent behaviour to other physical traits such as size, strength or longevity. In mammals, both mice and elephants are well adapted to their environment yet vary greatly in these three traits. It is the evolutionary history and the ecological requirements which dictate the size, strength and longevity of organisms. The same may be said of intelligence.

For any given organism, the nature and sophistication of its intelligence is determined by its environment. If intelligence comprises a spectrum of phenomena, it is a complex, infinitely multifaceted one indeed. It is not some easily measured quantity which expresses itself merely as the ability to reason logically. Very few of humanity's great insights were derived as a result of logical deductions. Only their justification – their veracity – was secured by the application of reasoning after the fact. The original inspiration involved a much more fuzzy perception of subtle patterns, characteristic of advanced intelligence systems.

Intelligence: The Basic Definition

Before proceeding, we need to define intelligence in broad and basic terms. For the purposes of the present discussion, *intelligence* is considered to be a property of advanced information systems. Just as *information* is a basic, physical property of the universe, so is *intelligence* a product of the evolution of information systems.

Intelligence is a state or a condition. As a property of advanced information systems, it can be ascertained only by observing the dynamics or behaviour of the system. That is, "intelligence" can only be ascertained in terms of "intelligent behaviour". For example, it is impossible to assess the true intelligence of a child when it is asleep. We assess the intelligence of a child by observing how it responds to its environment (including the questions posed by a psychologist).

Intelligence is an irrelevance to a system in a static state. On the other hand, a dynamic system in a changing environment may be able to remain stable only by virtue of engaging in intelligent behaviour.

All that is required to maintain a system in an organised state – static or dynamic – is information. This is true at least in a relatively constant environment. In a changing environment, however, *intelligence* is required to retain a system's integrity by adjusting it to the environmental changes.

Intelligent activity, for the most part, involves an ability of a system to analyse its environment, and then to make an intelligent response. An intelligent response may result in one of three states:

1. The system has enhanced its own *survivability*.
2. The system has enhanced its own *reproducibility*.
3. If the system is goal oriented, it has enhanced the *achievement* of that goal.

The above broadens the concept of intelligence as it is generally used in everyday life, while at the same time attempting to define the term "intelligence" in fairly precise terms. However, because one is dealing with a phenomenon which has evolved, its origins prevent us from drawing too fine a line between the intelligent and the non-intelligent: There exist phenomena which are borderline. These we will consider to involve sub-intelligent, or *proto-intelligent*, behaviour.

A pocket calculator, for example, engages in information processing. So do a number of physical systems such as membranes selecting the kinds of molecules which may pass through them. Likewise, other physical systems appear to be able to remember previous events and alter their response to environmental inputs, as, of course, so may a computer.

Therefore, certain systems capable of organising information, processing information or learning may be said to exhibit proto-intelligent behaviour. To achieve true intelligence, however, a system must fulfil one of the three criteria described above.

Finally, all intelligent systems engage in *information processing*. In addition, more advanced forms of intelligence exhibit the capacity to *learn*. Learning, in the present discussion, is defined as the ability to modify intelligent activity on the basis of previous experience (real or vicarious).

Thus, there is a much broader spectrum to be considered than the one which compares fish intelligence to human intelligence. This is the spectrum which ranges from non-intelligent information systems to highly advanced intelligent systems able to learn prodigiously.

Beyond Information: The Evolution of Intelligence

If we examine the occurrence of organisation in the universe, we immediately detect a hierarchy of organisation. Fundamental particles organise into nucleons. Nucleons organise to form atomic nuclei, and then, in combination with electrons, form atoms. Atoms organise into molecules, and molecules into large polymers. Homo- and heteropolymers create more complex structures such as membranes, protein systems, photosynthetic apparatuses, which in turn, organise into subcellular systems. Subcellular organelles such as microsomes, mitochondria and chloroplasts appear to be derivatives of primitive organisms which became assimilated and organised to create "advanced" cell types a billion (10^9) years ago which in turn set the stage for the evolution of multicellular organisms. And so it goes on.

Organisation builds on pre-existing organisation. Not only bits of matter, but force fields and flows of energy become organised as well. On earth, the information content of systems has kept, and continues to keep, increasing, converting the free energy available from the sun into information, creating initially the biosphere, and most recently, human global society – which the French philosopher Teilhard de Chardin calls the "noosphere".

Along parallel lines, Klaus Haefner (1991), at the University of Bremen, has explored the idea that the entire universe is made up of information processing systems – ranging from the smallest physical particles to human societies and technological systems – and that all such system evolve.

It is the purpose of the next several chapters to expand and refine these concepts; to analyse the evolution of non-intelligent into proto-intelligent systems, and to study this emergence and further progression of biological intelligence. All these must become a part of our general understanding of "intelligence" – an understanding crucial for a realistic analysis of the phenomenon of intelligence, in general, and the future of machine intelligence, in particular. Such an understanding also becomes a prerequisite to the development of a general theory of information.

Literature Cited

A Bundy (1988) Artificial intelligence: Art or science? *R. Soc. Arts J.* 136(5384):557–569.

GJ Chamberlin and DG Chamberlin (1980) *Colour: Its Measurement, Computation and Application*, Heyden, London.

R Forsyth and C Naylor (1985) *The Hitch-Hiker's Guide to Artificial Intelligence*, Chapman and Hall/Methuen, London.

K Haefner (1991) Evolution of information processing systems, Project Evolution of Information Processing, University of Bremen, Germany.

EW Menzel (1986) How can you tell if an animal is intelligent? in *Dolphin Cognition and Behaviour: A Comparative Approach* (RJ Schusterman, JA Thomas and FG Wood ed), pp. 167–181, Lawrence Erlbaum Associates, Hillsdale, NJ.

AH Munsell (1946) *A Color Notation*. 15th edn, (1988) Macbeth Division, Kollmorgen Instruments Corp., Baltimore, MD.

JL Pollock (1989) *How to Build a Person: A Prolegomenon*, The MIT Press, Cambridge, Mass.

I Rosenfield (1988) *The Invention of Memory*, Basic Books, New York.

G Scarrott (1986) The need for a "science" of information, *J. Inform. Technol.* 1(2):33–38.

E Schrödinger (1944) *What is Life?* Cambridge University Press.

T Stonier (1986a) Towards a new theory of information, *Telecom. Policy* 10(4):278–281.

T Stonier (1986b) What is information? in *Research and Development in Expert Systems III* (MA Bramer ed), pp. 217–230, Cambridge University Press.

T Stonier (1988) Machine intelligence and the long-term future of the human species, *AI & Society* 2:133–139.

T Stonier (1989) Towards a general theory of information II: Information and entropy, *Aslib Proc.* 41(2): 41–55.

T Stonier (1990a) Towards a general theory of information: information and entropy, *Future Computing Systems* 2(4): 409–427.

T Stonier (1990b) *Information and the Internal Structure of the Universe*, Springer-Verlag, London.

· 2 ·

The Spectrum of Intelligence

Introduction

The first chapter introduced several cardinal principles which comprise the intellectual foundation of the present work. The first of these is that any system which exhibits organisation contains information. This conceptualisation of information – that information is a basic property of the universe and is as "real" as are matter and energy – from here on in will be taken for granted.

The second premise states that intelligence is a property of advanced information systems. Systems exhibiting intelligence not only engage in information processing, they are also able to analyse their environment and respond to it intelligently. Intelligent activity is defined as activity which leads to one or all of the following outcomes: It enhances survivability; it enhances reproducibility; if it is goal oriented, it enhances the attainment of that goal.

Intelligent activity may include processing information, storing information and learning behaviour. However, as we shall discuss in this chapter, these activities, by themselves, comprise merely proto-intelligent behaviour. Proto-intelligence and intelligence represent the outcome of evolutionary processes. As such, both between them and within each category one may observe *spectra of phenomena*.

The idea that intelligence involves a *broad* spectrum of phenomena requires an expansion of what is usually thought of as "intelligence". The evolution of information systems from non-intelligent to proto-intelligent and, finally, to systems clearly exhibiting intelligence, involves fuzzy demarcations with substantial overlaps. We are forced to make almost arbitrary decisions when we are classifying intelligent systems. Certainly, in the light of our limited knowledge, any taxonomy of intelligence proposed at this time will be open to debate at some point in the future. The author's own professional (biological) background may have led to the prejudice that *all* forms of life – all living systems – exhibit significant intelligent behaviour. Probably, in the long run, it will not matter so much as to where, exactly, the lines are drawn, as it becomes clear that one is dealing with phenomena which evolved from relatively simple information systems to the highly complex – from fundamental physical particles to a global collective intelligence.

Human Intelligence

Older notions about "intelligence" – many still held by the lay public – tend to be extremely anthropocentric: Only human beings possess *real* intelligence – animals may have some, but it is so inferior when compared to humans that it hardly counts.

Further, the common notion of "intelligence" tends to focus almost entirely on the individual human being. Thus we administer IQ tests to individuals. We would never dream of measuring the IQ of a society. Yet, human intelligence is a manifest property exhibited not only by an individual, but also by a group of people, by entire countries, or even by global society as a whole. One of the major differences between the human species and other organisms is the fact that humans were able to develop an effective collective memory. This was done through developing an oral and subsequently a written cultural tradition which passed information from one generation to the next. By being able to store information and retrieve it across both time and space, the human species was able to develop a collective store of information. This process, in due course, became institutionalised. In western Europe, for example, monasteries, churches, archives, museums, universities and libraries became a part of, and reinforced, cultural traditions. Most of these technologies also developed in other advanced civilisations around the world.

The above institutions represented a means of storing and retrieving information but not necessarily of organising or developing it. This changed with the advent of monks and scholars and later professional librarians whose job it was to take information and organise it into logical categories. It was this step of organising information in libraries and archives which improved the retrieval capabilities and hence the overall efficiency of the collective brain.

The second half of the twentieth century saw an enormous improvement in the ability to store and retrieve information by electronic means. Electronic databases now not only allow more information to be stored per unit space, but more importantly the computer permits much faster information storage and retrieval. The emergence of compact laser disks has made it cheaper to hold the contents of a sheet of paper on a disk, than on paper. Furthermore, the time to access any chunk of such information can be measured in milliseconds –comparable to the time it takes to recall information inside our heads.

This is a great contribution to our collective memory: We have entered an era which will see all major printed databases –library catalogues, the entire content of encyclopedias, dictionaries, government statistics, telephone directories, professional society memberships, train timetables, airline schedules, stock market quotations, etc. – become available to all homes via the telephone or other networks, twenty-four hours a day, with a markedly increased ease of access.

The psychology of a mob differs from that of the single individuals composing that mob. In like manner, so does the intelligence of a social group differ from that of its individual members. Furthermore, in general, a group is much more capable of solving problems – therefore in engaging in intelligent behaviour – than the average individual within such a group. There may be exceptions to this, but the matter will not be discussed further in this chapter: The phenomenon of collective intelligence is worthy of deeper considerations and will, therefore, be explored further in Chapters 4 and 5. Suffice it here to state that if intelligence comprises a spectrum, human *collective intelligence* represents the high end of the spectrum of known phenomena.

Whether *individual* human intelligence – ie, an individual human being, isolated educationally from all human culture, but stimulated and nourished sufficiently to attain normal functioning – is a match for the collective intelligence of a group of wild dogs or a troop of baboons remains a matter of speculation. In fact, at present, so does the question of the relative individual, native intelligence of humans versus certain species of dolphins, and possibly even other animals with larger brains than humans, such as elephants. However, individual human beings raised in a normal human environment, absorbing information from their cultural surroundings, will be considered as next in line in the spectrum of intelligent phenomena. We are probably correct in assuming that many other animals "see" without "understanding" – absorb information without being able to interpret its meaning, lacking the richness of the information environment existing inside the human brain – an information environment capable of providing context, hence *meaning* to new information inputs.

Sub-human Intelligence

This book is not meant to be a text on human intelligence. Many such books already exist emanating from psychology and related fields – more recently from the artificial intelligence community. At the time of writing, three works thoughtfully summarise a great body of knowledge: C. Blakemore (1988), P.N. Johnson-Laird (1983), and H.C. Longuet-Higgins (1987). Although it will become necessary in a later chapter to discuss human intelligence in order to compare and contrast it with machine intelligence, in this chapter we will ignore individual human intelligence except for the assertion that in the spectrum of known intelligences, individual human intelligence ranks below human collective intelligence and above animal intelligence (with one or two possible exceptions).

As discussed in the first chapter, most people intuitively believe higher animals to be intelligent. Undoubtedly this reflects the fact that higher animals are able to engage in one form of higher intelligent activity – learning. Trained dogs, circus seals, street monkeys and aquarium dolphins all demonstrate that certain animals possess the capacity to learn complex routines. This intuition, however, is not shared by all. The author has held numerous discussions with a wide range of scientists and related professionals. The majority will draw the line in one of two places. Most accept that animals capable of learning exhibit some form of intelligence. Some, however, consider a creature to be intelligent only if it is able to interpret what it has learned. The ability to interpret presupposes that the animal has some model of the world in its head which becomes altered.

This view would appear to provide a much more rigorous, if limiting, definition of intelligence. At first glance it would seem to exclude all animals with the possible exception of higher primates and perhaps certain dolphins. But does it? A bee can be trained to find a dish of sugar solution at a specific location. It can be retrained to find it at another location. It can communicate that information to other bees so that they fly unerringly to the new find. How could this be possible if bees did not have a model of the world in their brains?

As we shall discover in a later chapter, bees not only must possess some sort of model of the world in their brains, they are able to modify that model on the basis of semiotic activity – utilising abstract visual and auditory symbols to communicate. Surely by the above criterion, a bee exhibits intelligence.

In fact, a bee's intelligence extends to the ability to learn to anticipate events which have not yet occurred. That is, on the basis of past experience, they are able to anticipate future events which are normally well outside the range of ordinary experience in nature (to be discussed in Chapter 4). Their model of the world, therefore, must include not only a spatial component, but a temporal one as well.

The brain of a bee is about the size of a pin head. Its intelligence cannot be as advanced as that of mammals. Yet it engages in intelligent behaviour. Once more, we are forced to conclude that intelligence involves a spectrum of phenomena.

Our closest taxonomic relative are the chimpanzees and bonobos. Their intelligence is not only much greater than that of a bee, it begins to approach our own. One feature of advanced animal intelligence is the ability to use tools in a goal-oriented fashion – a behaviour observed in many animals – and, more advanced still, to *create* tools. It was Jane Goodall (1971) who first established that chimpanzees in the wild not only used tools, but actually *fashioned* them. Her report and others indicate that these apes use twigs and rods to "fish" for termites in termite mounds or obtain honey from beehives, used sticks to probe trees for possible insects, and sponges made from chewed leaves to sop up rain water in tree hollows not directly accessible to the mouth or to wipe remnants of brain from inside the skull of a killed baboon, used leaves as toilet paper, stout sticks as levers to pry open banana boxes or enlarge the opening of an underground bee's nest, used rocks as hammers, and rock, sticks, serrated leaves and branches as weapons. It was Goodall who observed that both the fishing sticks and the leaf sponges involved modifying natural objects to use as tools. Primitive as such tool making may be, it must involve a chain of problem-solving reasoning to achieve a desired goal.

Another set of field observations reviewed by H. Kummer (1982) has demonstrated that monkeys are capable of stealth and deception – a form of behaviour which can occur only if animals possess a high degree of insight into the social situation at hand. Two examples will suffice:

A young female hamadryas baboon in oestrus repeatedly mated with a young male behind a rock where her adult male troop leader could not see her. Between matings she moved to peek at the leader, or even, on occasion, went to him and presented herself before returning to her hiding place to continue intercourse with her young mate.

In an experiment to test the "loyalty" of female gelada baboons, individual females were confined with individual males who were not their mates. Their mates were kept on the other side of a concrete wall where they could not see but could hear what was going on. When females began to groom the illicit males, the latter would restrain themselves and remain quiet, in contrast to the loud vocalisation which normally accompanies this activity.

Another set of observations which attest to the social intelligence of non-human primates is described by Menzel (1975). In reviewing his own and Jane Goodall's studies he observes that older chimpanzees can actively inhibit most signs of emotions if they so choose. This means that a chimp who has discovered a source of food in the presence of a stranger or a dominant chimp, doesn't rush over for a quick meal. Instead, "he waits as long as he has to until the coast is clear; or he might even get up, lead the other animal somewhere else, and then (while the follower is otherwise engaged) circle back for the hidden food". Menzel is certain that the other chimps in such a group, sometimes assess this deceptive behaviour with uncanny accuracy: "The less eager and obvious he tries to act, the more closely the followers might keep him under surveillance".

The studies of Frans de Waal (1989) on various primate groups in zoos make entertaining and enlightening reading. It becomes very difficult not to conclude that higher primates have developed levels of social intelligence which approach our own.

In the laboratory, as we become more proficient in communicating with chimpanzees, it becomes apparent that they are capable of a much wider range of intellectual skills than was previously thought.

The work of the Premacks (1972) with a chimp named Sarah demonstrated that chimps could, by using a variety of plastic tokens, learn not only a substantial reading and writing vocabulary of "words" – at least 130 of them – but that in the case of Sarah her understanding extended beyond the meaning of words to concepts of "class", sentence structure and the rudiments of logic. Earlier works by the Gardners (1969) with a chimp called Washoe using sign language established that the chimp could develop a vocabulary of at least 100 "spoken", ie, signed, words. An independent observer, A. Kortlandt – himself a prominent primatologist –became deeply impressed by watching Washoe "reading" an illustrated magazine. When, for example, she saw an advertisement for vermouth, she signalled "drink"; when spying a picture of a tiger she signed "cat". As Kortlandt (1973) observed: "It was fascinating to see a chimp 'thinking aloud' in gestural language, but in perfect silence, and without being rewarded for her performance in such a situation".

Although much of the earlier work leaves room for criticism, critics such as the Rumbaughs, using computer keyboard communications systems, themselves conclude that: "Apes are capable of language-relevant, if not true language, behaviours". (Rumbaugh and Savage-Rumbaugh 1978). These authors also point to a phenomenon which appears to occur some time during the course of training: The feeling that one has started to communicate, even if in a limited way, with the chimpanzee. Part of this feeling follows unexpected word usage and linguistic innovation on the part of the ape – the sense that the chimp is experimenting with language to explain something to the trainer.

In any case, our efforts to communicate with chimps under laboratory conditions is strictly a human-centred activity within a human-created artificial environment – expecting the animals to engage in quasi-human activities. We set the rules of the game to our advantage – sometimes we even move the goal posts. Whether or not chimpanzees or other animals, operating in their own natural habitat, possess a "real" language as linguists would define it is not as important as the recognition that animals may possess extremely sophisticated systems of communication, systems which involve a great deal of highly complex information processing on the part of both sender and receiver. As Menzel concludes: "Chimpanzees perceive the world and interpret each other's behaviour in ways that are not ridiculously different from the ways that we ourselves use, especially when we are silent and non-sedentary".

As we develop increasingly sophisticated methods, both our unjustified anthropocentrism and our justified scientific scepticism will recede as we rediscover what Charles Darwin already understood over a century ago: The differences in intelligence between us and higher animals are differences of degree, not of kind.

Sub-human Self-consciousness

The foregoing provides evidence that the higher apes engage in advanced intelligent behaviour. Almost everyone agrees that these animals are intelligent. Few, however, are prepared to grant that their level of intelligence is sufficient to allow one to ascribe to them the property of self-consciousness. However, this once again demonstrates our anthropocentric prejudices. As the primatologist Russell H. Tuttle (1990), professor of anthropology at the University of Chicago, has emphasised [p. 119]: "Of all the arrogant conceits in which humans have indulged, among the greatest must be counted the claim that only we are aware of ourselves, have individual identities, and think about what we are doing, have done, and will do".

In this book, self-consciousness is defined as a special form of intelligence which is able to perceive a discontinuity between the system itself and the rest of the universe. As such, the system perceives a uniqueness about itself, ie, it recognises itself.

By this definition chimpanzees clearly possess self-consciousness, whereas monkeys may or may not. This assertion is based on the behavioural response of animals seeing their own reflection in a mirror. Monkeys when catching a glimpse of themselves in a mirror respond as if they see another strange monkey. They may engage in threat behaviour. Some appear never to learn, for no matter how frequent the encounter, the self-image is treated as another monkey. Chimps, on the other hand, both in the wild and under controlled experimental conditions in the lab, are puzzled by a mirror. In due course, they learn to recognise themselves. The most convincing experiment demonstrating this recognition is as follows: A mirror-wise chimpanzee is anaesthetised. While unconscious, a red patch is painted over an eyebrow or an ear tip, where the ape cannot see it without the aid of a mirror. After recovery, the chimp is returned to its quarters with access to a mirror. Upon seeing its face reflected in the mirror, it engages in behaviour exploring the red patch. This includes rubbing the spot and then smelling the fingers. It returns to the mirror repeatedly to examine the changed image (Gallup 1975, as reviewed by Tuttle 1990).

A fish, such as a grouper, exhibiting strong territoriality will continue to attack its self-image in a mirror until it has broken the mirror. It may turn out as we devise other tests, not using mirrors, that monkeys possess a self-image somewhat intermediate between a fish and a higher ape.

Human infants appear to have a well-developed sense of self-identity by about 18–20 months (as reviewed by Blakemore 1988). At that age, a baby will touch a spot of rouge on its nose when it looks at itself in the mirror. It does not respond that way at an age of nine or ten months. Furthermore, at about a year-and-a-half, it will start to use words such as "I", "me" and "my". This is as true of deaf children signing to deaf parents as it is of their vocal counterparts.

Earlier, at 8–12 months, infants develop a fear of strangers – a feat which implies that they are able to recognise and remember different faces – an obvious prerequisite to recognising and remembering their own.

Donald R. Griffin (1984) considers that: "When animals devote elaborate and specifically adjusted activities to communication . . . it seems rather likely that both sender and receiver are consciously aware of the content of these messages". Griffin cites earlier workers such as A. Jolly and N. K. Humphrey, who suggest that consciousness arose in primate evolution when societies developed to the stage where it became crucially important for each member of the group to understand the feelings, intentions and thoughts of others. To become "natural psychologists", they needed to acquire internal models of the behaviour of their companions. It would seem inevitable that sooner or later comparison between others' and self states would lead to a clear sense of personal identity. Griffin suggests that such a process may occur in non-primate species as well. That is, that it could apply to any animal living in mutually interdependent social groups.

Only a strident anthropocentrism would keep us from recognising that humans are not unique in achieving states of consciousness which lead to self-recognition. If it turns out (when all the evidence is in) that we do it better, or more profoundly, then that would merely reinforce the thesis that intelligence, in its myriad manifestations, comprises a broad *spectrum* of phenomena.

Dolphin Intelligence

Dolphins and whales are a prime example of mammals living in the kind of mutually interdependent social groups considered by Griffin. Their intelligence is still an anomaly. What is clear is that these creatures have very large brains, and that certain species of dolphins are extremely fast learners. Both are properties which we associate with higher forms of animal intelligence.

Another indicator of dolphin intelligence is its brain growth after birth. Ridgeway (1986) estimates that the bottle-nosed dolphin *Tursiops truncatus* ranks somewhere between our nearest primate cousins (chimps and gorillas) and us.

At least part of the problem in evaluating the intelligence of cetaceous mammals is that they took to the seas somewhere between 70 and 90 million years ago, while the advanced areas of the brains of land animals tended to evolve only around 50 million years ago. This would account for the fact that while whale brains, for example, have retained all the conservative characters seen in primitive land mammals, they differ markedly in the evolution of the more recent neo-cortex (Morgane et al. 1986). Ridgeway (1986) has pointed out that the dolphin's reliance on sonar requires the ability to process sound images rapidly, and has suggested that much of the enlargement of the dolphin's brain auditory system –perhaps even the entire cerebrum – relates to this need to process auditory information rapidly.

In line with this suggestion are the reports of Herman and co-workers (Herman 1986) on teaching visual matching to a dolphin named Puka. Dolphin eyesight has been an enigma until recently. It now appears that dolphin visual resolution is well developed, similar to that described for many terrestrial animals. Its visual activity underwater is best at 1 metre or less, while in air it is best at distances exceeding 2.5 metres. The dolphin eye is well adapted to the underwater medium and operates efficiently under conditions of both bright and dim lighting. Herman reports that early attempts to teach Puka visual matching met with no success until the researchers decided to give auditory "names" to the visual test objects. The dolphin, now having a name for each of the two different brightnesses, was able to match the correct alternative target to the correct target. As Herman states [p. 227]: "By naming the targets we may have offered a way for the dolphin to represent the visual information as an auditory code, thereby allowing it to process the task through its auditory centres". The key here is "auditory code". Dolphins clearly are able to utilise arbitrary symbols to represent objects or properties (brightness) of such objects. Symbolic representation, therefore, is a property of dolphin intelligence – a fact that should not surprise us in view of the many lines of evidence suggesting the power of the dolphin brain.

Symbolic representation is, of course, a prerequisite for developing a language. On the basis of extensive investigations Herman [pp. 246–247] has concluded that "dolphins processed both semantic and syntactic features of . . . sentences . . . [thereby] arriving at an interpretation of the underlying instruction". Dolphins are able "to interpret the function of an early word in a sentence on the basis of a later-appearing word or words". Both linear and inverse grammatical forms can be learned by dolphins, and dolphins are able to comprehend both novel sentences and novel structures. It is clear from Herman's study that dolphins, like humans, are able to master two completely different language media – the auditory and the visual – and that their cognitive skills are broad. We will examine cetacean intelligence in greater detail in a subsequent chapter.

Instinctive Behaviour

There are some who do not consider "instinctive" behaviour as truly "intelligent". This is not an unreasonable position –clearly, the two, instinctive and learned, behaviour are not on a par. However, both are part of a spectrum of intelligence. Both fulfil the criteria for intelligence posited earlier. That is, instinctive behaviour, although it may not involve higher forms of thinking, involves information processing and under normal ecological circumstances has as its outcome an increase in the probability of both survival and reproduction.

A fly, unlike a bee, seems to possess little or no learning capacity. Its behaviour appears to involve merely a series of reflex responses (see Reichardt and Poggio 1981). Yet when it avoids being swatted or lays its eggs in a mouldering carcass, it is engaging in intelligent behaviour – even if it is unable (presumably) to "understand" the significance of its actions. Its intelligence is so limited that it appears unable to alter its responses when the situation calls for it. For example, in nature a fly is unlikely to be attacked from two different directions simultaneously. Swatting a fly with two hands coming from two different directions simultaneously so overloads a fly's nervous system that it almost invariably gets killed.

A spider has programmed into its brain the information for weaving a beautiful, intricate web characteristic for that species. This information is stored in its brain and is inherited. One is tempted to suggest that rigid behaviour patterns which are inherited are analogous to the read-only memory (ROM) devices of computers, while those involving learned behaviour are analogous to random-access memory (RAM) devices. An intermediate behaviour pattern such as the imprinting phenomena observed among higher vertebrates, would correspond to programmable read-only memories (PROM). Such a concept would imply that the evolution of the brain would have involved an increase in the number of ROMs and PROMs, followed by an even faster increase, in higher mammals, of RAMs. We will compare computers and human brains in later chapters.

Are Brains Necessary for Intelligent Behaviour?

Lower invertebrates lack brains. They do, however, possess nervous systems capable of analysing their environment and responding to it. Furthermore, invertebrate nervous systems may exhibit learning behaviour, although it involves only that most primitive of all learning behaviours – conditioned reflexes.

The California sea snail *Aplysia* has a nervous system consisting of a mere 18,000 neurons (the human brain has 10 million times as many). Yet *Aplysia* can learn (as reviewed by Blakemore 1988; Marcus and Carew 1990). The slug has a gill which it pushes out into the water. If the gill is touched, it activates a reflex mechanism consisting of twenty-four sensory nerves plus six motor neurons which instruct the muscles to contract, thereby causing the gill to be retracted rapidly. If the gill is touched lightly but repeatedly the slug gradually stops retracting it – the animal has been "habituated". However, if the slug is poked elsewhere, or the gill is insulted with a strong chemical, the reflex reaction immediately returns to its former strength. Like Pavlov's dogs, trained to salivate at the sound of a bell, *Aplysia*'s gill can be taught to retract in response to some other non-specific stimulus. That is, *Aplysia*'s reflex can be trained to become a *conditioned* reflex.

Learning is a property of higher intelligence – one obviously does not need a brain to engage in simple forms of learning.

Is a Nervous System Necessary for Intelligent Behaviour?

When it comes to ascribing intelligence to non-human organisms, many information scientists will draw a line at this point. They may concede that simple invertebrates possess intelligence by virtue of the fact that such creatures possess a nervous system, that they are motile, and that they can learn. As we move to single-celled animals, things become fuzzier. Plants are definitely out. So thoughtful a roboticist as Hans Moravec (1988) states that: "We need make only the grossest comparisons of the plant and animal kingdoms to appreciate the fact that mobile organisms tend to evolve the mental characteristics we associate with intelligence, while immobile ones do not" [p. 16].

Plants, however, are able to analyse their environment in many ways and respond "intelligently". Furthermore, some plants are able to move rapidly in response to certain environmental stimuli, involving an extremely rapid transmission of information from the site of contact to the site of response. The best example of this is the Venus fly trap, which rapidly closes its opened leaf in response to objects moving on its upper surface. In this manner it traps flies and other insects to supplement its meagre nitrogen supply in the bogs of North Carolina.

The detection system of a Venus fly trap allows it to discriminate between a piece of dirt falling onto its leaf, and an insect moving about. It takes energy to open up the leaf and set the trap. Evolution has selected for a system which does not waste energy on a piece of dirt. The detection and catching of insects makes this organism appear to behave more like a predatory animal than a plant. It is a plant nevertheless, and manages to catch insects without recourse to a nervous system.

Similarly the Touch-me-not collapses its leaves and stems in response to injury or mechanical stimulation such as cattle browsing. The speed and distance the impulse moves along the leaves, twigs and stems is determined by the intensity of the stimulus. Again, this plant also has nothing which resembles the neurons of an animal's nervous system. The transmission of information involves a different mechanism. Other plants exhibit movements, although not as dramatic, as for example, the heads of sunflowers turning to face the sun – facing east in the morning, and west in the evening.

In addition to these more obvious responses to environmental inputs, plants have a more subtle repertoire of response to environmental stimuli. Plants perceive where light is coming from and grow their shoots towards it, while the leaves of trees may position themselves so as to achieve maximum absorbtion. Germinating seeds under the ground analyse the gravitational field so as to send the shoots up and the roots down. Seeds are able to ascertain when is the optimum time to germinate by analysing several environmental factors simultaneously – moisture content, soil temperature and temperature cycles, among others. Some of these systems are so sophisticated that they are still not properly understood. For example, many plants contain the information for flowering during certain times of the year. They do this by detecting the relative length of the day or night. Plants contain a variety of sophisticated systems for detecting not only light, gravity, moisture and other aspects of their environment, but also how these relate temporarily. The information for carrying out these tasks is transmitted from one generation to the next. A seed, like an egg, contains the information necessary for becoming an adult organism, ready to survive in a complex, dynamic environment, and then pass on that information to the next generation.

What *individual* plants cannot do is *learn*. With the exception of those discussed above, plants lacking a nervous system exhibit no rapid reflexes. Lacking reflexes, they are not capable of that most primitive of all learning phenomena – conditioned reflexes. It is probably for this reason that most scientists currently consider plants as lacking all intelligence.

In the present work, we will consider self-organising systems that *learn* as representing more advanced information systems than those that do not. Keep in mind that many people do not consider sea slugs as possessing intelligence. For them, only animals which exhibit consciousness possess intelligence. In our scheme, animals that can recognise themselves represent higher levels of intelligence than those that can not. In line with this thinking, organisms that cannot learn are not relegated to the "non-intelligent" category, but instead are classed as possessing a more primitive level of intelligence. Furthermore, the *collective* intelligence of any given species – plant, animal or microbial – is capable of learning in the traditional sense: New information about the changing environment is acquired by the species as a whole. Selecting from among a series of hit-and-miss mutations, the forces of evolution select those which are adaptive to the new environment, then store this new information in the genetic material of each species. This matter will be discussed in greater detail shortly. However, it is a powerful argument for considering that all biosystems possess some measure of intelligence.

Intelligence in Biological Subsystems

A biological subsystem which processes information to achieve homeostasis, thereby maintaining the stability of the system, is exemplified by the complex biological and behavioural feedback loops which control the amount of salt and water in our body fluids (Stricker and Verbalis 1988). Normally, thirst appears to be controlled by an osmoregulatory system which involves a simple, single negative feedback loop. The brain contains certain sensors called "osmoreceptors". When these become dehydrated, they activate a central system which induces the sensation of thirst. This results in a behavioural response: We drink fluids until the dehydration is corrected, and the goal of the system, to maintain a reasonably constant volume of body fluids, has been attained.

Suppose fluid intake has been excessive. The surplus water is then excreted in the urine. Excessive drinking causes the concentration of solutes in the extracellular fluids of the body to fall below the allowed tolerance of one or two per cent. This leads to an *inhibiting* of the secretion from the pituitary gland of vasopressin, the anti-diuretic hormone which promotes water conservation in the kidneys. Thus the kidneys release water. At the same time, thirst is also further inhibited.

If we eat salty food such that the concentration of sodium in the body's fluid exceeds a threshold, the body interprets this as a deficiency of water because the brain's osmoreceptors once more signal that the body is in a relatively dehydrated state. The loop is the same as described in the first paragraph above.

What happens when we are in an accident in which we lose blood? Or to simplify matters, what happens when we donate a pint of blood to a blood bank? The body is short of a pint of fluid. The first priority is to stabilise the blood pressure. There is a neural input into the brain from the stretch receptors embedded in the smooth muscle wall at various sites of the circulatory system. These "baroreceptors" send signals which cause the pituitary to release vasopressin. Vasopressin, as discussed above, is an anti-diuretic which causes the kidney to retain water. It also acts as a vasoconstrictor causing the blood vessels to constrict, thereby increasing the blood pressure. Finally, the same signals appear to stimulate thirst, as well.

Drinking plain water, however, is a poor substitute for the loss of blood. The lost blood also contained sodium. Experiments with rats have shown that the thirst is abated well before the quantity of lost fluid has been replaced. However, rats given access to a concentrated salt solution as well as plain water will consume a mix of the two so as to both restore the lost body fluids and maintain the right osmotic pressure. The stimulus for sodium appetite appears to involve a number of other hormones – renin, angiotensin, aldosterone, oxytocin – acting at times in combination to stimulate positive behaviour, or alternatively, to counteract the inhibitory effect of hormones, or nerve centres of the brain. Obviously, these involve complex feedback loops because the body is now attempting to reset the system in respect to two sets of parameters: The first is to replace the lost body fluid and restore normal blood pressure. The second is to retain normal osmotic pressure by ensuring that the water intake is balanced by an appropriate sodium intake.

Higher animals contain many examples of such self-regulating subsystems which not only *detect* altered organisational states, but then *process* the information and *act* on that information to return the system to its original state. Clearly this must be considered a form of intelligent behaviour.

Almost all detectors, for example, baroreceptors detecting pressure changes and osmoreceptors detecting changes in osmotic pressure, have their antecedents in single-celled organisms. The modern single-celled organism has behind it a couple of thousand million years of evolutionary experimentation. Living single-celled animals have had time to evolve new systems, to modify them, to lose them, to evolve them once more, to combine and recombine disparate systems, etc. Thus we are dealing with exquisitely organised, integrated systems, capable of continuously monitoring the external environment, the internal state of the system (the cell itself) and the interaction between the two. Multicellular organisms evolved by extending many of these systems from an intra- to an inter-cellular dimension. The basic principle, however – feedback loops exchanging messages and acting on those messages – has remained a prerequisite to all levels of intelligence. This leads to the following axiom:

All intelligent behaviour involving the interaction between a system and its environment is based, at least in part, on an exchange of information involving feedback loops.

Proto-Intelligence

If the phenomenon of intelligence is to be viewed as a spectrum of phenomena, what is the underlying mechanism which created such a phenomenon in the first place? What lies at the base of the phenomenon of intelligence? All living systems including the subsystems of advanced biosystems exhibit some level of intelligence as defined in the present work. The question then must be asked: May inorganic, non-living systems exhibit intelligence?

Leaving aside "machine intelligence", which will preoccupy us in later chapters, let us consider the case of a crystal of manganese dioxide dropped into a solution of potassium permanganate. The crystal, instead of dissolving, becomes the focus of an autocatalytic reaction which converts the solution of potassium permanganate into manganese dioxide.

The ability of a crystal of manganese dioxide to convert its external environment into more of itself demonstrates that an inorganic system may reproduce. As such the crystal has fulfilled one criterion for ascertaining intelligent behaviour – the enhancement of reproducibility.

A seed crystal of salt dropped into a supersaturated solution of salt or a seed crystal of silicon dropped into a cooling mass of molten silicon will also trigger off reactions which result in the precipitation of salt crystals, or the growth of the seed crystal into a large crystal of silicon. Again, the criterion of reproducibility has been fulfilled. Does this mean that crystals possess intelligence? We are now at the borderline of our spectrum. We need to make a decision as to how we delimit our spectrum. When we define the "visible" spectrum of light, we define it in terms of light being visible to the human eye. We exclude portions of the ultra-violet – which happen to be visible to bees, for example.

Similarly, our definition of intelligence will *exclude* individual crystals. Instead, we will consider them to be *proto-intelligent*. That is, crystals, being highly organised entities which possess considerable information and engage in substantial information processing, lack true intelligence: Under usual circumstances, they fail to duplicate themselves. When they do reproduce, they are engaging in intelligent behaviour. However, once the reaction is completed, the crystals return to their wholly inanimate state, totally subjected to the vagaries of fate which their environment may impose on them. Nevertheless, if only briefly, crystals may exhibit "flashes of intelligent behaviour". For this reason we invoke the concept of *proto-intelligence*.

The concept of proto-intelligence is important: It is important in its own right. It is important to any analysis of intelligence. And it is a prerequisite for the analysis of machine intelligence.

Proto-intelligence may be defined as phenomena which involve aspects of intelligent behaviour but exist only temporarily, or if permanently, only partially satisfy the criteria for intelligence. For example, memory is an integral part of the learning process. Many non-living systems exhibit the property of memory: "Memory metals" and other materials which "remember" previous shapes and processes, a disturbed pendulum returning to its resonant frequency, many computer systems – both hardware and software – all of these exhibit various levels of memory and as such, constitute a form of proto-intelligence.

Still more primitive in organisation, involving fewer components, are molecules, atoms and subatomic particles. As Haefner (1991) has pointed out, these entities manage to maintain their identity – a proton behaves as a proton, an electron as an electron and a hydrogen atom as a hydrogen atom. It is the ability of these entities to maintain their physical integrity, to engage both in information exchanges and in information processing, which implies that they are stable information systems which exhibit aspects of intelligence. In the present work, their inability to reproduce themselves, unlike biological systems, puts these inanimate entities into the lower forms of intelligence –that is, proto-intelligent systems.

Reproduction in biological systems is based on the transmission of information across generations via a stable genetic material (DNA or RNA). The selection of new characteristics (mutations) to adapt the system better to the environment involves a learning process. That is, just as a rat learns its way through a maze by trial and error, then remembers the successful moves, so does a species learn by the trial and error of random mutations, then *remembers* the successful ones by incorporating this beneficial information into its genome (DNA or RNA) for future use. The importance of biological reproduction relates to the ability of biosystems to *learn* to adapt to their environment. This is why *all* living things may be said to possess intelligence, while inorganic systems posses only proto-intelligence.

Therefore, the ability of a system to reproduce itself, or be reproduced externally, is a vital component of *intelligence* because without reproduction, the system has virtually no chance to evolve. All evolution involves a learning process, and the capacity to learn may be as useful a guide as any for ascertaining whether a system exhibits true (rather than proto-) intelligence.

The concept of proto-intelligence must be an integral part of the concept of the evolution of intelligence. The evolution of the lung in animals living on dry land was preceded and derived from the evolution of the swim bladder in fish. The evolution of bones, important for survival on land, was preceded by the evolution of bony fish. Fish don't need hard bones to function well in water. Sharks, which possess only relatively soft cartilage, have fared very well for hundreds of millions of years swimming around in the oceans. Fish moving upstream into fresh water, however, faced an uncertain supply of vital calcium. What more logical solution than to create a calcium "bank" by depositing calcium compounds among the cartilage? Thus the cartilaginous mechanical structures may be considered as "proto-bones"; similarly, a swim bladder can be considered to be a "proto-lung", and certain fins of fishes as "proto-legs". The move from an aquatic to a terrestrial environment is a most remarkable step upward in the evolution of life on this planet, involving not only the vertebrates but the invertebrates (insects were probably the first land animals), plants and the earliest of all invaders, micro-organisms.

We recognise that there is a difference between animals that spend their life on land, and those that spend their life in water. However, there are numerous amphibians which represent an intermediate state. In a like manner, the evolution of information systems into intelligent systems probably involves intermediate stages. It is here that the concept of proto-intelligence becomes useful. We look for phenomena that, in themselves, do not satisfy our criteria for intelligence, but which are related. We would not look to the eye of a fish to evolve into a lung, nor its blood vessels to become bones; instead we look to its swim bladder and its cartilage. Similarly, we look to information systems exhibiting limited aspects of intelligence as constituting the phenomena of proto-intelligence from which intelligent systems evolved.

The above discussion has identified several phenomena which may be classed as proto-intelligent:

1. Survivability, as demonstrated by the stability of atomic particles.
2. Reproducibility, as exemplified by the growth of a crystal.
3. Memory.

Other phenomena will be identified as we delve more deeply into the subject. However, one form of proto-intelligence which is so basic as to make impossible any informed discussion of intelligence without it, is *feedback*. All intelligent systems process information along at least one major feedback loop.

Feedback loops have their antecedents in the form of regular cycles which, under certain circumstances may represent a form of proto-intelligence. Such cycles may be observed in the organisation of an atom, a swinging pendulum, a resonating electronic system, a planet swinging around a star, the stability of Bénard cells, cyclic chemical reactions – that is, any cyclic phenomenon with a regular periodicity involving two counteractive forces: centrifugal/centripetal, electrostatic/electromagnetic, oxidative/reductive, etc. Like a gyroscope spinning, regular oscillations tend to maintain the stability of the system even when the environment changes. It represents a major mechanism in the survivability of a system. In some proto-intelligent systems, the oscillations dampen down in time and finally disappear. The system collapses. In others, such as atoms, the organisation is maintained indefinitely by a complex interaction of internal forces. In contrast, in biosystems, internal rhythms are maintained by the controlled inputs of an external source of energy. Plants do it by utilising sunshine, animals by eating plants or other animals. Similarly, mechanical or electronic systems function by having available a source of energy.

A grandfather clock is a prime example of a piece of machinery which constitutes a proto-intelligent system. It is a goal-oriented object. Its goal (imposed by its human designer) is to move the hands of the clock in small, even exact, and continuous steps. It processes information in that the time it takes for a weight to descend is converted into the movement of the hands of the clock. It achieves this goal by regulating the input of energy by means of mechanical gears and levers and a steadily swinging pendulum, so as to achieve a constant output. However, the clock contains no system which compensates for changes in the environment. The steady, gravitational pull of the weight, moves the steady, ticking machinery. If the weight becomes insufficient, as it does when it reaches the end of the chain, the clock stops. If the weight becomes too heavy, the clock tries to run faster and may break. An increase in temperature causes the pendulum to become longer, and the clock slows down. The reverse happens if the outside temperature cools.

The grandfather clock exhibits aspects of intelligence: It is goal-oriented. It processes information. It regulates (in limited fashion) the throughput of energy. It converts energy into information. And its pendulum exhibits memory (in so far as it will return to its basic frequency of oscillation if disturbed). However, it is totally dependent on the right combination of externally imposed factors in order to achieve its goal. And it cannot learn. For this reason one may class a grandfather clock as a proto-intelligent device.

The grandfather clock exemplifies a system which has many of the attributes of intelligence, yet it should be classed as a proto-intelligent system. When we examine machine intelligence in later chapters, we will see that the divide becomes increasingly blurred. The problem is a familiar one to biologists trying to define taxa: "When is a variant a new species?" – a problem which has its counterpart at all levels of classification.

For example, in vertebrate taxonomy, the class "mammals" differs from the class "reptiles" from which it evolved, in that mammals in general, possess hair, give rise to live young and are warm blooded, while reptiles have scales, lay eggs and are cold blooded. However, the armadillo, a mammal, has scales; the duck-billed platypus, another mammal, lays eggs, while certain snakes and other reptiles give birth to live young; and certain dinosaurs are believed to have been warm-blooded. The reason for this overlap is that mammals evolved not once, but independently several times from the reptiles, and the products of various lines of evolution exhibit an overlap of characters.

In like fashion, the evolution of intelligent systems from proto-intelligent systems must have occurred on numerous occasions, involving quite different kinds of advanced information systems – resulting in the insoluble taxonomic problem of defining unequivocally what is a proto-intelligent system, and what is an intelligent one. We must recognise, therefore, that the bottom end of the intelligence spectrum is blurred: It becomes impossible to create a clear demarcation between advanced information-processing systems which exhibit proto-intelligence and those which could be classed as truly intelligent.

Intelligence and the Control of the Environment

Thus we can define only the limits of the known spectrum of intelligence: At one extreme is a cube of sugar dissolving in a cup of tea. Although highly organised, the cube is totally controlled by environmental events and exhibits zero intelligence. At the other extreme is a technologically advanced society deciding to divert the waters of a river so as to irrigate a plain to provide an assured food supply for the entire population.

In considering the limits of the spectrum of known intelligence, as well as the various stages in between, there emerges, therefore, a new principle: The intelligence exhibited by a system, may, at least in theory, be measured as a ratio, or *quotient*, of the ability of a system to *control* its environment, versus the tendency of the system to *be controlled* by the environment.

Using the environment to best advantage is one way of exercising control over the environment. A system *adapting* to a stable environment may be considered as having developed a form of partial control: It is a way of both exploiting the environment for the benefit of the system, and reducing the likelihood of the system being destroyed by its environment.

The key concept, therefore, is this: *Intelligence is a measure of the system's ability to respond effectively to changes in the environment, thereby enhancing its survivability, or reproducibility.*

In biosystems this involved initially various forms of adaptation which allowed systems to develop internal homeostatic mechanisms to offset changes in the external environment. Later, higher forms of intelligence were able to influence their environment directly and control such changes. Ultimately, such systems began to restructure their environment.

Restructuring of the environment is exemplified by ant hills, bird nests and beaver dams. However, the epitome of this process of environmental control has been achieved by contemporary human society: The reader, looking up from this text, is likely to see very little that has not been created by human hands. Even outdoors, the trees and meadows reflect human intervention. Only a virgin forest, a desert, the mountains, the oceans and the clouds and the sky have been left relatively untouched.

The evolution of human civilisation may be viewed as a process which results in an ever increasing control over its environment. One must be clear that the environment of any given society includes not only its physical environment (soil, rainfall, natural resources, etc.), but also its biological environment (plants and animals, pests and diseases) and its social environment (neighbours, trading partners, enemies). For example, a society may have assured itself of a steady food supply, only to fall victim to a plague, or be decimated by warlike neighbours. The appearance, development and demise of a wide range of cultural institutions during the evolution of human societies represents efforts on the part of those societies to maximise control over their total environment.

From termite mounds to human cities, *Life* utilising *Intelligence* as its tool has been striving to create surroundings of its own choosing, thereby reducing the uncertainties of an indifferent environment. A measure of the effectiveness of intelligence, hence of intelligence itself, is the success with which the system is able to create its own favourable environment.

Literature Cited

C Blakemore (1988) *The Mind Machine*, BBC Books, London.

GG Gallup, Jr (1975) Towards an operational definition of self-awareness, in *Socioecology and Psychology of Primates* (RH Tuttle ed), pp. 309–341, Mouton, The Hague.

RA Gardner and B Gardner (1969) Teaching sign language to a chimpanzee, *Science* 165:664–672.

J Goodall (1971) *In the Shadow of Man*, Houghton Mifflin, Boston, Mass.

DR Griffin (1984) Animal thinking, *Am. Sci.* 75(5):456–464.

DR Griffin (1984) *Animal Thinking*, Harvard University Press, Cambridge, Mass.

K Haefner (1988) The evolution of information processing, Faculty of Mathematics and Informatics, University of Bremen, Germany.

K Haefner (1991) Evolution of information processing systems, Project Evolution of Information Processing, University of Bremen, Germany.

LM Herman (1986) Cognition and language competencies in bottlenosed dolphins, in *Dolphin Cognition and Behaviour: A Comparative Approach* (RJ Schusterman, JA Thomas and FG Wood ed), pp. 221–252, Lawrence Erlbaum Associates, Hillsdale, NJ.

PN Johnson-Laird (1983) *Mental Models*, Cambridge University Press.

A Kortlandt (1973) Comments following GW Hewes Primate communication and the gestural origin of language, *Current Anthropol.* 14(1-2):5–24.

H Kummer (1982) Social knowledge in free-ranging primates, in *Animal Mind – Human Mind* (DR Griffin ed), pp. 113–130, Springer-Verlag, New York.

HC Longuet-Higgins (1987) *Mental Processes*, The MIT Press, Cambridge, Mass.

EA Marcus and TJ Carew (1990) Ontogenetic analysis of learning in a simple system, in *The Development of Neural Bases of Higher Cognitive Functions* (A Diamond ed), pp. 128–145, New York Academy of Science.

E Menzel (1975) Natural language of young chimpanzees, *New Sci.* (16 Jan):127–130.

H Moravec (1988) *Mind Children*, Harvard University Press, Cambridge, Mass.

PJ Morgane, MS Jacobs and A Galaburda (1986) Evolutionary Morphology of the dolphin brain, in *Dolphin Cognition and Behaviour: A Comparative Approach* (RJ Schusterman, JA Thomas and FG Wood ed), pp. 5–29, Lawrence Erlbaum Associates, Hillsdale, NJ.

AJ Premack and D Premack (1972) Teaching language to an ape, *Sci. Am.* 227:92–99.

D Premack (1971) Language in chimpanzees, *Science* 172:808–822.

WE Reichardt and T Poggio (ed) (1981) *Theoretical Approaches in Neurobiology*, The MIT Press, Cambridge, Mass.

SH Ridgeway (1986) Physiological observations on dolphin brains, in *Dolphin Cognition and Behaviour: A Comparative Approach* (RJ Schusterman, JA Thomas and FG Wood ed), pp. 31–59, Lawrence Erlbaum Associates, Hillsdale, NJ.

D Rumbaugh and S Savage-Rumbaugh (1978) Chimpanzee language research: status and potential, *Behaviour Res. Methods and Instrumentation* 10(2):119–131.

EM Stricker and JG Verbalis (1988) Hormones and Behavior: the biology of thirst and sodium appetite, *Am. Sci.* 76:261–267.

RH Tuttle (1990) Apes of the World, *Am. Sci.* 78:115–125.

F de Waal (1989) *Peacemaking Among Primates*, Harvard University Press, Cambridge, Mass.

· 3 ·

The Origin and Early Evolution of Intelligence

Introduction

". . . you can never get hold of the real beginning of anything" (Teilhard de Chardin 1956, p. 64).

The phenomenon of *life* – that is, the origin and evolution of living organisms on this planet – represents the best example of the origin and early evolution of the phenomenon of true *intelligence* known to us. Until recently it represented the only example. This has changed with the advent of machine intelligence – a matter to be discussed in later chapters. In this chapter we will explore the origin of proto-intelligent systems into pre-biotic ones, then look at certain aspects of simpler forms of intelligence as exemplified by plants and micro-organisms.

The Preconditions for Intelligence

The most basic assumption one can make about the phenomenon of intelligence is:

Intelligence is a property of advanced information systems.

That is, just as information is a property of the universe, so is intelligence a property of advanced information systems.

A system contains information if it exhibits organisation. The more information a system contains, the greater and more complex will be the organisation of that system. Advanced information systems exhibit many complex organisational features, some of which set the stage for proto-intelligence. Of these, five basic processes must have been well established before complex proto-intelligent systems could appear. These are:

1. Resonance.
2. Duplication.
3. Differentiation.
4. Recombination.
5. Feedback.

Resonance: A major feature of many organised systems is that they exhibit resonances. Resonances produce oscillations. These result in regular cycles – a range of phenomena observed from subatomic to human social systems. Regular cycles favour *stability*: Like a spinning gyroscope, it becomes much more difficult to displace or distort a cycling system than a static one. However, a resonating system also allows minor *variations*. Each recursive cycle permits the introduction of variations into the cycle. The more complex the system – the more numerous and complex are the cycles and subcycles – the easier it becomes to introduce variations.

The stage becomes set for advanced information systems. If "variation" represents the first half of the mechanism of evolution, "selection" represents the second half: Systems which work survive; those which do not, do not. The resonating systems evolve into feedback loops, not only between the various components of subsystems and systems – thereby assuring their organisational stability – but also between the system and its *environment*. The system begins the rudimentary task of detecting changes in its environment and responding to it. This is the birth of intelligence.

Duplication: One of safest ways of introducing variations into a system without destroying it is for the system to duplicate – to have divided (or multiplied) into many identical units, and then, and only then, "experiment" on some of these subunits. After such cloning, a variation lethal to one of the multiple units need no longer be lethal to the whole.

Differentiation: Duplication followed by a process of variation affecting the individual (duplicated) parts leads to differentiation.

This is how insects evolved: From a multi-segmented arthropod such as a millipede in which all the segments have legs and are generally similar, to an insect in which only the middle section, the thorax, has legs. Other segments became altered so that instead of legs, insects produced antennae or wings (See review by Laughon and Carroll 1988). As the vertebrae in our backbone attest, we humans can also trace our ancestry back to segmented animals.

If each segment, initially similar, evolved to carry out a specialised function within an individual organism to allow a higher survival value, then a beehive illustrates that the same may happen *across* individuals, initially similar. More primitive insects consist of individuals which, except for the sexes, are identical. Bees, on the other hand, evolved societies in which classes of individuals became *anatomically* differentiated in order to carry out specific functions. In addition to being physically different, there are further behavioural differences. For example, workers involved with the care of larvae carry out tasks different from those workers whose main job it is to gather pollen and nectar. In ant societies this differentiation of individuals evolved even further to result in several castes, anatomically distinct from each other, each adapted to carry out a specific task. Both the ant colony as a whole and the beehive are so highly integrated that some naturalists have considered these conglomerates to be equivalent to a single, differentiated organism (rather than a society), and that the individual ants or bees are more analogous to individual cells than to individual organisms – a matter to be explored further in the next chapter.

Nature confines itself not merely to duplicating structures –it also duplicates processes. For example, the process of evolution itself, based on variation and selection, reappears over and over again at each higher level of organisation. Similarly, the mechanism described so clearly by Teilhard de Chardin – two lines of evolution diverge, then merge to combine into entirely new forms – happens over and over. For example, such a mechanism appears not only during the process of evolution, but also represents the basic processes which underlie the immune response of our own bodies to invaders of the bloodstream. By combining in many different ways, a few hundred, or at most a few thousand genes are able to code for the millions of different antibodies which comprise part of our immune mechanism.

Recombination: It is probably true to say that the process of *combination* and *recombination* is the primary source of major evolutionary advances (rather than the steady build-up of point mutations). For example, the "eukaryotic" cell which possesses that complex cell organelle, the nucleus – an organelle lacking in the more primitive "prokaryotic" cells – has a complexity of structure which, it is now believed, implies that the eukaryotic cell is derived from combinations of more simple (prokaryotic) cell types. For example, in photosynthesising plant cells, the chloroplasts are thought to represent evolutionary derivatives of formerly independent, photosynthesising cyanobacteria. In both plant and animal cells, the mitochondria (which comprise a cell's "powerhouse"), similarly, represent derivatives of bacteria which in ancient times were independent (Margulis 1970).

The eukaryotic cell became the fundamental building block of multicellular organisms. Prokaryotic cells, in the case of colonial bacteria, are able to produce colonies with differentiated cells – the whole colony behaving more like a single organism. However, evolution could not traverse the path to more complex multicellular organisms until it could utilise the more advanced eukaryotic cells as building blocks. This probably reflects the fact that the integrity of prokaryotic cells is maintained by an external cell wall, while that of eukaryotic cells is maintained by an internal cytoskeleton (Kabnick and Peattie 1991). Replacing an external wall with an internal skeleton allows for much greater freedom with respect to substances and particles moving in and out of the cell. This, in turn, set the stage for improved communication between cells – all such primitive communication involving the exchange of chemicals. Improved communication between the cells comprises the first step in the further integration of evolving systems. The second involves the creation of feedback loops.

The principle of divergence and recombination is repeatedly evident not only during the course of evolution (at the phylogenetic level), but also during the development of an embryo into an adult individual (at the ontogenetic level). The human body develops from a single (eukaryotic) cell into a myriad of cell types – different kinds of blood cells, liver cells, muscle cells, heart cells, brain cells, etc. Not only are the cells making up different tissues, organs or systems different from each other, *within* each tissue, organ or system, different cell types exist. Yet these myriad of differences combine to form a co-ordinated, incredibly complex unit – a unit so complex, that it is still not fully understood how it works (its physiology), or how its form came into being (its morphogenesis).

In the very early stages of human embryo development, after the fertilised egg has divided only a few times, each cell appears to be the mere *duplicate* of every other cell: Any cell can be isolated and give rise to an entire organism (the cells are totipotent). Very soon, however, as cell division proceeds, cells begin to *differentiate*, and seem to have their totipotency restricted, first to being able to produce large categories of cell types (the cells are still pluripotent), then, as the embryo becomes more and more complex, the potency is further restricted until finally most cells can only produce their own cell type (unipotent), or, in some instances, cannot even divide at all, as in the case of mature red blood cells in the human circulatory system, or mature nerve cells in the human brain.

The process of differentiation involves the activation and inactivation of various genes. That is, the information stored in the DNA of the cell is released and processed in relatively small packets, in a tightly controlled time sequence. Which packets are activated, which are shut down, and which are inhibited from being activated in the first place (repressed), is dependent on sequences of chemical messages, some originating from the cell's own metabolic machinery, some originating from neighbouring cells, and others arising from cells at some distance from the receptor cell. This last situation involves hormones – the *chemical messengers* – which continue to play such a vital role in integrating the trillions of diverse cells of the adult human body into a coherent whole.

Each cell in the developing embryo is, therefore, exposed to a gradient of chemical messages, emanating from its own, its various neighbours, and more distant sources of metabolic activity. This explains the principle first stated by the German botanist Herman Vöchting (1878): "The function of a cell is determined by its morphological position". That is, *where* a cell is located in the body of a plant or animal determines what kind of cell it is going to become.

Note that the gradients of various messages yield unique *combinations* of messages so that relatively few kinds of substances, in a multiplicity of combinations, can create such an amazing diversity of differentiated cells. What is crucial to the understanding of the whole process is that the chemical messages may be of different kinds: Some may instruct a cell to divide, others to enlarge, still others to differentiate – in some cases leading to the point of death – while a fourth kind of message may instruct the cell simply to be quiescent and not do anything. Most important are the messages which tell a cell to produce or release hormones, neurotransmitters or other chemicals which themselves act as messages for other cells. It is this mechanism which creates *feedback loops* and allows for *integration*. It is in this manner that the diverse processes can be integrated into a coherent whole.

Feedback: Feedback loops are a prerequisite to intelligence. Feedback loops stabilise *complexity* and allow a system to interact with the environment in a way which enhances *survivability*.

A simple example will suffice: The shoot of a tomato plant produces certain hormones and vitamins which are transported to the root tips. Without these substances the roots cannot grow. Conversely, the root produces other hormones and amino acids, vital for healthy shoot growth. Damage to one part of the plant, either root or shoot, causes the other part to "wait" until the damage is repaired, and normal balanced growth and development can once again resume.

The growth of a tomato plant exemplifies the role feedback loops play in maintaining the organisation and integrity of a complex system.

Finally, vital to any analysis of intelligence is the concept of *hierarchy*. Both the phenomenon of *information* and the phenomenon of *intelligence* exhibit hierarchies of complexity. That is, complexity builds on pre-existing complexity. Without this understanding – that there exist many levels of complexity which can be graded into a hierarchy – it becomes impossible to develop either a general theory of information, or of intelligence.

Proto-Intelligent Systems

The principles described in the previous sections form a constellation of phenomena and processes which constitute the prerequisites to the emergence of intelligent systems. At this point it may be helpful to introduce the concept of the *corpuscle*, as Teilhard de Chardin (1956) introduced it [pp. 19–25]: Complexity does not mean simple aggregation, nor the undefined repetition of units. Complexity implies combination, which knits together a certain fixed number of elements within a closed whole of determined radius, such as an atom, molecule, cell, plant or animal. Such a unit Teilhard de Chardin calls a corpuscle. This is in contrast to units which arise by aggregation and crystallisation in which the arrangement remains incomplete: One can always add on from the outside. This form of non-corpuscular organisation applies equally to a microcrystal and a giant star. There is no inherent unit, no self-limiting boundary – only an accidental "rounding off" of the system.

Combination produces groups which are structurally complete even though such groups may themselves duplicate and therefore may be indefinitely extensible from within. Teilhard de Chardin considers [p. 20] that the corpuscle is: "a unit truly and doubly 'natural' in the sense that while organically limited in its contours so far as its own existence is concerned it also, at certain higher levels of internal complexity, manifests strictly *autonomous phenomena*" (italics in original).

Although it is not entirely clear from Teilhard de Chardin's treatise exactly what he means by "autonomous", presumably it refers to internal processes which have been sufficiently insulated from the external environment to allow their operation to proceed independently of that environment. That is, the boundary provided by the corpuscle excludes the environment from directly controlling the processes internal to the corpuscle. Presumably this is as true for electrons orbiting around the nucleus of an atom (but within its atomic confines) as it is for the enzyme-controlled metabolic reactions within cells, or the heat regulating system of our bodies which buffer such enzyme reactions.

Using Teilhard de Chardin's concept of the corpuscle as our point of departure, it must be clear that to reach the levels of integrated complexity required to achieve the corpuscular state, feedback loops are required. The internal organisation of such a corpuscle must also have previously undergone an evolutionary process which involved duplication, differentiation and recombination. These then, are the processes we must look for in pre-corpuscular systems to find examples of proto-intelligence.

Clay Minerals and the Origin of Life

Duplication, differentiation and recombination characterise the processes by which clay minerals arise. What is interesting about clay minerals is that, in recent years, a whole new line of investigations has centred on the possibility that the origin of life, in its earliest stages, was based on a symbiotic interaction between clay crystals and organic compounds (Cairns-Smith and Hartman 1986).

In reviewing what has become known as the "Clay Hypothesis", Hartman (1986, pp. 10–12) points out that all contemporary life forms involve, first, nucleic acids, which are the chemical basis of replication and mutation, and, second, proteins, which mediate the general metabolism of the cell. This represents the dichotomy between genotype and phenotype, and is much too sophisticated a system to have arisen all at once. Furthermore, the search for simpler, more primitive systems must go beyond nucleic acids and proteins: It is likely that inorganic crystals would have had a major role to play in such pre-biotic systems (Cairns-Smith 1986).

About half of all sedimentary rocks on earth are made of clays. Clays are abundant in other parts of our solar system as well, and clays are ancient. They are the product of both degradation and synthesis. Weathering of rocks involves not only grinding rocks into small bits, but also the dissolving of various minerals in these rocks and their crystallisation from supersaturated solutions. Clay crystals build up through polycondensation. They are continuously generated from very dilute, yet supersaturated solutions – the product of the weathering of materials such as feldspars, which in turn are continuously generated through geological processes.

Clays, because of their enormous surface area, are ideal for filtering, for chromatographic processing and for catalysis. This means they can act like the primitive equivalent of proteins, organising "metabolic" events: For example, Mortland (1984) has described such a system, composed of a Cu^{2+}-smectite and the well-known co-enzyme pyridoxal phosphate. This "pseudo-enzyme" has been shown to deaminate DL-glutamic acid and glutamine, but not the closely related aspartic acid and asparagine. As Pinnavaia and Mortland (1986) point out: "The deamination of glutamic acid is not a particularly interesting reaction in itself. But the work demonstrates the activity of the silicate structure in the catalytic process and suggests other important reactions might be feasible such as transamination and decarboxylation". As such, it "is relevant to the possible role of clay-transition metal cation complexes in pre-biotic chemistry and chemical evolution".

These and other observations indicate that clay mineral –protein complexes are able to perform the "phenotypic" functions of biological systems if, and this is a big if, they are properly organised and co-ordinated. That is, a great deal more information would need to be added to make such pre-biotic, semi-organic systems work like living cells. Part of such an information requirement could be met by the availability of a "genotype" master system. What is required is a system which may be stably reproduced, yet exhibits the possibility for variation.

Before a genetic apparatus could be harnessed to act as both master regulator of the phenotypic systems and as perpetuator of the information which assured the survival and reproduction of such complexes, there had to exist some stable information reproducer in the first place. This leads to the concept of the "naked gene" which Mackay defines [p. 142] as a system in which: "A message is simply reproduced". A naked gene, originally, need not relate to anything. Mackay also showed that, basically, a crystal matrix has the characteristics of an abacus on which it is possible to write an arbitrary message. Clay crystals, like abacuses, are combinatorial structures with a large number of metastable states on which it is possible to write a large number of arbitrary messages.

We are used to messages being carried on unidimensional carriers. The words on this printed page are strung along in one direction, like beads. This is equally true for data stored on a computer tape, or music on an audio tape. It is still true when compressing data, or music, onto a disk – the information remains in linear form even if it is now in the form of a coil. Likewise, DNA and RNA are unidirectional message carriers. As Mackay points out, both "human language and the genetic code, depend on messages written and read in a linear sequence".

Crystals, on the other hand, can be two-dimensional or three-dimensional message carriers. Two dimensions makes it easier to reproduce the information. However, it is more difficult to access and edit information, unless the two-dimensional matrix is broken up into easily accessible rows and columns. Three-dimensional information systems become more difficult still, unless, like in a book, they are made up of easily separable leaves.

To get a feeling for crystal genes, envisage a brick floor made up of yellow and red bricks to form an arbitrary horizontal pattern. If the nature of the crystal growth is such that normally only a yellow brick stacks on top of a yellow brick, and a red one on top of a red brick, then the two-dimensional pattern would be reproduced faithfully in the third (vertical) direction. Assume now that the nature of the interbrick bonding is such that cleavage of the whole crystal can occur only in the horizontal plane, ie, in a plane perpendicular to the axis of growth. Once fractured, the bottom half can continue growing upward, as before, while the top half can grow downwards – both perpetuating the original yellow/red pattern. (Actually, the two surfaces, top and bottom, would not look identical but would represent mirror images of each other.) Any stable irregularity (such as substituting a red brick with a yellow or even a blue one would be efficiently transmitted from one generation to the next as long as growth was only in one direction (vertical), and cleavage occurred neatly only in a place perpendicular to the axis of growth (ie, horizontally). In such a system, the information being replicated would be a two-dimensional pattern. The information carrier, however, would have a robust, three-dimensional structure, with the information carried within it highly redundant. Such a system may be nowhere near as sophisticated and efficient as the enormous amount of information perpetuated in living cells, but in the pre-biotic world of a few thousand million years ago, robustness was probably more important than elegance.

With the above as background, Cairns-Smith has considered a number of systems [pp. 143–152] which would provide a class of objects which could act as "proper crystal genes". He concluded that there are four general requirements which are critical:

1. *Disorder*, to provide information capacity.
2. *Order*, for replicative fidelity.
3. *Growth*, to duplicate the information.
4. *Cleavage*, to complete the replication process.

As one of the pioneers of the *clay hypothesis*, Cairns-Smith has raised some profound questions about the origin of life, and provided thoughtful answers and useful analyses, such as the one above. Of the four general requirements, however, one needs to be cautious about how one interprets the first: *Disorder* does not provide information! Mačkay's naked gene needs no disorder to exist and multiply – only order, growth and cleavage. Disordering it, would in fact destroy it. As discussed in a previous work (Stonier 1990), information is a function of organisation: Information is *inversely* related to disorder and the entropy which measures this state. However, disorder can provide the mechanism for altering the structure of a system so as to allow a "mutation" to appear. If there existed no possibility for introducing *variations*, then there would be no possibility for the system to evolve. Given that such variations in crystal systems may involve specific individual loci, where, for example, one atom or atomic grouping is replaced by another, it might be conceptually more helpful to restate Cairns-Smith's first requirement as: "*disorder*, to provide *mutations*". That is, the term "information capacity", derived from the communications engineers, should be replaced by the more relevant term "mutation", used by biologists. It would also be more lucid if this, the first of the four requirements, be made the last.

To sum up, small molecular units such as silicic acid and hydrated metal ions can combine in a multitude of ways and can give rise to a large number of stable combinations. Clay crystals, therefore, may be classed as aperiodic crystals whose essentially crystalline character provides both regularity and stability. Clay crystals were plentiful in pre-biotic times. As such, they could have performed, even if only in a much less efficient manner, functions currently carried out by nucleic acids. Other clay minerals, in an analogous fashion, and again with less efficiency, would have been able to carry out the catalytic functions currently carried out by proteins. Clay pseudogenes and clay pseudo-enzymes, coupled to a mixture of organic compounds in an aqueous medium would have set the stage for numerous interdependent systems whose complexity finally exceeded that threshold, which we call *Life*. In each case, stable interacting subsystems would maintain their stability by means of feedback loops. In due course, the integration of such subsystems into larger systems, then supersystems, would likewise depend on the establishment of further feedback loops.

In this manner, *hierarchies of complexity* emerged, reaching levels of thermodynamic improbability impossible to describe with mere astronomic numbers. However, in each case, the *feedback loop* remains the basis for stabilising the integration of complex subsystems: In contemporary living systems no nucleic acid synthesis can occur if there are not available the right amount and type of protein enzymes. Conversely, no protein synthesis takes place if there are no messages emanating from nucleic acids. There can be no advanced levels of dynamic organisation without feedback loops.

The progression from clay to life on this planet probably involved the following steps:

1. The formation of a wide range of clay minerals.
2. The simultaneous formation of a limited number of organic compounds, some perhaps extensively polymerised.
3. The, originally erratic, production of an extremely wide range of organic compounds including large homo- and heteropolymers as a result of the catalytic interactions between the clay minerals and salts and the simpler, primitive organic compounds in aqueous systems.
4. The regular production of complex organic heteropolymers, including proteins, nucleic acids and membranes.

5. The formation of coacervates brought about by the mixing of aqueous systems and fatty polymers creating microenvironments bounded by membranes.

6. The emergence of self-organising systems and the creation of what could be considered as clearly proto-biotic chemical systems.

7. The emergence of self-duplicating organic molecules within such self-organising coacervates, setting the stage for:

8. The earliest organic life forms.

The first, second and, in a limited way, probably the third step, took place within and on the surface of most, if not all, the bodies of our planetary system. On the basis of their analysis of carbonaceous chondrites – meteorites containing carbon compounds and repre-senting left-over bits of matter from the earliest stages of the evolution of the solar system – Chang and Bunch (1986 p. 129) concluded: "The coexistence of clays, mineral salts and organic matter in the oldest objects in the solar system is remarkable. That these objects show evidence of aqueous activity in a planet-like environment so early in solar system history is truly significant". With the exception of the Earth, all the other bodies in our planetary system appear to have been frozen at level 2 or 3 – although we need to explore the solar system systematically before we can rule out the existence of later stages. Chang and Bunch point out that the mineralogy and geochemistry of some of the moons of Jupiter and Saturn would provide important clues to the interaction of minerals and organic chemicals in a pre-biotic setting.

With the planetary conditions just right, steps 4 to 7 evolved, setting the stage for the origin of life. The synthesis of membranes in steps 4 and 5 would have resulted in complex coacervates which would compartmentalise matter into aqueous (hydrophilic) and oily (lipophilic) systems – a prerequisite for the creation of cell membranes and the internal structure of the living cell.

Whatever was involved in step 8, it is becoming clear that the first living cells were able to grow and divide only because they were able to ferment organic molecules formed *non-biologically* in an environment virtually entirely devoid of oxygen (Schopf 1978).

We may still be uncertain about the final steps leading to the creation of cells, but what should become apparent is that organised systems such as molecules and crystals, containing a substantial amount of information to begin with, organise further, building complexity upon complexity and increasing the system's information content further. The *exponential* increase in information content of the various systems as they evolved created hierarchies of organisation until finally there emerged the phenomenon of life, and by definition, intelligence.

Intelligence, as we stated earlier, is a property of advanced information systems. In order for such advanced information systems to come into existence, there must have existed a substantial natural history preceding the formation of such advanced systems. *Intelligence was preceded by proto-intelligence.*

Furthermore, the demarcation between the two becomes fuzzy: For example, the emergence of a system of self-duplicating molecules within a larger, self-regulating system might be considered as *either* proto-intelligent or as intelligent. In view of this fuzziness of demarcation exhibited by proto-biotic systems, it appears probable that life arose not once, but on numerous occasions.

Plants: Advanced Biosystems

Some years ago there appeared a book entitled *The Secret Life of Plants* (Tompkins and Bird 1973). This book was a maddening mixture of scientific fact and fiction. It was unfortunate that so much folklore and misleading material was included in the book because it has been known for a long time that plants exhibit a wide range of sophisticated behavioural adaptations (see for example Bonner and Galston 1952). For most behavioural scientists, however, the life of plants is indeed a great secret.

The term "behaviour" is usually defined as "response to stimulus". "Instinctive behaviour" is usually considered to involve a "biologically programmed response to stimulus". By such a definition plants engage in "instinctive behaviour". Even though plants lack a nervous system, they have a variety of senses which first analyse the environment, then respond intelligently on the basis of a variety of effector mechanisms which have been genetically programmed.

The problems of survival for plants are quite different from those of animals. Plants manufacture their own food. The need to move information rapidly from one part of the body to another – a prerequisite for achieving locomotion – is not important to plants (with minor exceptions such as the predatory Venus fly trap, and a few other specialised cases such as the Touch-me-not). Much of the exchange of information among the various parts of the plant body is achieved by hormones – the chemical messengers. Unlike transmission mediated by a nervous system which is able to move information from one end of the animal body to another in a fraction of a second, plant hormones involve a time scale somewhere between minutes and weeks. Furthermore, plant hormones do not trigger specialised tissue such as muscle tissue; instead movement in plants involves the enlargement or multiplication of cells, a process which involves a time scale ranging from hours to years. It is the lack of tissue specialised for rapid response such as nerves and muscles – tissues which allow animals to engage in behavioural responses as fast as the blink of an eye – which makes plants so slow and ponderous in their behavioural responses. This slowness, however, should not blind us into believing that plants do not engage in instinctive – that is, biologically programmed – behaviour.

A few examples will illustrate the point: Plants are *geotropic*. That is, just as some animals have been programmed to go under the ground (eg, moles) and others up into the trees (eg, gibbons), so the vast majority of plants have been programmed to send their roots down and their shoots up. The gravity detectors consists of tiny grains – cell organelles called statoliths – which are found in cells at the root tips and shoot tips. These statoliths tend to sink to the bottom of cells and bring about a redistribution of growth hormones by affecting the synthesis, transport or destruction of hormones in the local region. These hormones primarily affect cell elongation just behind the tip. In roots, elongation of the upper surface causes the tip to bend downward. In shoots, the opposite occurs as the distribution of hormones causes the lower surface to extend – forcing the growing tip upward.

Plants are *phototropic*: Shoots are positively so, therefore grow toward the light; roots exhibit negative phototropism – growing away from light. As with geotropism, phototropism relies on cellular organelles near the tip which act as photoreceptors and which affect the distribution of growth hormones, again, by altering local transport, synthesis or their rate of destruction. Incidentally, at the molecular level, the transport of organic substances, such as hormones, and of inorganic ions, as well as many other aspects of basic cellular physiology, are very similar in plants and animals – sometimes virtually identical.

Some plants have evolved special organs to facilitate the response to light and gravity. The coleoptile in grasses is such an organ. Grasses are among the most advanced of land plants from an evolutionary point of view. The seeds of grasses, such as oats, are relatively small with a limited supply of stored food. Anything which helps the germinating seed to push its shoot up rapidly through the soil towards light would aid survival. Although a shoot needs to grow, its main function is photosynthesis – a function denied the plant underground. By encasing the young, vulnerable germinating shoot in a protective sheath which is able to detect very low intensities of daylight (it is red blind) and is equally sensitive to gravity, the germinating seedling is assured of an optimum behavioural strategy for raising its shoot. Once above ground, the leaf breaks through the coleoptile to achieve its photosynthetic function.

The oat coleoptile is richly endowed with both gravity and light detectors, and produces large quantities of growth hormones. It was, in fact, while working with the oat coleoptile that Fritz Went in the 1930s first provided unequivocal evidence for the existence of plant hormones – a classic piece of work which can trace its lineage of experimentation and observation back half a century to Charles Darwin.

The grasses illustrate another behavioural strategy, adapting them to an environment which includes grass-eating herbivores: Instead of growing from the top down as most plants do, they grow from the bottom up. That is, their growing centres (meristems) are at the bottom of the shoot (rather than at the tip), thereby minimising damage from grazers or, for that matter, from lawnmowers.

Another case of biologically programmed behaviour in plants is the ability of many plants to flower at the same time – for example, in the spring – thereby assuring reproductive efficiency. This example parallels the instinctive behaviour of many animals which engage in unlearned – that is, biologically programmed – mating behaviour during certain specific seasons of the year. In many instances, the mechanism appears to be virtually identical in plants and animals: Both plants and animals have mechanisms for detecting the appropriate season by measuring the length of day/night cycles. An induction period of a sufficient number of days of the right length alters the hormonal status of the organism. This basic mechanism, then, results in a wide repertoire of behaviour: Male stickleback fish develop red bellies, build nests and become extremely aggressive; red roughed grouse males stake out territories of heather which they defend vigorously; female deer go into oestrus while their potential mates, having grown large antlers earlier, have been bashing each other about for some time. Plants merely flower.

It is easy for students of behaviour to overlook plants. Yet the photoperiodic detection mechanism in plants is exquisitely sensitive: In a greenhouse of tobacco plants, a nightwatchman checking his station, turning on a 40 W bulb in the middle of the night for only a few minutes, will prevent those plants from flowering.

Finally, one must emphasise that whereas most behaviour in *plants* is dependent on hormones, hormones also play a crucial role in the behaviour of animals. Returning to the molecular dimension, it is probably no mere coincidence that one of the most important of plant hormones, indole acetic acid, is a close chemical relative of the neurotransmitter serotonin. Probably both substances are concerned with the transport of crucial ions across membranes.

Both the biological microworld of comparative molecular chemistry and the macroworld of ecology provide ample evidence for the need to extend traditional concepts of intelligence and behaviour to embrace *both* kingdoms.

The Collective Intelligence of Micro-organisms

A respectable analysis of the evolution of intelligence in biological systems ought, logically, to move from plant intelligence to animal intelligence, and from there to human intelligence. However, we will eschew this logic and omit discussing animal and human intelligence at this point for three reasons. First, the matter has already had some coverage in the preceding chapters, and more will be discussed in greater depth later on. Second, there is a general awareness of animal and human intelligence, and the purpose of the present work is to expand our existing definition of intelligence. Third, and this is an extension of the second reason, we have focused on crystals and plants because the common perception by both laymen and professionals is that neither of these can be classed as possessing intelligence. In fact, the suggestion that plants are intelligent, and rocks exhibit flashes of intelligent behaviour, is generally greeted with amusement, if not derision and hostility. The most that the vast majority of intelligent people usually (and not always) concede is that creatures which move exhibit some measure of intelligent behaviour.

Mobility, however, cannot be the only criterion of intelligence: A tree, although stationary, possesses a greater intelligence than an amoeba: It has by far more sensing systems with which to analyse the environment. As discussed above, a plant can detect moisture and send its roots towards it; it can detect light and send its shoots up towards it; it can detect gravity to guide its shoots up and its roots down as a good first order approximation where the former will find light and the latter moisture. Plants can detect the seasons and interpret these, then act on this information by flowering, shedding their leaves, germinating or just plain hibernating. Most important, a single plant can withstand a much wider range of adverse environmental conditions than can any individual, motile protozoan swimming around in a pool of water.

The matter is more complex, however. As a *group*, any given species of protozoan is likely to outlive any individual plant, a statement which can be applied with even greater certainty to the oldest of all known cell forms – bacteria.

Contrary to how traditional bacteriologists view bacteria – as pure colonies of single cells growing on agar in Petri plates – in the real world, bacteria live in complex multicellular communities (see review by Shapiro 1988). Some communities may consist of a mixture of many different species. Others may consist of a single species forming complex colonies. Myxobacteria, for example, never exist as single cells. Even when adverse conditions force them into dormancy, the colonies form multicellular cysts which germinate to yield a ready-made colony of thousands of individuals.

As the colony grows and the population becomes more dense, the individual bacteria migrate. However, they do so in a co-ordinated fashion, secreting trails of extracellular slime which mark the highways along which thousands of cells migrate, in colony-co-ordinated rhythmic pulses. Part of the colony differentiates to form cysts; in some species colonies form elaborate, psychedelic fruiting bodies. When the colony migrates, it does so as an intact unit – any cell which moves a few nanometres beyond the edge rapidly returns to be enfolded once again by the colony.

These various activities are under genetic control. A. D. Kaiser and his colleagues have shown that the species *Myxococcus xanthus* has two different genetic systems for regulating movement: An A (adventurous) system which allows individual cells to move and an S (social) system which regulates the movement of groups of cells. A defect (a mutation) in either system leads to an abnormal colony structure. If both systems become defective, the cells cannot spread at all. At least twenty-three different genetic factors have been identified in the A system, and at least ten in the S system. When two motility-defective mutants are combined in the same petri dish, they regain motility as long as the two mutant types remain closely associated.

Work with other bacteria has shown that the organisation of colonies into distinct concentric zones involves the formation of rings, not at specific positions on the agar on which they are growing, but at specific times during the growth of the colony. As Shapiro points out: "Both biological clocks and the temporal control of development . . . are important features of higher organisms".

Bacteria as a group have been around for a few thousand million years and are so widely dispersed on this planet that some scientists refer to them as the "global organism". As S. Sonea (1988), the author of that term, has reviewed, one reason for the universal success of this apparently vulnerable, microscopic form of life is that bacteria have evolved a number of mechanisms for exchanging genetic information, which include the use of viruses and plasmids as genetic tools. This allows bacteria to gear up rapidly to new metabolic opportunities, or adapt to new requirements imposed by the environment. Such genetic mechanisms represent the bacterial equivalent of the two-heads-are-better-than-one phenomenon encountered in human intelligence systems.

A single bacterium, therefore, represents a biological system near the bottom end of the intelligence spectrum. However, the conglomerate – all the bacteria and their genetic transfer mechanisms together – represents a biological system with a much higher level of intelligence – possessing a much more sophisticated system for analysing the environment and then responding intelligently – than any one, individual bacterium. The *collective intelligence* of bacteria – that is, bacteria viewed as a global organism – comprises a manifestation of intelligence substantially greater than that of any one, individual multicellular organism.

We will discuss the phenomenon of "collective intelligence" in greater depth in the next two chapters. However, it is important, at this point, to indicate that the collective intelligence of bacteria represents an example of an *advanced* form of intelligence, a form which is capable of *learning*. The DNA or RNA of the bacteria becomes modified according to the experiences the organisms have had in the past, and such experiences become incorporated into the information storage system of each organism – its genetic material. That is, if we define "learning" in traditional psychological terms – as enduring change in knowledge or behaviour resulting from experience – then the DNA/RNA, as the species' store of knowledge, becomes modified as a result of its environmental experience. If one expands the concept of "behaviour" to include metabolic behaviour, then clearly the bacteria behave differently as a result of their changed genetic status.

Literature Cited

J Bonner and AW Galston (1952) *Principles of Plant Physiology*, WH Freeman, San Francisco.

AG Cairns-Smith (1986) The four crystal genes, in *Clay Minerals and the Origin of Life* (AG Cairns-Smith and H Hartman ed), pp. 143–152, Cambridge University Press.

AG Cairns-Smith and H Hartman (ed) (1986) *Clay Minerals and the Origin of Life*, Cambridge University Press.

S Chang and TE Bunch (1986) Clays and organic matter in meteorites, in *Clay Minerals and the Origin of Life* (AG Cairns-Smith and H Hartman ed), pp. 116–129, Cambridge University Press.

H Hartman (1986) The clay hypothesis, in *Clay Minerals and the Origin of Life* (AG Cairns-Smith and H Hartman ed), pp. 10–12, Cambridge University Press.

KS Kabnick and DA Peattie (1991) Giardia: a missing link between prokaryotes and eukaryotes, *Amer. Sci.* 79:34–43.

AS Laughon and SB Carroll (1988) Inside the homeobox, *The Sciences*, New York Acad. Sci. March/April 1988, pp. 42–49.

AL Mackay (1986) The crystal abacus, in *Clay Minerals and the Origin of Life* (AG Cairns-Smith and H Hartman ed), pp. 140–143, Cambridge University Press.

L Margulis (1970) *Origin of Eukaryotic Cells*, Yale University Press, New Haven, Connecticut.

MM Mortland (1984) Deamination of glutamic acid by pyridoxal phosphate-Cu^{2+}-ion-smectite catalysts. *J. Molec. Catalysis* 27:143–155.

TJ Pinnavaia and MM Mortland (1986) Aspects of clay catalysis, in *Clay Minerals and the Origin of Life* (AG Cairns-Smith and H Hartman ed), pp. 131–135, Cambridge University Press.

JW Schopf (1978) The evolution of the earliest cells, in *Life at the Edge* (JL Gould and CG Gould ed), pp. 7–23, WH Freeman, New York.

JA Shapiro (1988) Bacteria as multicellular organisms, *Sci. Am.* 258(6):62–69.

EW Sinnot (1960) *Plant Morphogenesis*, McGraw-Hill, New York.

S Sonea (1988) The global organism, *The Sciences*, New York Acad. Sci. July/Aug 1988, pp. 38–45.

T Stonier (1990) *Information and the Internal Structure of the Universe*, Springer-Verlag, London.

P Teilhard de Chardin (1956) *Man's Place in Nature*, Collins, London (English translation, 1966; Fontana Books, 1971).

P Tompkins and C Bird (1973) *The Secret Life of Plants*, Avon Books, New York.

H Vöchting (1878) *Uber Organbildung im Pflanzenreich*, Max Cohen, Bonn.

· 4 ·

The Evolution of Collective Intelligence in Animals

Introduction

The selective pressure to gain greater control over the environment led to combinations and recombinations of existing and newly formed information systems. At all stages in the evolution of intelligence, once true intelligence had become established, there emerged the phenomenon of *collective intelligence*.

This concept of collective intelligence is crucial to the understanding of "intelligence" as a phenomenon. It becomes impossible to develop a general theory of intelligence without understanding collective intelligence. Briefly, the phenomenon may be defined as follows:

A system may be said to exhibit "collective intelligence" when two or more "intelligent" subunits interact to engage in intelligent behaviour.

As discussed earlier, one criterion by which we recognise intelligence is by intelligent behaviour. Behaviour is defined traditionally as a response to a stimulus. Intelligent behaviour involves responses which enhance the system's survivability or reproducibility. Therefore a *collective* intelligence must exhibit intelligent behaviour. This may involve two human beings "putting their heads together" to solve some problem of mutual concern, or a group of small ants transporting a large insect, or various nerve centres of the human brain collaborating to interpret an external stimulus.

Collective intelligence, like *unitary* intelligence, also involves a spectrum – but in at least *two* dimensions. The first involves the *quality* of the individual intelligences of the subunits. This may range from proto-intelligent subsystems combining to form the simplest type of bio-intelligence, to individual human beings combining to create human society and culture. The second involves the *number* of subunits. These may be extremely large: For example, in human systems they may range up to billions (10^9) if one considers human global society, and trillions (10^{12}) if one considers individuals neurons plus the numerous other cells of the body required for normal neuronal functioning.

In addition to the above two dimensions, there is a third factor, as important as the other two: The extent and sophistication of the *integrative systems* which allow the individual units to act as a coherent whole.

Without a thorough grasp of the concept of collective intelligence, we cannot understand the past emergence of higher forms of intelligence nor forecast the future of intelligence in general, and machine intelligence in particular. The evolution of collective intelligence in the form of cultural traditions also becomes crucial to the understanding of human history – a matter which will be discussed in the next chapter.

Collective Intelligence in Insect Societies

Probably the most easily understood illustration of collective intelligence is to be found among insect societies, a matter elaborated most clearly by Nigel Franks at the University of Bath (Franks 1989). Thousands of insect species live in advanced social orders often characterised by exquisitely integrated co-operative behaviour. Included in this last category are some well-studied species which have become classics in the insect literature. These include the honey and bumble bees, various kinds of ants – army ants, driver ants, leafcutter ants, slavemaker ants, weaver ants – and the fungus-growing termites. Among the most dramatic of these is the integrated behaviour of colonies of army ants (reviewed by Franks 1989; Hölldobler and Wilson 1990; Schneirla and Piel 1948).

Social Ants

The army ant bivouac is made up of live ants co-operating to form a more or less cylindrical hollow cluster or "nest". It may hang from a low branch as strings and filaments of ants, hooked together leg to leg. A close-up suggests some kind of an animal with a creepy "fur". This is, of course, the ants themselves acting as the outer tissue of the nest. This outer tissue is made up of workers major and intermediates, while minims concentrate around the queen within. In spite of substantial fluctuations in temperature at the floor of the tropical rain forest, the ants are able to regulate the temperature inside the nest to within 1°C of optimum. From this nest they engage in daily foraging raids. A colony of the species *Eciton* can maintain a steady compass bearing as each day they raid in a different direction – up to 200 m from the nest. Each day the direction of the raid is rotated by about 123° to avoid raiding the same areas two days in succession. This keeps up for 15 days after which the whole colony migrates to a new site.

The above behaviour optimises the utilisation of food resources. It also correlates perfectly with the breeding cycle. The queen, who lays of the order of 6,000,000 eggs in her life time, engages in prodigious egg laying just after migration – about 100,000 in a few days. It is this clutch of eggs which hatches and allows the larvae to reach adulthood by the end of the 35-day cycle.

Whereas the human brain contains of the order of 10^{11} neurons, each ant contains only 10^5 neurons in its brain. Each individual, in a colony of 500,000 possesses only little or no knowledge of the dynamics of the colony which engages in optimal foraging strategies, regulates nest temperatures to within 1°C of optimum, and organises the transport of prey very much larger than any individual ant. The half a million individual ants are welded into an integrated behavioural unit by means of a highly efficient, chemical, visual and tactile communications system. The limited intelligence of each individual is programmed to respond appropriately to each communication. Take, for example, the maintenance of the nest temperature, crucial to the normal, rapid and carefully timed development of the larvae. As Franks points out, the hundreds of thousands of ants generate more than enough heat as a result of metabolic activity. If the outside temperature drops, the colder individuals on the outside of the nest huddle in towards the centre, closing up ventilation gaps and raising the temperature. The reverse happens when temperatures rise.

Even more dramatic is to watch the small ants transporting a large prey insect back to the nest. Franks postulates: "a remarkably sophisticated solution is achieved through the use of a simple algorithm: if there is a prey item in the trail moving below the standard retrieval speed, and you are not carrying an item, then help out; otherwise continue". Ants join the transport team only when the speed of movement is too slow, and ignore others which are doing all right. All teams are comprised of individuals who have selected themselves. Each ant has enough intelligence to judge whether a team needs it or not. In contrast, it does not have enough intelligence to survive should the ant become isolated. The colony, on the other hand, is able to survive and reproduce indefinitely (providing it doesn't meet up with an ecological disaster).

This feature is a characteristic of most of the social insects. In weaver ants, for example, Hölldobler and Wilson (1977) have reported that individual ants perform no more than fifty distinct behavioural acts – the majority involving communication – creating, however, a highly effective working unit of great survivability: a fossil colony was found in East Africa in 1963 which dated to over 15 million years ago. As the authors pointed out "the effectiveness of the colony is obtained by the rigid programming of the relatively simple components of individual behaviour, which secure a complex but lockstep pattern of co-operation during group activities".

Franks sums up the trend in the evolution of insect intelligence as follows: from individual, hard-wired, yet high-grade processing units such as solitary wasps, to societies of great numbers of simpler individuals linked by increasingly sophisticated patterns of communication. Army ants represent the culmination of this trend.

The Collective Intelligence of Honey Bees

More sophisticated and more intelligent than individual army ants are the individual honey bees. These are probably the best studied of insect societies, and a wealth of information, both practical and theoretical, has accumulated over the centuries, including more recently a great deal of insight into the various modes of communication among the bees (Gould and Gould 1988).

A bee which has discovered a rich source of food is able to convey this information in very precise terms to fellow workers, primarily by engaging in a "dance" – a mix of a series of formal movements and sound signals.

1. The dance contains a part in which the worker bee wags her tail while moving forward in a straight line. This indicates the *direction*. In the case of the dwarf bee, the dance occurs on a horizontal surface and the forward movement indicates the direction in which the bees should fly to find the source of food. In most other bee species the dance is performed *inside* the hive, in the darkness and on a *vertical* surface. Here the direction of the forward dance relates to the direction of the sun. Envisage a hypothetical clock. If the food is in the direction of the sun, the bee wags straight up into 12 o'clock. If the food is 60° to the right of the sun, the bee wags straight in the direction of 2 o'clock. If the food is to the left, at a right angle to the sun, the bee wags to 9 o'clock. If the source is in a direction exactly opposite to the sun, the pioneer bee dances straight towards 6 o'clock, etc.

2. The pioneer indicates how far the source is. The wagging dance has two components. As just described, the first part involves a straight run. The second part involves returning to the point of origin by returning in a semi-circle. This return portion of the dance alternates between left and right, thereby creating a series of flat figure eights. By altering the tempo of the whole dance, the bee indicates the distance from the source. If the source is close to the hive – and what is "close" to a bee varies from species to species – the figure eight is so distorted as to approach a single circle – the so-called "round" dance, in which the bee appears to be rotating back and forth along a circle. During the waggle straight dance, the bee also vibrates its wings to produce a sound. The length of the train of sound emitted during a straight run of the dance tells the distance (see review by Wenner 1964).

3. How *extensive* the food source is, is conveyed by the vigour of the dance: The richer the source, the livelier and longer the dance – and the more it arouses other bees. Part of this liveliness involves sound: There is a correlation between the rate of pulse production and the strength of the sugar concentration in the food source supplied.

If several plants are in bloom at the same time, those providing the richest, most favourable food source cause the most intense dances

– stimulating the largest number of workers to fly there for collection. Upon their return, the first generation of recruits are also engaged in dancing, causing still more bees to forage among the new source. Ultimately, as the source dries up, the dances slow down or stop and the worker bees follow other, competing signals promising a better harvest.

Bee communication systems are inherited. Young bees reared in isolation are able to perform the waggle dance and transmit other related information without ever having been taught to do so by watching mature worker bees. Furthermore there are dialects among bees. For example, it is possible to obtain a mixed hive of Austrian and Italian bees which live together in perfect harmony. There is a problem, however. The Italian bee – *Apis mellifera* – has a dance intermediate between the "round" dance (for nearby food sources) and the "straight waggle" dance. The Austrian bee – *Apis mellifera carnica* – has a different perception of distance; this causes the bees to get their signals mixed up. An Austrian bee aroused by an Italian waggle dance will fly too far because, for example, at a distance of 200 feet, the Austrian bee still engages in a round dance while the Italian utilises the straight waggle dance.

Parenthetically, it is important to realise that although the dance of the bees represents, for humans, one of the most dramatic aspects of bees communicating information to each other, a number of other systems have been identified as well (reviewed by Gould and Gould 1988). For example, the bee carries back to the hive both the odour of the flower, and the odour of the general location, either of which provide clues for potential recruits. So does the nectar regurgitated by the forager bee. Bees also mark sites by means of Nasinov's pheromone, a scent which acts as a powerful attractant to foraging bees. Thus inter-organismal integration in a beehive is achieved by linking individual members through systems of communication which involve sight, sound, smell and taste, as well as a number of other semiotic interactions not described here.

To understand bees requires an understanding of the *beehive*. That is, it is easier to understand the intelligent behaviour of bees by considering the *beehive* as a kind of super-organism, and the bees merely as individual cells.

This idea, that a social insect colony may be considered as a "super-organism", was first put forward by William Morton Wheeler in 1928. It was further considered by the present doyen of insect behaviourists, Edward O. Wilson (1971), and more recently it has been reviewed by Seeley (1989). It is an important concept from the point of view of understanding the closely related concept of collective intelligence. Wheeler coined the term to denote insect societies which were organised into highly integrated units whose features were analogous to the physiological processes taking place within individual organisms. Seeley classified a group of individuals as a super-organism when the individual organisms "form a cooperative unit to propagate their genes, just as we classify a group of cells as an organism when the cells form a cooperative unit to propagate their genes". In more primitive insect societies, individuals engage in intense intragroup conflict as they compete for "reproductive success" – who will lay the eggs which hatch to propagate the individual? In contrast, individual members who are part of a super-organism rarely, if ever, engage in intragroup conflict. Harmony resides inside a beehive – food and aid pass freely among the members in ways which promote the economic success of the colony as a whole. The whole represents an integrated biological machine which promotes the success of the colony's genes – keeping in mind that the drones, the fathers of the workers, are haploid, producing sperm cells with identical genomes. Thus the workers and their future queen sisters are all cloned to be genetically very similar.

The beehive therefore parallels the human body, which also promotes the success of its genes – keeping in mind, however, that the germ cell giving rise to an egg or sperm possesses a genome which is *identical* (not merely similar) to all the other cells of the human body.

In a colony of bees, two levels of biological organisation exist simultaneously – the organismal and the super-organismal. What integrates the former so as to create the latter is an extremely complex network which facilitates a myriad of information interactions. There is no centralised control. However, the individual bees are in constant communication with each other – the hive is filled with bees tapping, buzzing, dancing, stroking, tugging, bumping, shaking, waggling, puffing, releasing scents, and so forth, giving rise to the expression "a beehive of activity". In addition to the direct exchange of information between individuals or groups of bees, there are the cues provided by the environment. For example, if the hives gets too hot, that is a signal to start fanning – if too cold, the signal indicates a need to increase metabolic heat by the isometric flexing of the wing muscles. Thus the bees exhibit a collective intelligence in analysing their environment and responding to it collectively.

As with the army ant, a relatively small number – perhaps only a few hundred, probably several thousand – relatively simple algorithms programmed into the small brain of the bee suffice for the apparently complex behaviour of the individual organisms, and for the subtlety and wide repertoire of adaptive responses exhibited by the super-organism.

The beehive, like the army ant bivouac, is a paradigm for collective intelligence, demonstrating two points:

1. Collective behaviour may have a genetic basis.
2. Higher forms of intelligence arise from the synchronised interaction of simpler units of intelligence.

The building up of more complex phenomenon from simpler phenomena is basic to understanding any complex system in any sphere of knowledge. In the evolution of intelligence it is also a universal phenomenon, occurring repeatedly at all levels of the intelligence spectrum – a matter to consider in greater depth, later. For example, chimpanzees, whose brains are very close to ours and very far removed from that of a bee, solve the same problems of finding a source of food and communicating it to other members of their troop. However, the communications systems of apes are not restricted to a limited set of genetically programmed signals. Instead, they develop a wide range of signals – learning both by imitation and by experimentation and innovation – to communicate with their conspecifics. Similarly, the understanding of apes at the receiving end of a communication is not limited to a few stereotyped algorithms. Instead, they attend not only to the signals of the sender, but evaluate the situational context of these messages – including, as we discussed in Chapter 2, the possibility that these messages might involve a deliberate deception.

The Collective Intelligence of Dolphins

Anyone who has seen dolphins on display, when pairs or several dolphins swim together, engaging in various manoeuvres in unison, will recognise that these animals enjoy acting together as a team. What is not apparent from such a set of observations is the possibility that social cohesion in dolphins may be much greater than that experienced by humans.

We shall examine human collective intelligence in the next chapter. However, it is worth noting that humans are the most socially integrated of all primate species. For example, it is hard to envisage a platoon of chimpanzees, marching in unison, sharply obeying the commands from the drill sergeant – the whole platoon acting as a single ape. Perhaps military manoeuvres on the parade ground represent the extreme in human social cohesiveness, but there are other aspects: Individual self-consciousness is normally heavily intertwined with group identification. A soldier may identify his own self with his regiment, or perhaps only his own squad of men. In battle, a "one for all, and all for one" ethos may greatly enhance the chances of survival of both individuals and the group even though it may involve risking one's own life for the benefit of the group. It is an attitude which is characteristic of high morale units and greatly prized by military commanders.

The comradeship and social cohesion of soldiers at the front is also exhibited by individuals who work together in dangerous circumstances – for instance, coal miners or fishermen. A range of such group loyalties exist for all humans. These may extend from members of the immediate family only, to large nation-states, even to a global sense of humanity. However, we all tend to tie our self-identity to some group or other. We may consider ourselves Europeans or Asians or North Americans; we may think of ourselves as New Yorkers or Californians, Londoners or Lancastrians, Berliners or Bavarians; or we may identify ourselves with a particular tribe or clan or family or work group – all of us, however subtle, tend to think of ourselves in terms of some group.

We were meant to. The success of the human species, compared to other primates, rests, at least in part, on the fact that we became the most co-operative – the most socially cohesive – of the primates. Our consciousness of self is intertwined with our group identities.

With dolphins, it is probably even more so. Jerison (1986), analysing dolphin cognition and intelligence, points out [p. 163] that "although something analogous to self as we know it may occur in dolphins its expression is likely to be different from ours". Jerison goes on to argue that: "When knowledge of the external world is based on echolocation, the sensory data . . . in a large-brained species may generate an especially unusual self. Information from echolocation can be sensed at the same time by several individuals, and . . . the perceptual worlds of a *group* of dolphins . . . could occasionally share an immediate experience of 'self' in their perceptual world". In other words, a dolphin's cognition of "self" may, at times, be a group self rather than an individual self. Jerison uses the term "the extended, communal self", emphasising that this would be *in addition* to the individual self characterised, among other things, by the vocal "signature calls" emitted by all dolphins as individuals.

Such an extended, communal self becomes, like a well-drilled army unit, an extremely efficient instrument for carrying out a group attack – for example, against large sharks. As such, dolphins represent another instance of environmental circumstances favouring the close interaction of intelligent subunits combining to create a collective intelligence.

Social Intelligence vs Collective Intelligence

The above discussion of dolphin collective intelligence is meant to illustrate two points: First, that among mammals, there exist non-primates whose collective intelligence is at least as sophisticated, and probably more so, as that found in the higher primates, including humans. Second, by emphasising the work of Jerison and other researchers that dolphins may share a genuine sense of group-self, we come to distinguish between "social intelligence" and "collective intelligence".

Social intelligence is an advanced form of intelligence which allows an animal – itself capable of a complex and varied repertoire of behaviour patterns – to analyse and respond correctly (intelligently) to possible behavioural responses of other members of the group. Perhaps the epitome of non-human social intelligence is that already described in Chapter 2 – the deception practised by monkeys engaged in illicit mating behaviour, or chimps trying to cover up that they have found a desirable source of food. Social intelligence is exhibited by individuals coping with their social environment.

Collective intelligence is also an advanced form of intelligence. In higher mammals it may prove to be epitomised by dolphins. Collective intelligence involves group intelligence in which individuals submerge their individual identity as the group copes with its social, biological and physical environment.

Note that the army ants discussed earlier lack the sophisticated social intelligence of higher mammals. Social insects are programmed genetically to respond to signals from conspecifics. Proof that such a system involves low *social* intelligence derives from the numerous observations on ant parasites living in their colonies (as reviewed by Hölldobler 1989). A wide range of arthropods make their homes inside ant nests. In some cases, for example, certain rove beetles not only eat the food meant for the ants, they eat the ant larvae as well. The low social intelligence of ants allows these interlopers to fool the ants completely. For example, begging behaviour on the part of the beetle causes an ant to regurgitate droplets of food for them. The parasites, of course, are able to mimic not only the behaviour of their ant hosts, but also the chemical signals (pheromones) vital to the social integration of the nest.

Another example illustrating the low social intelligence of social insects is found in mixed beehives: Italian and Austrian bees sharing the same hive confuse each other because they have been programmed to respond differently to the same signals. Social insects, unlike social mammals, need not *understand* the behaviour of their cons-specifics to engage in appropriate behaviour. On the other hand, there is nothing to be found among higher animals that approaches the total integration of individual behaviour exhibited by an army ant bivouac or a beehive.

Social insects therefore, rank low in social intelligence, while they rank very high in collective intelligence. Large-brained social mammals, on the other hand, rank very high in social intelligence. We have yet to discover just how extensive is their collective intelligence, an intelligence based primarily on mutual understanding and empathy rather than genetic programming.

The Origin of Societies

The antecedents of advanced animal societies may be found at the very beginning of life's evolutionary scale: Single-celled organisms frequently cluster in a manner which parallels the social organisation of higher animals. That is, each single cell remains, and seems to operate, as an individual, yet the totality of cells may combine into a coherent societal unit.

One of the most remarkable cases is that of the colonial diatoms (reviewed by Bonner 1980). These are microscopic, mobile cells which move rapidly inside a branching tube of extracellular material secreted by the diatoms themselves. Anchored to a rock or some other substratum, this branching tube looks like a delicately branched seaweed and may be several centimetres across. Other well-established examples involve social bacteria. Like social insects, these have castes which differentiate individual cells during their reproductive phase. Within a fruiting body, individual cells may differentiate into reproductive spores or non-reproductive support cells. Such social bacteria also engage in co-operative feeding. They secrete large amounts of enzymes collectively to digest prey which they could not possibly attack singly.

Somewhat higher up the evolutionary scale are the slime moulds. Many forms go through a cycle where they alternate between motile, individual feeding cells and aggregates called "plasmodia" which represent a giant multinucleate single "cell". This, in turn, may cleave and differentiate into a highly complex fruiting body made up of huge numbers of cells. The whole fruiting body is capable of migrating as a unit, consisting of a foot, a stalk and a head containing the cells differentiated into reproductive spores. Here again, one sees a kind of caste system reminiscent of the social insects.

A very different group of bacteria, the cyanobacteria (formerly classed as the blue-green algae), include species whose colonies contain highly differentiated cells. The cyanobacteria represent a very ancient group of bacteria. They are capable of both photosynthesis and nitrogen fixation. The former is adapted to conditions when the earth's atmosphere contained only half its present amount of oxygen. The latter is adapted to a still more ancient time when the earth's atmosphere contained virtually no oxygen at all. To engage in nitrogen fixation, all oxygen needs to be excluded because oxygen poisons the system. To achieve this, specialised cells are formed with thick walls coated with mucilage which insulate the cell from oxygen, while, at the same time, the cell's metabolism is designed to trap and inactivate any oxygen molecules which do get through. Colonies of cyanobacteria, therefore, are designed to survive in a purely inorganic environment in which most cells reduce carbon dioxide to organic carbon compounds by means of photosynthesis, while a few others have specialised in reducing atmospheric nitrogen. Both cell types represent intelligent systems. Together they comprise a collective intelligence so powerful as to have survived at least one, and perhaps two or three, billion years. The association of these two cell types is stabilised by simple biochemical feedback loops. The photosynthesising cells cannot grow without the amino acids and other reduced nitrogen compounds provided by the nitrogen-fixing cells. The latter cannot fix nitrogen if they are not provided with the products of photosynthesis, both to provide the energy needed, and to provide the reduced carbon skeletons to be fleshed out with reduced nitrogen.

The key to stabilising the association of two or more intelligent subunits into an effective collective intelligence is to create an *interdependence* between subunits. Such interdependence involves feedback loops. The more complex the subunits, the greater the possibility for more and diverse feedback loops – hence the greater the chances for more complex associations. Bacteria consist of cells which lack nuclei and other cell organelles and are classed as "prokaryotic", in contrast to the modern "eukaryotic" cells which emerged less than a billion years ago. The divide between these two forms of life is much more profound than the difference between plants and animals. Apparently, only the eukaryotic cells possess the complexity required for evolving into multicellular organisms.

Multicellular organisms represent the evolutionary outcome of genetically integrating individual cells which possess the genetic information to differentiate into a variety of cell types. In the case of the slime moulds described above, any and all of the cells are capable of differentiating into foot, stalk or reproductive cells – the nature of the differentiation being determined by the position the cell finds itself. In slime moulds, this process of integration and differentiation takes place only during a relatively small part of the organism's life cycle – the greater part of its life cycle involving *individual* cells foraging for themselves. At the other extreme are multicellular organisms, such as human beings, whose life cycle entails only a very small part being spent as a single-celled organism, viz., the fertilised egg before it begins to divide and become a multicellular embryo.*

Something as highly integrated and complex as the human body is, however, still no more than a genetically integrated unit made up of potentially independent subunits. With the exception of cells comprising the mature nervous system and cells whose differen-

---

* One might also consider the sperm and the unfertilised egg as part of a single-celled phase of the life cycle. However, one could present arguments against this view.

tiation involves the loss of vital cellular components – eg, mature red blood cells which have lost their nucleus – all other cells can be cultured as individual cells in laboratory tissue cultures, or can be converted to uncontrolled, individual units within the human body as cancer cells.

Under normal circumstances, however, the fertilised egg has been genetically programmed to divide repeatedly until it has produced the many trillions of cells comprising the adult body. At the same time, the genetic programme causes cells to activate or shut down metabolic systems which bring about the differentiation of cells into blood, bone, liver, skin, nerves, etc. In the middle of the nineteenth century, the German botanist Vöchting coined the adage: "The fate of a cell is a function of its position" – an adage which predates the modern understanding that it is gradients of chemical messages, secreted by other cells, which determines a cell's metabolic behaviour, and hence its direction and extent of differentiation.

In principle, the genetically programmed response of cells to chemical signals emitted by other cells, and the genetically programmed response of ants to chemical signals emitted by other ants, is the same. What determines whether or not one has a collection of many individuals forming a society, or an integration of those individual units into a coherent organism depends on the environmental pressures. In many instances having many individuals acting on their own is advantageous. For example, if an organism lives in an environment which is fairly stable and allows easy access to food – such as an ocean bay, a lake or wet forest soil – individual organisms may be able to move about, find sources of food and multiply fast enough to avoid being totally devoured by predators. On the other hand, no amount of scouring the surface of moist earth will allow individual organisms to both extract water from deep beneath the soil and obtain maximum amount of light from high above the soil. For that you need an organised unit such as a tree.

It becomes obvious that it is the environmental requirements which determine the form life takes under any given circumstance. This is best understood in terms of survival and reproducibility. Some circumstances favour totally independent individuals, others a society of individuals, and, in the long run, the environment favours integrated organisms. The progression from individual bacteria to human beings represents two thousand million years of evolution of the biosphere as a whole. It also represents the evolution of collective intelligence, as subunits became integrated into units, which in turn evolved to become superunits – ultimately generating hierarchies of intelligent systems – the spectrum of intelligence which comprises our world today.

The formation of groups of units into "societies" represents the first step in the formation of collective intelligence, which, in turn, precedes the total integration of individual units into a coherent superunit.

The Emergence of Culture in Animals

In his book *The Evolution of Culture in Animals*, Bonner (1980) defines animal society as "A cohesive group of intercommunicating individuals of the same species" and culture as "The transfer of information by behavioural means, most particularly by the process of teaching and learning" [p. 76]. Bonner goes on to point out that social animals are communicating animals, and the extent of communication is the one aspect of animal societies which is directly related to culture. "Culture is simply not possible without communication" [p. 113]. Bonner cites two reasons for animals to form groups: The first involves the ability to gather food more effectively or to hunt more effectively; the second involves more effective means of protection from predators. One could add to that something which covers perhaps both, such as the modification of the environment witnessed in beavers building dams, termites building mounds and, for that matter, all social insects building nests as discussed earlier.

"The forces moulding animal societies were parallel but by no means identical with those moulding culture" [p. 102]. Bonner lays great stress on the evolution of learning and teaching, where he points out that there is a continuum from the simplest kind of imitation which may not involve any teaching at all, to the other end of the spectrum where human parents and teachers give complex instructions to a child. Complex teaching is, from an evolutionary point of view, a recent invention. It is basic to cultural evolution. In contra-distinction to having a student who is instructed, or even an apprentice who merely imitates, is learning by trial and error. Experience may be the best teacher – it is also the most expensive and may, at times, be fatal.

However, learning by experience must have been a prerequisite to learning from conspecifics. In fact, adaptive behaviour can be found in protozoans such as *Stentor* which exhibits both "sensitisation" and "habituation" to stimuli. In that sense, *Stentor* is able to learn from the experience of various stimuli and its environment and decide whether to react strongly or ignore any given particular stimulus. There is no evidence, however, that one protozoan instructs another protozoan about the environment. By the time we get to bees, however, as we have seen, one bee may tell other bees where to find a particularly good source of food. Clearly, there is instruction here. However, the method of instruction is frozen, as is demonstrated by mixed hives of Italian and Austrian bees which confuse each other's signals because the signals are wholly under genetic control. In vertebrates, unlike insects, there exist remarkable powers of imitation.

Bonner postulates that if the earliest forms of learning involved simply imitating the behaviour of conspecifics, in particular, parents, then the earliest forms of teaching must have involved parents reinforcing positively the offspring's effort to imitate them [pp. 131–132]. He then goes on to discuss five forms of cultural transmission by imitation:

1. Physical dexterity.
2. Relations with other species.
3. Auditory communication within species.
4. Geographic location.
5. The transmission of inventions or innovations.

Oyster catchers have two methods of getting at a mussel: Either the bird brings the mussel on shore, then hammers with its bill at a soft spot, or, while the mussel is open under water, the bird quickly reaches in with its bill and snips the adductor muscle. It takes the young a long time to learn either technique. Both behaviours appear to be innate: The young exhibit both kinds of behaviour in rudimentary form. However, whether they become hammerers or stabbers, appears to be dependent on what their parents and other members in their surroundings are doing, thus one can find cultural patterns determined by what behaviour is present at the time the young are learning.

There are numerous other examples of learned behaviour which is transmitted. Galapagos finches use thorns to remove grubs from trees. Sea otters and other animals use rocks to break abalone or other shells. Goodall (1971) has reported that chimps fishing for termites use sticks fashioned by stripping off the leaves. This practice appears to be learned by imitation, and represents an instance in non-human primates of not only using tools, but also of making them. At the Yerkes Laboratories, chimps taught how to use a drinking fountain transmitted that know-how to other members watching them.

In the South African park of Addo live some of the most dangerous elephants in Africa. The reason for this is that in 1919 a small population of 140 elephants were hunted at the request of local citrus farmers. The farmers engaged a famous hunter, Pretoreus, who shot the elephants one by one and reduced the herd to somewhere between 16 and 30 individuals. At that point, the elephants had become so wary of humans that they remained in the thickest bush during the day and moved stealthily about at night. Pretoreus gave up. In 1930, the elephants were given sanctuary. However, four decades later they were still hiding and would attack human intruders. This behaviour appears to involve cultural transmission because only very few, if any, of the 1919 animals who actually experienced the trauma of the killings could still have been alive at that point.

The opposite to the culture of fear learned and transmitted by the elephants of Addo is the culture of tameness exhibited by many animals isolated on the islands of the Galapagos: One can walk right up to a bird and touch it. The same is true for Galapagos penguins and marine iguanas – but only if approached on land: In the water, where these animals may encounter sharks, the presence of a human swimmer induces a typical flight reaction.

Mobbing behaviour by European blackbirds can be shown experimentally to depend on what the young blackbird learns early on. Thus, it was possible to trick a learner into mobbing not the natural enemy of blackbirds, the owl, but an innocent Australian honey-guide. The learner thus tricked, in turn, was made to teach others and thus a small flock of blackbirds was created which had developed a tradition of mobbing Australian honey-guides. A number of examples of bird songs and whether they sing a particular song with a local dialect depends on the young learning the particular tune from older conspecifics. Similarly, specific routes for migrating birds (and for monarch butterflies) involves learned behaviour, such learning determining which particular locality an individual will migrate to.

One of the more remarkable examples of animals learning a useful trick and transmitting it is exemplified by the blue tits. These small pleasant birds discovered that the shiny caps of milk bottles can be pried open to reveal cream, or milk, which they could then drink. This discovery, and the technique of getting at the milk bottles, spread through England at a rate of about 5 miles per year (see also review by Gould and Gould 1988, pp. 220–221).

In a similar fashion, but under controlled conditions, there is the example of Imo, the genius young female macaque who, in the Japanese monkey studies, discovered that sweet potatoes, when washed with sea water (and perhaps salted by it?) tasted better. She also devised a way to clean up a pile of wheat thrown on the beach. She would scoop up the wheat and the sand together, then toss the whole thing into water: The sand would sink while the seeds floated to be easily scooped up and eaten. Her discoveries were quickly picked up by other juveniles and slowly spread through the troop. The last to acquire the new technique were the old, senior alpha males.

Bonner points out that there are strong selective forces which favour the process of cultural transmission. It is a system which can respond much more rapidly to environmental changes than can the traditional genetically determined evolutionary changes. Envisage how long it might take for blue tits to evolve genetically the inclination to pry off the tops of milk bottles to get at the cream.

Social insects exemplify the extreme of genetically determined behaviour patterns. Primates and other large-brained mammals such as elephants and dolphins would represent the other extreme in the animal kingdom in which both individual and collective intelligence analyses the environment continuously then sets up modes of behaviour patterns to exploit new resources or avoid new dangers.

Bonner believes that these general pressures provided the impetus behind the spectacular changes that produced a larger brain so rapidly in the evolution of the hominids. Bonner also postulates that the genetic changes which produced such a large brain, which in the human line is a vastly different phenomenon from that which occurred either in the great apes or in the proto-human Australopithecines, could be very slight indeed. It could involve merely a simple modification of a few genes which govern the duration of the development of some parts of the organism. This delay – a process called *neoteny* – could have been applied to the developing brain in *Homo*. That is, the human brain would continue to develop for a relatively longer period than in the great apes. Such a gene alteration may have been based simply on the growth hormones secreted by the pituitary gland, or that the receptors in the brain cells which respond to these hormones had been altered during a late stage in the development of the brain so rather than its further growth being terminated – as in apes – it continued its development. This implies that great changes in the capacity to engage in intelligent behaviour could have been produced by relatively minor changes in the genetic apparatus of the animal involved – in this case, us.

Communication and Collective Intelligence

It must be obvious that collective intelligence cannot exist without effective two-way communication between the various subunits. The colonial insect behaviour described above shows that such communication may consist of a number of systems. In the case of the bee waggle dance, the communication involves sight. But as we have seen, it also involves sound. Feeding freshly collected nectar to nest mates, and marking sources of nectar with pheromones involves the transmission of chemical signals. Chemicals are even more important in ant behaviour – individual ant movement away from the nest being largely determined by trails of various species-specific chemicals.

Communication by means of trails of chemicals is but one example of nature's use of "pheromones" to govern collective behaviour. In the case of the fire ant, Wilson (1971, p. 218) postulates that almost the entire social organisation of the colony might be mediated by as few as ten such pheromones. Wilson defines pheromones as substances exchanged among members of the same animal species which regulate their behaviour or development. Unlike *hormones*, which are the "chemical messengers" between the cells, tissues, organs and systems comprising the *internal* environment of an individual organism, *pheromones* act across individuals, regulating and co-ordinating the behaviour and the interactions of members within *groups* of individuals.

Even more far-reaching than substances acting as chemical messengers across the individuals comprising a single species are the many instances of flowering plants sending out scents attractive to insects such as moths, butterflies and bumblebees, whose own anatomy has co-evolved to fit the anatomy of the flower. Clover and bumblebees are a classic example, the long proboscis of the bumblebee matching the anatomy of the flower. The bumble bee gets its nectar, the clover is assured of cross-pollination. There is evidence that in many instances the nectar provided by the flowers stimulates the reproductive physiology of the insect dependent on it for food. That is, co-evolution not only involved adapting the flower and insect anatomies to each other, but also their respective physiologies. If the concepts of "hormone" and "pheromone" are well established, we ought to add the idea of "ecopheromone" to cover chemical messengers between species comprising part of an ecosystem.

All of the above represent instances of collective intelligence evolving at various levels of complexity. A team of humans and dogs engaged in hunting represents another example of an interspecific collective intelligence – humans and dogs communicating by means of subtle visual signals, some auditory ones and perhaps olfactory cues by human scent emission.

All of these phenomena have applicability to human beings. Sight, sound, smell, touch – all of these form part of the biological communication systems among human beings. It is these flows of information between the various subunits which integrate the subunits into that functioning collective intelligence which we call human society.

A Short Comment on Intelligence, Genes and Evolution

It is currently fashionable in biological circles to assess the mechanism of evolution in terms of the properties of genes (for example, Dawkins' "selfish gene"). Universal evolution operates (ie, varies and selects) at many levels of complexity – not merely at the level of DNA molecules. To view human bodies or beehives merely as successful carriers and replicators of specific genes has an element of truth in it, but at the same time is a misleading oversimplification. Both bodies and beehives represent levels of organisation, ie, information, which are the inevitable consequence of the evolution of intelligent systems. This will become apparent once genetic engineering reaches maturity. At that point, genes will have lost further control. For it will be us, with our human collective intelligence, who will determine which genes we want, which not. It will not be genes experimenting with humans to assure the reproductive efficiency of the gene, but human *intelligence* which will decide the fate of each gene. Irrespective of whether we do it wisely, it will be a clear case of superior intelligence (human) overriding biological information systems (DNA). Intelligence may be the product of biological evolution, but, just as *Life* itself is the product of the evolution of inert *Matter* and *Energy* – then superseded it – so will *Intelligence* supersede *Life*.

Literature Cited

JT Bonner (1980) *The Evolution of Culture in Animals*, Princeton University Press, NJ.

DJ Coffey (1977) *The Encyclopedia of Sea Mammals*, Hart-Davis MacGibbon, London.

NR Franks (1989) Army ants: A collective intelligence, *Am. Sci.* 77:138–145.

J Goodall (1971) *In the Shadow of Man*, Houghton Mifflin, Boston, Mass.

JL Gould and CG Gould (1988) *The Honey Bee*, Scientific American Library, WH Freeman, New York.

DR Griffin (1984) *Animal Thinking*, Harvard University Press, Cambridge, Mass.

BK Hölldobler (1989) in *Life at the Edge* (JL Gould and CG Gould ed), pp. 111–121, WH Freeman, New York.

BK Hölldobler and EO Wilson (1977) Weaver ants, *Sci. Am.* 237(6):146–154.

BK Hölldobler and EO Wilson (1990) *The Ants*, Springer-Verlag, Heidelberg.

HJ Jerison (1986) The perceptual world of dolphins, in *Dolphin Cognition and Behaviour: A Comparative Approach* (RJ Schusterman, JA Thomas and FG Wood ed), pp. 141–166, Lawrence Erlbaum Associates, Hillsdale, NJ.

TC Schneirla and G Piel (1948) The army ant, *Sci. Am.* 178(6):16–23.

RJ Schusterman, JA Thomas and FG Wood (1986) *Dolphin Cognition and Behaviour: A Comparative Approach*, Lawrence Erlbaum Associates, Hillsdale, NJ.

TD Seeley (1989) The honey bee colony as a superorganism, *Am. Sci.* 77:546–553.

AM Wenner (1964) Sound communication in honey bees, *Sci. Am.* 210(4):117–123.

WM Wheeler (1928) *The Social Insects: Their Origin and Evolution*, Kegan Paul, Trench and Trubner, London.

EO Wilson (1971) *The Insect Societies*, Harvard University Press, Cambridge, Mass.

Information Technology, Collective Intelligence and the Evolution of Human Societies

Introduction

One of the best ways of demonstrating the existence and importance of collective intelligence in humans is to contrast the announcement of the discovery of the X-ray in the 1890s with a corresponding event in the 1980s – the announcement of the discovery of the W-boson (as reviewed by Pais 1986). Conrad Roentgen performed the experiment by himself, and his first publication announcing the discovery of X-rays carried only his name as sole author. In contrast, the report providing clear evidence for the existence of the W-boson was signed by 135 authors coming from twelve European and two North American institutions. Furthermore, while the nineteenth-century scientists tended to work in makeshift laboratories of their own making, their late-twentieth-century counterparts tend to work in government- or institution-supported laboratories of great sophistication. The group which announced the discovery of the W-boson working underground at CERN, the European Nuclear Research Centre, required not only the ingenuity and expertise of many hundreds of minds at CERN working on the administrative, technical and scientific aspects, but thousands more working across the world to provide the scientific, technical, administrative, political and financial back-up necessary for so large an enterprise expending hundred of millions of dollars of public funds.

The political decision to spend such large resources on any one particular set of experiments reflects a series of collective decisions involving many governments and other agencies and organisations.

Each government, in turn, represents an example of collective decision making, for even the most authoritarian of modern states involving a single dictator relies on a variety of collective information inputs on the one hand, and the collective administrative implementations on the other. Modern society is designed to analyse and solve problems collectively, and likewise society tends to implement solutions collectively. Over the past ten millennia or so, our human collective intelligence has grown from hunting– gathering bands relying almost entirely on oral communication and relatively simple cultural traditions (ceremonial dances, totem poles, etc.), to contemporary nation states and transnational enterprises such as CERN whose institutions, artefacts and sophisticated methods could (and has) filled whole libraries with books.

Cultural Evolution

One of the major differences between the human species and other organisms is the fact that humans were able to develop an effective collective memory. This was done through developing an oral and subsequently a written cultural tradition which passed information from one generation to the next. This allowed humanity to store and retrieve information across both time and space.

To Herbert Spencer we credit the idea of cultural evolution. His life's work of amassing a huge body of anthropological data, then abstracting and organising it, was not adequately appreciated at the time. His controversial theories became unfashionable. It is gratifying that some anthropologists are making the effort to re-examine his works in depth, and applying modern interpretations to the wealth of information provided by Spencer's studies (see Carneiro 1981).

Culture in the present context is defined as a society's communal database upon which it draws to define belief systems and accepted modes of behaviour patterns. Cultural evolution differs from biological evolution in at least three fundamental respects:

1. It is goal oriented.
2. It can be Lamarckian.
3. Its rate of change is vastly accelerated.

1. The emergence of human consciousness as a result of the evolution of the primate nervous system introduced a discontinuity into the process of evolution. No longer was evolution dependent on random variation, followed by the selection of successful variants. Human cultural evolution became goal oriented. Instead of waiting for the environment to have an impact on the system (in this case human society), the system analysed then altered the environment so as to enhance the system's survivability. After ten thousand years of human cultural evolution, a planet which originally could sustain, at best, several million hominids, now sustains several billion people.

2. Lamarck postulated that the neck of the evolving giraffe became extended because its ancestors had stretched their necks to reach the leaves higher up on the trees. It was the stretched neck, according to Lamarck, which was inherited by all subsequent descendants. In contrast, Darwin and Wallace derived the great insight that the variations in biological systems were random. It was the selection of successful variants which gave evolving systems their apparent direction: Giraffes with longer necks had a higher chance of survival, therefore were more likely to reproduce.

In contrast to biological evolution, in human cultural evolution, the Lamarckian mechanism *can* operate. If an individual wishing to get to the top of a tree invents a ladder, then all descendants of that individual can use that ladder. Hence "the inheritance of *acquired* characters" – a heresy in biological evolution – is a basic feature of cultural evolution.

3. This also accounts for the speed of cultural evolution: Instead of bumbling around for generations, relying on random variations which only incrementally solve the mismatch between a biological system and its environment (in this case short-necked ungulates and tall trees), goal-oriented cultural evolution allows a non-incremental solution (eg, a ladder) to appear in one generation.

Richard Dawkins (1976) has suggested that specific ideas, beliefs or technologies are transmitted within the context of human culture as discrete entities he calls "memes". The transmission of memes parallels the transmission of genes in the context of biological systems; that is, selection favours memes which exploit their cultural environment, being in competition always with other memes. If nothing else, Dawkins' suggestion provides a conceptual tool for analysing at least one mechanism of human cultural evolution – always keeping in mind the profound difference between the origin of new genes, by mutation brought about by environmental agents external to the system (such as cosmic radiation), and the origin of new memes, arising internally from a goal-oriented intelligent system (human culture) attempting to master its environment.

The Role of Information Technology in Cultural Evolution

Since the dawn of humanity, social evolution has been driven by technological evolution (Stonier 1981). What makes information technology (IT) so interesting theoretically is that, from here on in, IT will drive technological evolution just as technology has been driving social evolution.

Kenneth Cooper, chief executive of the British Library, has been quoted (1986) as saying that in his generation, academics' lives were revolutionised by three developments – jet travel, direct telephone dialling and photocopying. Cooper expects the information revolution to have a more profound impact yet.

Not only in academia is the emergence of adaptable, cost-effective communication devices producing changes in the modes of operation. Virtually all large businesses and industries have discovered that effective decision-making requires more and more people – often flung across the globe. Productive processes are no longer confined to a single nation, but tend to rely on components produced by many countries. Likewise, the financial structures of the world are now all based on systems which favour a rapid and irresistible global flow of money. The key to the rapid development of new telecommunication systems during the last quarter of the twentieth century is the increasingly close interrelationship between information, communications and economic activity. What the French call "telematique" (telecommunications plus automatic data handling) has become paramount in commerce and industry.

By the end of the 1980s, among the most significant of developments was the fact that magnetic disk technology was approaching the critical cross-over point where it had become cheaper to hold the contents of a sheet of paper on a disk rather than on the paper. In the 1990s, laser disks promised a hundred-fold, if not a thousand-fold, reduction in the storage cost coupled with a hundred-fold increase in capacity. Not only will storage continue to become cheaper, but the time to access any chunk of such information can now be measured in milliseconds, that is, it has become comparable to the time it takes to recall information inside our heads.

These developments will trigger off a bigger upheaval in the way we handle information than any since the invention of printing. Humans have for centuries stored information outside their skulls – in filing cabinets, books, and so on. But the access time was exceedingly slow. There will come a time, early in the next century, when there will be no technical obstacles to putting the contents of the entire British Library (including pictures) on a set of optical disks or comparable devices. Both individually, and collectively, human beings will have increased substantially their effective intelligence.

China and Europe: A Case Study in Collective Intelligence

It has always been a mystery why at some time around the seventeenth century Europe began to outpace the other great ancient civilisations such as China. If one looks at the technological achievements of the Chinese by the beginning of the present millennium, they were indeed remarkable. During the Middle Ages, European culture acquired from China a wide range of technologies, either directly or indirectly – rice, the wheel-barrow, the cross-bow, gunpowder, the compass, paper and the printing press, to name but a few. The Silk Route from Xi'an in western China to Venice in southern Europe was a great facilitator not only of an exchange of goods, but also of ideas. For example, the first "fancy" loom, the *Chinese draw loom*, probably entered southern Europe via the Silk Route.

Added to the above were the Mongol conquests, which, after the conquest of China, spread Chinese technology across Asia to the gates of Europe. It was Chinese engineers working for Genghis Khan, for example, who brought down the Arabs, the best armed and most proficient armed force of the time, by flooding the valley of battle – causing the heavily armoured horses and riders of the Arabs to struggle in the quagmire while the light Mongol horsemen rode circles around them.

Had the Portuguese ventured into the Indian Ocean a century earlier, they would have encountered a superior Chinese navy, which, however, had been withdrawn for political and economic reasons by the time the Portuguese ventured around the Cape of Good Hope.

Not only during Europe's Middle Ages, but very much earlier did China exhibit its enormous technological capability. The Grand Canal, opened in AD 610 took about a thousand years to build and extended well over a thousand miles from Beijing to south of Shanghai. A uniform forty paces wide, cutting across both the Yangtze and Yellow Rivers, it incorporated many technological features not seen in Europe for another thousand years. Perhaps the oldest known instance of biological control of insect pests is recorded in the Guangzhou (Canton) area well over 1,500 years ago: Colonies of weaver ants would be collected, sold and installed in citrus fruit groves to clear the area of other, damaging insects (Hölldobler and Wilson 1977). China's agricultural practices were unexcelled.

Another example of early Chinese high technology may be viewed inside Beijing's Museum of Chinese History, facing Tiananmen Square, which contains a model of a seismograph invented by the scholar Zhang Heng in AD 132. Still earlier, in the third century BCE, Emperor Qin, best known in the West for the grandiose army of terracotta soldiers unearthed at his tomb, built the Great Wall of China – reputedly the only human artefact visible from the moon – as well as the Lingqu Canal, and the Dujiangyan irrigation system (actually started around 250 BCE) which watered the fertile plains of Sechuan and is still in use today, twenty-two centuries later. Emperor Qin, who by conquest united all of China in the third century BCE, probably built the Lingqu Canal for military purposes. However, by connecting the Haiyang and Lijang Rivers, he tied the Yangtze River system to the Pearl River system, thereby assuring the economic integration of South China into the rest of the country.

Silk weaving, according to legend, dates back to the year 2640 BCE when the Empress Hsi Ling Shi wove a robe for her husband, Huang Ti. The list of examples demonstrating both the power and the antiquity of Chinese technology goes on and on. The question arises, therefore: How is it that after about the seventeenth century, Europe managed to outpace China?

A number of explanations have been put forward: One of these points to the turmoil of seventeenth century China. This can hardly be an explanation if one considers the Protestant/Catholic fratricide of Europe's Thirty Years' War, a war which, in part, involved an eighty-year conflict between Holland and Spain (both ended by the Peace of Westphalia in 1648). On top of that, add the British Civil War, and the Imperial conflicts involving Holland, France and England later in the seventeenth century.

The opposite explanation has also been suggested: China was a large, integrated country not subject to the incessant warfare which characterised Europe. Therefore its science and technology did not receive the competitive stimulus which its European counterpart did. This probably contains some, but not much truth: Galileo was a military engineer studying the trajectories of cannon balls. However, Europeans had been battering each other for millennia; there is no evidence that during the first millennium AD when China was relatively peaceful, while Europe was an incessant battle-ground, that progress in Europe's science and technology was in any way keeping up with China.

A third explanation makes more sense: By the late Middle Ages, mercantilism had taken over in much of Europe. Trading between groups is one of the chief facilitators of flows of ideas. Probably the movement of goods inside China was at least as extensive as that inside Europe. However there was one major difference between trade within China and trade within Europe: The ruling aristocracy of China, perhaps recognising a potential threat when they saw one, ensured that China's merchant class had no power and no prestige. Being a merchant was a lowly profession, looked down upon. In contrast, the late Middle Ages saw the rise of a powerful merchant class in Europe which, by the middle of the seventeenth century, had acquired enormous prestige.

The important role of status in transferring new ideas is best illustrated in an experiment conducted on monkeys: Monkeys caught in the wild were trained to operate a "banana vending machine". After having acquired the skill of obtaining bananas from the machine, individual monkeys were released among the original troop along with the vending machine. The trained monkey operated the machine in the wild. If it was a high status monkey, the rest of the troop watched carefully and other monkeys rapidly learned the technique. If the trained monkey was of low status, however, the troop never learned – the more senior monkeys just took away the bananas.

This experiment should be considered as an allegory – comparing the flows of technology transfer in seventeenth-century Europe with that of China.

There is, however, a much more important factor which contributed to the accelerating pace of Europe's science and technology – the *printing press*! For Europe (unlike for China), the introduction of printing represented a major new form of information technology, greatly increasing the capacity of human collective intelligence. Although Johann Gutenberg is frequently credited with the invention of the printing press in the 1440s, the technology had existed for some time in Europe and Asia. Gutenberg perfected certain aspects but it was a technology already so widely diffused that within thirty years there were 236 printing presses in Italy (Venice became a major printing centre), 78 in Germany and 68 elsewhere. By 1500 the number of printing presses in Europe had more than doubled again. During the sixteenth century, publishing became distinct from printing. Antwerp, already a major trading centre, also became a centre of book publishing, where the firm of Plantin possessed twenty-two presses and employed up to 160 workmen – a major industrial enterprise for the early sixteenth century. Actually, Plantin received some of its working capital from King Philip II, so that it was an early version of Her Majesty's Stationary Office (HMSO), the Government Printing Office. The same could be said of the Aldime Press in Venice, which was patronised by the Pope, and Estienne, the French publisher, subsidised by the French kings.

The most important books in terms of size of editions consisted of books of devotion: Catholic breviaries, or the Huguenot Psalter, which in 1569 involved an edition of 35,000 copies. In the long run, of greatest significance were school books like Erasmus' *Colloquia* for Latin students, or the De Villedieu's *Doctrinal* for teaching grammar, textbooks such as Besson's *Theatre of Instruments*, and others written by Ramelli, Veranzio, Branca and Zonca connecting the arts and crafts of the classical period. Even more important were the new works on metallurgy, mining and chemical technology by Biringuccio, Agricola, Ercker and Lohneiss. Unlike their medieval predecessors, the craftsmen of the late sixteenth century were in a position to consult the descriptions and instructions of their colleagues all across Europe.

It is also doubtful whether a Royal Society could have been founded and flourished if printing scientific papers were not a mature technology.

Printing presses had existed in China and the Far East long before they entered Europe. The Korean Pavilion at Expo '86 in Vancouver, exhibited such a press, which pre-dated Gutenberg by well over a century. It also exhibited a manuscript produced by this press – and therein lay the clue as to why the printing press proved so important to Europe's collective intelligence and remained so insignificant to China's: It takes many years of dedicated study to learn to read a pictographic language such as Chinese. The K'anghsi dictionary of Chinese in AD 1716 listed 40,545 characters (Ong 1982). To become truly literate in Chinese normally took twenty years. Only Mandarins and scholars could invest such an amount of time. In contrast, in late medieval Europe a universal phonetic language – Latin – consisting of twenty-six letters (plus ten digits for Arabic numerals) was a natural for the printing press. It was possible to learn to read in a matter of weeks. Thus not only was the Church composed of members (including monks) who were generally literate, much of the aristocracy and merchant class, became literate as well. Furthermore, scribes who could read and write became cheap and plentiful. The European printing presses rapidly found a large market for their output.

Europe's collective intelligence, then, achieved two major advances denied the Chinese. First, printed texts could move information around much more accurately and faster by producing many copies simultaneously, and at the same time, act as an important information store – a collective memory. Secondly, *mercantilism* acted as an increasingly effective vehicle for technology transfer; that is, mercantilism greatly improved the trans-European nervous system, shunting information and new ideas across the length and breadth of Europe.

If the emergence of a superior collective intelligence following the Renaissance in Europe accounted for its eventual ascendency over the rest of the world – including China – China's older successes must also be ascribed to their earlier superior collective intelligence. Such a case is easy to make: Following Qin's unification of China, the great Han Dynasty (206 BCE to AD 220), selected highly educated bureaucrats by competitive exams, established a university at the capital Xi'an, and encouraged intellectuals. With the invention of paper, new ideas were spread across the country.

It may be appropriate to mention at this point that there is no evidence to indicate that *individual* Chinese or European intelligence is superior, one over the other. Contrast, however, the efficiency of spreading ideas by means of handwritten manuscripts among a tiny elite of literati in Ancient China, with the mass spread of the printed word to the vast majority of ruling, clerical and commercial groups, in seventeenth- and eighteenth-century

Europe. By the late nineteenth century, mass-literacy was a basic tenet of western culture and accounted for its success both in military and economic terms: Armies of illiterate peasants or horsemen were never a match for armies consisting of soldiers able to read instructions and commands. To operate and maintain the advanced machinery of death requires a literate soldiery. On the civilian side, the same may be said for the quality of the labour forces which underpin all economies.

The ascendencies of cultures, one over the other, in the past has been largely a question of luck, determined by the availability of natural resources plus the effective utilisation of technology. The latter both reflected the status, and contributed to the growth, of a culture's collective intelligence.

BP: Before Printing

In focusing on the importance of the printing press as a piece of intellectual technology which contributed so greatly to the collective intelligence of European society, we should not lose sight of the profound impact on human society made by the precursors of the printed word – the alphabet, the written word, and human speech itself.

At the time of this writing, the sequence of events following the emergence of the original human mother language – *proto-World* – appears to be as follows (see review by Shevoroshkin 1990): On the basis of archaeological finds, coupled to a basic analysis of human DNA strands, it would appear that modern *Homo sapiens* (ie, *Homo sapiens sapiens*) originated in East Africa around 100,000 years ago. It is about this time that proto-World was spoken. These early, modern humans began to migrate, and the languages which evolved from proto-World – first as dialects, then as discrete languages – conform strikingly to the migratory paths taken by our early ancestors.

The first split involved the Khoisan-speaking people – the Hottentots, Bushmen and other tribes of southern Africa – the oldest linguistic phylum of them all. A second split resulted in Congo-Saharan, accounting for the peoples of central and northern Africa. Probably by 35,000 years ago a derivative of proto-World was evolving among the settlers of the Middle East to give rise to other, later proto-languages includes Nostratic, Sino-Caucasian, Austric, Indo-Pacific and Amerind. This last was spoken by the earliest migrants from Asia into America, some 12,000 years ago. A later wave, about 9,000 years ago, spoke a Sino-Caucasian derivative called Na-dene. Last to arrive, about 6,000 years ago, were the Eskimo-Aleutians who spoke a language akin to Altaic, a derivative of that ancient Middle East proto-language Nostratic. Altaic gave rise to Japanese, Korean and Turkic. Nostratic existed 14,000 years ago and, over the next 4,000 years, gave rise not only to Altaic in the Far East, but Uralic to the north, Indo-European to a broad band from Europe to India, and Afro-Asiatic, locally. Afro-Asiatic gave rise to Semitic, the precursor of Hebrew and Arabic. By 3,000 years ago, the Indo-European family had fragmented into five major language groups in Europe (Baltic, Slavic, Italic, Teutonic and Celtic), and in Persia and India, Iranian and Indic, each of which in turn gave rise to about 20 languages. Over the past two millennia, the Teutonic tribes of Europe's north and west fragmented further linguistically, into Gothic (extinct), German, Danish, Norwegian, Swedish, Icelandic, Dutch and English. Similar events took place in other parts of the world, accounting for the ethnic diversity of the many thousands of peoples and languages found on this planet.

Human speech emerged only after a long evolutionary process. Philip Lieberman, Professor of Cognitive and Linguistic Sciences at Brown University, has reviewed (1988) the stepwise, mutual stimulation and integration of brain development and vocal anatomy which occurred during the past several hundred thousand years, and which must have preceded the full flowering of human speech.

All apes, as well as human infants under the age of three months, lack the anatomical structures required for the full range of human speech sounds. This inability reflects mainly the location of the voice box – the larynx – which is situated high in the throat of these inarticulate groups, and low in adult humans. As Lieberman emphasises: "So critical is the overall configuration of the vocal tract to the generation of formant frequencies that only when the voice box has retreated into the throat is the capacity for speech virtually certain". Every mammal except *Homo sapiens* can breathe and drink at the same time. This useful facility is brought about by a larynx high in the throat which connects the nasal passage directly to the trachea – the windpipe – leading to the lungs, while food and water slosh around it on the way from the mouth to the oesophagus (which funnels the liquid down to the stomach). This blessing, of being able to drink and breathe at the same time, is extended to human infants for the first few months of their lives, when they haven't, as yet, got much to say for themselves.

In contrast, human adults, whose larynxes have retreated down into the throat, choke to death by the hundreds each year. Nature is never as careless as all that: There would be no selection in favour of some deleterious trait, unless that trait proved to provide strong selective advantage in some other way. In the case of the descending larynx, it is clear that in humans the relative importance of the two functions of the organ – which in mammals was primarily designed to facilitate drinking and only secondarily to act as a voice box – became reversed. There was strong selective pressure on the ability to modulate sound and thus articulate speech. In the present author's view, it seems highly improbable that such selective pressure would have been very strong, if there hadn't already existed a substantial system of communication and signalling. Such a system might well have been augmented by *miming*, which transcended the sophisticated signalling among higher primates, as part of their advanced social intelligence.

Mime, followed by speech, extended the *social* intelligence of the hominids into an increasingly effective *collective* intelligence.

Not only did the larynx move down into the throat, but the tongue also moved back, while the jaw shortened and lost some teeth. The mouth, therefore, became less efficient for eating, and better adapted for talking – another indicator that nature was putting a premium on speech.*

While the throat was evolving into an ever more efficient vocal apparatus, the brain, likewise, was evolving. For example, the manipulation of the throat and mouth muscles is centred in the frontal cortex of mammals. In apes, the motor area which controls these muscles is located towards the rear of the left side of the lateral frontal cortex, approximately where Broca's area is located

---

* For those who are offended by the teleological nature of these statements, please remember that any "motivation" ascribed to Nature represents a literary device. The concept of Nature is a human construct, largely referring to the universe outside of humanity, and certainly cannot be said to possess motivation. However, evolution is a real phenomenon occurring in the universe outside of humanity; hence, Nature exhibits evolution. Since the process of evolution is dependent on the sub-processes of variation and selection it may be imprecise, but not wrong, to say that "Nature selects for this . . . ", or "Nature does that . . .".

in the human brain. Broca's area is named after the French neurologist who discovered it back in 1861: People with lesions in this area, are unable to produce all the vowels and consonants which comprise human speech. Broca's area must have evolved into a refined speech controller from its earlier, primate function as a more crude controller of the throat and mouth musculature. As Lieberman states categorically: "Chomsky notwithstanding, the neural mechanisms associated with language have a counterpart in the brains of our predecessors".

Human speech gave its inventors an enormous advantage over their mute cousins. This shows up in the fossil record. *Homo sapiens sapiens*, originating in East Africa, invaded Europe and displaced Neanderthal man – not a stupid creature, but whose grunts were no match for the articulated instructions of his modern cousins. As Lieberman points out, vocal tracts as such do not leave a fossil record. However, the anatomy of the human speech apparatus is such that it requires a greater bend at the base of the skull. In contrast, "a straighter, unflexed basicranium is the hallmark of a non-human vocal tract. This is true for the skull of Neanderthal man . . . indicating that . . . that hominid was incapable of human speech" (Lieberman 1988). The oldest known skulls exhibiting a highly flexed basicranium were excavated from the 150,000-year-old Broken Hill site in Zambia. This is consistent with the idea that proto-World was spoken in East Africa around 100,000 years ago.

Why was human speech so important to the evolution of humanity? Because human speech had introduced a whole new dimension into the human collective intelligence. It represented a major discontinuity in the evolution of intelligence. The depth of its impact can be fathomed by looking at its effect: Human speech allowed communication across generations so that a store of collective wisdom could be built up much more rapidly than by other means (such as learning by imitation). Cultural evolution now became more important than biological evolution; the meme superseded the gene. In fact, it is likely that the great increase in brain size of the later hominids represented the high selective value placed on those of our proto-human ancestors who could learn and remember words, then articulate phrases and sentences. It was a time when the poet ascended over the brute.

The improvement in the collective intelligence brought about by the acquisition of human speech accelerated the pace of all forms of technological evolution. Human speech must have set the stage for the more effective domestication of plants and animals, one of the

most profound of technologies – the basis of the Neolithic
Revolution – which could assure a family a steady, year-round food
supply. Colin Renfrew (1989) has effectively argued that the spread
of the Indo-European language from Anatolia about 8,500 years
ago, was associated with the spread of farming: Farming tribes could
have increased their population density fifty-fold over the one
person per 10 square kilometres characteristic of hunter – gatherers.
Crowding out the technologically less developed tribes was
inevitable except where local strongholds allowed the earlier
indigenous people enough breathing space to assimilate the new
technologies, yet retain their original culture and language. This
could account for the pockets of non-Indo-European languages such
as Basque in the mountains of Northern Spain and Southern France,
which is a derivative of proto-North Caucasian, and which implies a
prehistoric migration about 4,000 years ago from Asia Minor
(Shevoroshkin 1990).

The Invention of Writing

The invention of a visual, "written" representation of words and
ideas occurred many times, but always in association with advanced,
late or post-Neolithic cultures: The first known, was that of the
Sumerians in Mesopotamia around 5,500 years ago. Human beings
had been drawing pictures for countless millennia as mnemonic
aids, for magical or religious purposes, and perhaps just for
aesthetic reasons. Such pictures differ, however, from script which,
as Walter J. Ong (1982) has pointed out: "is a representation of an
utterance, of words that someone says or is imagined to say" [p. 84].
Ong reviews the multiple origin of scripts [pp. 85–86]: Mesopotamia
cuneiform, 3,500 BCE; Egyptian hieroglyphics, 3,000 BCE; Minoan or
Mycenaean "Linear B", 1,200 BCE; Indus Valley script,
3,000–2,400 BCE; Chinese script, 1,500 BCE; Mayan script, AD 50;
Aztec script, AD 1,400. Ong stresses the importance of the written,
in contrast to the spoken, word: The spoken word is transient:
"When I pronounce the word 'permanence', by the time I get to the
'-nence', the 'perma-' is gone . . ." [p. 32]. You cannot "look up"
spoken words. But you can the written word.
     However, the written word was not brought to the full flowering
of its usefulness until the invention of the alphabet. Ong points out

[p. 89]: "The most remarkable fact about the alphabet no doubt is that it was invented only once". This occurred around 1,500 BCE in the Middle East. The Semitic people who invented it utilised only consonants and omitted the vowels, which could be inferred from the context. This was an ingenious method of compressing the text, but it made it much more difficult to learn.

It was the Greeks who created the modern alphabet by modifying the earlier Semitic alphabet to include vowels. This step caused a "democratising" of writing – it became easy for everyone to learn (Ong 1982, p. 90). Citing earlier work by Havelock (1976), Ong stresses that the development of this intellectual tool – this efficient transformation of transient spoken words to permanent record – "gave ancient Greek culture its intellectual ascendancy over other ancient cultures".

This is consistent with the concepts explored above, and represents one of Ong's main themes [p. 85]: Writing is not only important in its own right, but it "transforms speech and thought as well". As such, he considers: "Writing . . . was and is the most momentous of all human technological inventions".

Today, one can forecast the future success of a country by examining the systems comprising its collective intelligence. This includes its communication and transportation systems (eg, its per capita telephone statistics), its information storage and retrieval systems (eg, the number of its libraries and on-line databases), its funding of science and research, and, in particular, the vigour of its education system.

The Communicative Era*

One cannot fathom the deeper currents of human history without understanding the growth and development of collective intelligence.

In this century, the electronic revolution created a range of devices which extended the human nervous system: Radio and telephone became a long-distance extension of the ear; film, initially

---

* The material covered in this section has been extensively explored by the author in earlier works (see in particular Stonier 1983, 1985).

an extension of sight, became coupled to sound, while television, from the beginning, represented an extension of both. Finally, the computer emerged as an extension of the brain.

The electronic revolution set the stage for further developments in microelectronics. Under the impact of these new technologies western society has moved into a new era of human history: The communicative era.

This era is characterised by the following features:

1. There exists a highly developed and sophisticated communications/information infrastructure. This includes television, radio, telephones, tape-recorders, electronic databases – a host of new, or improved communication technologies. In addition, communication is further facilitated by an elaborate transportation system which allows a large number of people to move in and out, as well as within, any given country.

2. The economic manifestations of the communicative era can be summarised by the term "post-industrial", or to be more precise, the "information economy". The "knowledge industry" is the most rapidly growing sector, which has begun to dominate all other economic activities. The labour force is characterised by an increasingly higher percentage of information operatives, who now vastly exceed not only the number of those working on farms, but also those working in factories.

3. The social and political manifestations of the above are, first, an increasingly peaceful society, both intra-nationally and internationally; second, an increased tendency towards democratisation and consensus decision making.

4. As countries move deeper into the communicative era, virtually every cultural institution is affected by changes in outlook and belief systems. These include not only such institutions as war and the state, but also religion, the role of work, education, the family, sex mores, etc.

The new information/communications technology is changing business practices profoundly. It will alter the relationship between home and work. Similarly it will alter the relationship between home and school. Education itself will be profoundly affected: In addition to computers providing new pedagogic techniques (such as computer-assisted learning) and a variety of intellectual aids (such as pocket calculators or word processors), information technology will make available new sources of information and new modes of discovering things (see review by Stonier and Conlin, 1985).

The function of libraries will change. Libraries will become a part of integrated information and communications systems. Such computer-based networks will allow the transmission of text, voice, graphics, pictures, documents, etc. Electronic mail and electronic newspapers will become part of such systems.

Although these systems will initially be developed and used by libraries, archives, universities, government offices and commercial organisations, as the price drops, they will ultimately end up in every home. Therefore the relationship between libraries and the general public will change. For example, as a source of specific bits of information, libraries will become increasingly bypassed as home computers tie into global databases. At the same time, librarians will have to become increasingly sophisticated because their role will be more and more that of epistemologists and information theorists on the one hand, and knowledge counsellors on the other.

The Emerging Global Nervous System

The introduction of solid state microelectronics has meant that all forms of traditional electronic communications devices such as radios, television sets, telephones, etc. have been made more reliable, easier to maintain and operate, more durable, less breakable, less power consuming, faster to operate, more precise, more efficient, lighter and cheaper. The upshot has been a profusion of communications devices all over the world – television aerials protruding from thatched Thai River houses, transistor radios blaring from Nepalese hamlets in the Himalayas, video tapes sold in corner shops in virtually every major city – with global television emerging in the 1980s under the impact of cheaper video recording systems, cable TV, and satellite with increasingly cheap home antennas linking up signals. In the meantime, the world's telephone system has been doubling with each passing decade.

All of this has brought about the emergence of Marshall McLuhan's "Global Village". The Global Village concept can be illustrated by the following anecdote: In 1985 there was a tragic fire in a football stadium in Bradford in the north of England. Almost 60 lives were lost. The author's home was about half a mile from the scene of that fire, yet he knew much less about it than his son in New York who had seen it on television within a couple of hours of the event – and so had his daughter in Paris. A student staying at the university, about a mile from the scene of the accident, heard about it from her parents in Italy, who telephoned that evening to make sure that she was all right. The details of the event were known all over the world much faster than people were able to gather them locally.

Similarly, when the Space Shuttle "Challenger" exploded shortly after launch, the entire world was shocked and shared the grief of the people at Cape Kennedy who had watched the explosion. In both instances, the global nervous system informed a global collective intelligence. It tended to be a predominantly *national* collective intelligence which investigated the accidents and sought to prevent similar recurrences. However, even the national collective intelligence was augmented by advice from other nations, and the Bradford Fund for the relief of the victims and their families received donations from all over the world.

The world of finance represents another, very different, aspect of the globalisation brought about by the creation of a global nervous network. The flow of money, trade and finance represents an interactive system which includes the money market, the international monetary fund, petro dollars, stock markets around the world, etc. Banks and stock markets no longer move around money: They move around computerised information – no longer limited in any significant way by national boundaries. The magnitude of these flows was indicated already in 1984 when Henry Wallich, Governor of the US Federal Reserve Bank, reported that the daily transactions in the New York foreign exchange market in 1983 amounted to $26 billion – twice the US daily gross national products and ten times America's daily exports plus imports. It is not surprising therefore, that by the early 1980s, the French economist, Albert Bressand came to describe the "Worldeconomy" as a global cybernetic system.

The Emerging Global Brain

The Automatic Subject Citation Alert (ASCA) run by the Institute for Scientific Information in Philadelphia constitutes an enormous aid to scholars all over the world. It peruses the journals of the world and provides an alert to scientists and other scholars whenever a key word emerges in the title of a journal article, whenever an author has published such an article, or when certain key authors are cited in the back of the article. A scholar's own name may be included as key author, on the theory that anyone who publishes a paper citing his or her name is likely to be covering a topic of interest to the scholar. As a result of this entry it becomes possible to become aware of articles in obscure journals in all parts of the world.

We alluded earlier to the importance of the development of an oral, and subsequently written, cultural tradition passing information from one generation to the next. This process, in due course, became institutionalised. In western Europe, for example, monasteries, churches, archives, museums, universities and libraries became a part of, and reinforced, cultural traditions. Most of these technologies also developed in other advanced civilisations around the world.

The above institutions represented a means of storing and retrieving information but not necessarily of organising or developing it. This changed with the advent of professional librarians whose job it was to take information and organise it into logical categories. It was this step of organising information in libraries and archives which improved the retrieval capabilities and hence the overall efficiency of the collective brain.

As we are all aware, there has been an enormous improvement in the last few years with the emergence of storage systems which not only allow more information to be stored per unit space, but more importantly the use of computers to help in the retrieval of such stored information.

The emergence of computer-based literature searches represents the next step in moving from a simple, dumb memory to the kind of searching for interrelated information which represents one of the basic steps in higher forms of thinking. The improvement in having the literature searched by computer, looking for key words and key authors, has been of enormous help to practising scientists overwhelmed by the information explosion.

By adding inference machines to databases we create expert systems. The fact that organic chemists can consult molecular structures is another example of databases becoming increasingly sophisticated. It also represents a form of mechanised information analysis which previously occurred only inside of people's heads.

The linking of a multitude of databases, both across disciplines and across countries, coupled to the rise of transnational expert systems, constitutes the emergence of an increasingly efficient global brain.

The application of such artificial intelligence techniques will mean that for human beings a lot of information can be pre-sorted and pre-digested in a way that will aid decision making. Increasingly, human beings will rely on the equivalent of a global brain to do some of the preliminary thinking for them.

The analysis of complex systems, such as the weather, is increasingly depend on computers. Computers linked to monitoring systems consisting of weather satellites, ground and air measurements plus a global picture coupled to a reasonable theory of weather formation represent a major improvement in weather forecasting. This is merely continuing a process that has been going on for some time, and can be used as a model for the further evolution of a global brain.

At the moment, among the most advanced of these forms of technology is to be found in the military. The superpowers are able to maintain a global monitoring system that allows military officers to draw on a wealth of real time information. Coupled to computer-aided decision making, battlefields have become electronic battlefields, both at the tactical and the strategic level. With "star wars" systems, the electronic battlefield will have become global.

Much of the military use of the new information/communication technology involves simulation. Simulation has also been used in the civilian sector in, for example, training airline pilots. As global machine intelligence systems continue to evolve they will be able to simulate more and more complex issues – Not only the weather, or the metabolism of the human cell, but also complex economic and political systems. Increasingly, then, decision making at governmental levels will rely on the use of machine intelligence.

What one hopes for is that these separate brains will tend to coalesce so as to provide governments and other decision makers with a global rather than a parochial picture, and a global rather than a parochial approach to solving problems. It is true at the moment that the world seems to be divided into competing political and economic groups. However, an objective evaluation of what has been happening in the world with the emergence of communicative society shows that there are very strong integrative pressures working towards a genuinely global society. Among the strongest of these is the integration of trans-national electronic information/ machine intelligence systems.

The merging of computers and telecommunications into a highly efficient global network constitutes what George Bugliarello (1988) calls an extensive synergistic brain – a "hyperbrain". Bugliarello, president of the Polytechnic University, defines the hyperbrain as "an advanced global telecommunications and information network, with each terminal constituted by an intelligent station". Each node, rather than being a neuron, is a person comprising trillions of neurons. In due course, each person will be coupled not only to their personal computers, but also – as a logical outcome of human societal organisation – to thousands of other such human–machine intelligence nodes.

Once we understand the concept of collective intelligence, we can discern the emergence on this planet of a *global* intelligence. It will be made up of an ever-increasing number of nodes consisting of a mix of machine and human (both individual and collective) intelligence. It is the emerging global electronic network, acting as a global nervous system, which will integrate these nodes. In principle, this process does not differ from the evolution of primitive nervous systems into advanced mammalian brains: Relatively few nerve cells, relatively poorly co-ordinated, evolving into an organ consisting of trillions of cells so exquisitely co-ordinated that our understanding of how it works still eludes us. With the evolution of the global brain we are dealing with a parallel process, but at a much higher level of complexity: We are now dealing with the very top end of the known spectrum of intelligence.

We will discuss this matter in further detail in subsequent chapters. However, we might just pause a moment to pay tribute to one of the great minds of the late nineteenth and early twentieth century – H.G. Wells – who clearly foresaw emerging what he called "the mind of the race". In his day, terms like "information technology" did not exist. It was long before computers appeared, and well before anyone was even thinking about information as an abstract entity. Yet, one form of information technology was thoroughly familiar to all – literature – and Wells understood fully its significance: "it is no doubt true that literature is a kind of overmind of the race. . ." (Wells 1915, p.167).

Literature Cited

M Boden (1987) Artificial intelligence: cannibal or missionary? *AI & Society* 1(1):17–23.

A Bressand (1983) Mastering the "Worldeconomy", *Foreign Affairs* 61(4):745–772.

L Bugliarello (1988) Toward hyperintelligence, *Knowledge: Creation, Diffusion, Utilization* 10(1):67–89.

RL Carneiro (1981) Herbert Spencer as an anthropologist, *J. Libertarian Stud.* 5(2): 153–210.

K Cooper (1986) quoted in *The Times Higher Education Supplement* 11 April 1986, p. 11.

R Dawkins (1976) Memes and the evolution of culture, *New Sci.* 72:208–210.

R Forsyth and C Naylor (1985) *The Hitch-Hiker's Guide to Artificial Intelligence*, Chapman and Hall/Methuen, London.

NR Franks (1989) Army ants: A collective intelligence, *Am. Sci.* 77:138–145.

EA Havelock (1976) *Origins of Western Literacy*, Ontario Institute for Studies in Education, Toronto.

WD Hillis (1985) *The Connection Machine*, The MIT Press, Cambridge, Mass.

BK Hölldobler and EO Wilson (1977) Weaver ants, *Sci. Am.* 237(6):146–154.

P Lieberman (1988) Voice in the wilderness, *The Sciences*, New York Acad. Sci. July/Aug 1988, pp. 23–29.

GA Miller and PM Gildea (1987) How children learn words, *Sci. Am.* 257(3):86–91.

WJ Ong (1982) *Orality and Literacy – The Technologizing of the Word*, Methuen, London.

A Pais (1986) *Inward Bound*, Clarendon Press, Oxford.

C Renfrew (1989) The origins of Indo-European languages, *Sci. Am.* 261(4):106–114.

V Shevoroshkin (1990) How linguists have reconstructed the ancestor of all living languages, *The Sciences*, New York Acad. Sci. May/June 1990, pp. 20–27.

T Stonier (1981) The natural history of humanity: past, present and future, *Int. J. Man–Machine Stud.* 14:91-122.

T Stonier (1983) *The Wealth of Information: A Profile of the Post-Industrial Economy*, Thames/Methuen, London.

T Stonier (1984) Computer psychology, *Educational and Child Psychol.* 1(2):16–27.

T Stonier (1985) *The Communicative Society: A New Era in Human History*, Gold Paper No. 5, The Foundation for Public Relation Research and Education, London.

T Stonier (1986a) Towards a new theory of information, *Telecom. Policy* 10(4):278–281.

T Stonier (1986b) What is information? in *Research and Development in Expert Systems III* (MA Bramer ed), pp. 217–230, Cambridge University Press.

T Stonier (1989) Towards a general theory of information II: Information and entropy, *Aslib Proc.* 41(2):41–55.

T Stonier and C Conlin (1985) *The Three Cs: Children, Computers and Communication*, John Wiley and Sons, Chichester.

HG Wells (1915) *Boon, The Mind of the Race, The Wild Asses of the Devil, and The Last Trump*, T. Fisher Unwin, London.

· 6 ·

The Evolution of Machine Intelligence

Introduction

The idea that machines may possess intelligence reflects our collective historical experience with computers. Both the term "machine intelligence" and the term "artificial intelligence" are derived from work with computers. The contemporary conception is that computers show the possibility of engaging in intelligent behaviour, and when they do, we will have created an artificial intelligence – an intelligence based on information processing carried out by machines. Thus Marvin Minsky (1968) defines "artificial intelligence" as: "the science of making machines do things that would require intelligence if done by men".

Some experts working in the field consider that we already possess computer systems which exhibit intelligence. Others deny this strenuously.

Joseph Weizenbaum, for example, one of the computer community's most thoughtful commentators, has argued that: "an entirely too simplistic notion of intelligence has dominated both popular and scientific thought, and that this notion is, in part, responsible for permitting artificial intelligence's perverse grand fantasy to grow" (1984, p. 203).

At the other extreme, Donald Michie, also known for his pioneering work and philosophical considerations, writes jointly with Rory Johnston: "it has been demonstrated incontrovertibly that something new can come out of computers, and that new something is knowledge. That knowledge, in turn, can be original ideas, strategies and solutions to real problems" (1985, p. 12).

Writing in the late 1970s, Christopher Evans considered the intelligence of the computers of his time to be: "substantially above a tapeworm but still . . . below the earwig" (1979, p. 170); while, by the mid-1980s, Richard Forsyth, in reviewing machine learning, concludes with the statement: "The age of the creative computer is about to begin" (1986, p. 223).

Obviously the matter is still open to interpretation.

The position taken in the present work is as follows: Intelligence manifests itself as intelligent behaviour. There can be no intelligent behaviour without information processing. However, not all information processing involves intelligent behaviour. Intelligent behaviour has been defined in the first chapter of the present work. On this basis one can show that not only do some computers exhibit intelligent behaviour, but that *all computers possess proto-intelligence*. Furthermore, there have existed for centuries devices which exhibit proto-intelligence, and some which could be classed as genuinely intelligent.

Early Machine Intelligence

To some extent, all machines and devices designed to replace or augment human skills exhibit proto-intelligence. Take one of the earliest of human inventions – animal traps and snares. Here were systems designed to analyse their environment (detect the presence of an animal), then respond to it (by releasing the trapping mechanism), thereby fulfilling the system's goal.

The first town clocks appearing in the fourteenth century were only coincidentally designed to tell time (Szamosi 1986; Whitrow, 1975). They could easily be off by an hour. Their main function was to mimic the movement of the known planets, reflecting the general belief that a correct knowledge of the movements of the heavenly bodies was crucial to the success or failure of human enterprises. For example, one of the most elaborate of such town clocks was built in Padua in 1364: While the time dial was rather inconspicuous, it exhibited all sorts of astronomical data, including seven dials, one for each of the seven planets. It was the ability of clocks such as these to represent the movement of the planets mechanically which engendered such wonder and excitement.

Such elaborate astrolabes not only did the potential work of a team of astronomers working around the clock to set and reset the dials manually – they replaced their observations and calculations. Astrolabes could do what formerly could only be done inside an astronomer's head – they were, in fact, among the earliest of computing machines.

These marvellous devices of the fourteenth century did not arise out of nothing. As with all other evolving systems, there was a prior tradition – a set of relevant experiences. The first known mechanical clocks were constructed in China around the ninth century (Szamosi 1986, p. 96). Arab astronomers in the early eleventh century devised simpler astrolabes which showed not only the position of the fixed stars, but also the motion of the sun and the moon (Pacey 1975, p. 66). Later in that century, Islamic astronomers invented the equatorium, a more complicated device designed to calculate the position of the planets. The equatorium was being used in Spain by about 1025.

Basically, all of the above were mechanical devices designed to mirror the movement of the heavens. In so far as the description of such movements required calculations, these devices also constitute simple computers.

Let us now rush forward in time to the early nineteenth century. The Jacquard loom probably represents the first instance of industrial automation. That is, the device was designed to make decisions, rather than merely extend the human musculature. Although Jacquard is generally credited with inventing the device – being granted a patent in 1801 – the ideas leading up to the Jacquard loom had been simmering throughout the French textile industry for at least three-quarters of a century (Benson and Warburton 1986). In 1725 Basile Bouchon used a roll of paper with punched holes to indicate which lifts should operate. Other inventors and mechanics improved on it, including Falcon and de Vaucanson. It was Jacquard who adapted de Vaucanson's selection device and incorporated Falcon's chain of patterned cards. Jacquard's machine was first exhibited in 1804 in Paris but when it moved to Lyons, the weaving centre of France, the first looms were publicly destroyed and accepted only years later through economic necessity, presumably foreign competition.

Jacquard's device was patented in Britain by Francett Lambert in 1820 but the Jacquard was not established until Stephen Wilson managed to create an effective loom by sending an industrial spy to Paris to discover the details of this "new French drawing loom".

We need not trouble ourselves over the detailed mechanism of the workings of the Jacquard loom. Like the piano roll which could replace a piano player because the holes of the punched tape indicated which note was to be played, so the holes in the punched cards of a Jacquard loom determined which shaft would be raised, thereby creating the pattern of the weave. It would still require a human operator – a textile designer or a pianist – to decide which pattern of threads or musical chords the machine (loom or piano) should play, but once the decision was programmed into the system, the system would then govern the workings of the respective mechanical device.

Another example of early automation is the "governor" of a steam engine. Note that the name given to this device – governor – could be considered as semantic evidence of an intuitive perception by the eighteenth-century engineers that the governor was no ordinary bit of machinery.

The governor of a steam engine is an automatic device which regulates the speed of, for example, a steam locomotive. There are several types, but the best known is the flyball governor. In this device, two "arms" hang down from a vertical shaft. Attached to each is a heavy ball. These arms spin around the vertical shaft. The faster they spin, the farther out and up they move because of the centrifugal force exercised on the balls by the rotation. The arms may end up fully outstretched horizontally if the shaft rotates fast enough. As they move farther out and up, they lift up a ring around the shaft which is connected to a throttle. The faster the shaft turns – the shaft being driven by the steam engine itself – the greater the force on the spinning balls and the greater the lift of the upward ring; this, in turn, throttles the engine down.

The governor on a steam engine comprises one of the simplest forms of negative feedback. The faster the steam engine works, the faster the governor rotates. The faster the governor rotates, the more it throttles the steam engine down. As the steam engine slows down, the balls of the governor rotate more slowly and the arms drop. When the arms drop, the throttle opens up again. When the throttle opens up, the steam engine starts working faster again until the speed of the governor's balls causes a throttling down once more.

Most readers will be acquainted with a more recent, and more commonplace, example of this kind of feedback mechanism: the thermostat in people's houses. When the temperature rises in a house as a result of heat being supplied by a central heating system, the thermostat detects this and the expanding metals cause a switch to be forced open. When the electrical switch is forced open no further gas or oil is supplied to the boiler. The boiler shuts down. As the temperature in the house falls, the metal detector of the thermostat cools, and in due course, closes the switch once again. Once the switch is closed, the boiler is turned on again and the temperature will rise once more as the house is being heated.

Both the flyball governor on a steam engine and the thermostat in a house represent *negative feedback* loops which regulate the workings of an internal system. It is one of the most basic mechanisms of machine intelligence and must be considered as a form of proto-intelligence. Actually, one could argue that the governor engages in truly intelligent behaviour. It is goal oriented; its goal is to stabilise the speed of the engine. It achieves this goal by analysing the state of the system (for the governor, the rest of the steam engine is part of its environment). On the basis of that analysis it acts to correct the faulty condition – excessive or insufficient speed – and achieves stability in spite of externally imposed variations in steam pressure. Similarly, the thermostat analyses the temperature of the house, and responds so as to maintain a stable temperature.

Here one could argue that a house containing a thermostat which controls its internal temperature is, in actuality, an intelligent system. That is, the house possesses a system for analysing its internal environment, which is a reflection of its external environment (in so far as the temperature inside is a function of the temperature outside). On the basis of analysing the state of the system the house engages in corrective behaviour by activating or inactivating a heating system of its own. This represents "intelligent" behaviour on two counts. First, the house has wrested from the environment a measure of control – the temperature of the house is no longer totally at the mercy of the temperature of the environment outside. Second, by regulating the furnace, the house is engaging in behaviour which is enhancing its own survivability: If there were no thermostat on the furnace itself, the furnace might overheat and blow up, or alternatively, by automatically keeping the house warm in winter, it keeps the pipes from freezing, then bursting, causing great damage.

It may or may not be superfluous to remind ourselves at this point that when we talk about the intelligence of a house, we are not talking about *consciousness*. What we are examining here, is a low level of intelligent behaviour. Both the governor controlling the throttle of a steam engine and the thermostat regulating the furnace engage in making decisions which in earlier times were made by human beings. As such, they comprise early examples of machine intelligence.

Calculators and Computers Prior to 1940*

The oldest mechanical calculator known is the abacus. It has been around in China for a good couple of thousand years. When it comes to adding or subtracting a column of sums, adroit Chinese merchants are able to outpace easily pocket calculator operators. The architecture of the abacus (a collection of beads on a series of rods or wires) implies a prehistory – perhaps involving placing pebbles on a grid drawn on the ground. One is reminded of the game "Mankala", widely played in the sands of Africa, which involves moving pebbles or shells around a series of depressions in the ground. Although, the specifics of the game are quite different from those involving addition on an abacus, both involve mathematical exercises consisting of changing the location of pebbles, or their equivalent, in respect to some frame of reference. Just as there exists an evolution of languages (as discussed in the previous chapter), so must there exist an evolution of other intellectual tools, including mental games.

The abacus, then, is the oldest known mechanical calculator. It fulfilled humanity's requirements for manipulating numbers admirably well until around the seventeenth century, when European civilisation had advanced sufficiently far, scientifically and technologically, to require more complex and more rapid calculations. Some of the finest minds in Europe – Napier, Pascal and Leibnitz – began to address themselves to the problem.

Napier invented logarithms: For every positive number there existed another number – its logarithm – such that the multiplication of any two numbers could be achieved by adding their logarithms. Similarly, division could be achieved by subtracting their logarithms. This breakthrough set the stage for an abacus-like device to

---

* Much of the material in this section has been abstracted from Chris Evan's splendid book *The Making of the Micro*.

multiply and divide. Napier, in fact, experimented. He created sets of rods on which the multiplication tables were put in such a way that if you turned the appropriate rod (there was one for each of the ten digits) and added or subtracted whatever numbers came up on the exposed faces, it was the same as if you were multiplying. In so far as these rods rattled around in their wooden boxes, they were referred to as Napier's bones, and were considered to be magic by the people of the seventeenth century who, for the most part, had trouble adding.

Pascal invented another, quite different, piece of machinery: The world's first calculating machine – consisting of interlocking cogs, wheels and axles. You dialled the number you wished to add into the machine. The act of dialling caused the cogs and wheels inside to rotate appropriately, so that the result appeared in a little window by the time you had finished dialling. Royalty and scientists alike were astonished. Here was a machine which could accomplish what most people had great difficulty in doing in their head. Nevertheless, the machine – called the Pascaline – was a commercial flop. In those days, accountants were so cheap that it did not pay merchants to buy Pascalines.

Leibnitz improved the Pascaline by introducing a new kind of stepped wheel for multiplication. This ingenious device became the precursor for the mechanical and electro-mechanical calculators of the nineteenth and twentieth centuries.

Note how the above developments depended on a Scot, a Frenchman and a German – a good example of Europe's collective intelligence at work.

By the early nineteenth century there appeared the brilliant schemes of Charles Babbage, in collaboration with Lady Lovelace. The trouble was that their ideas were too far ahead of their time. Lady Lovelace's programming algorithms were not to make sense for another century, and neither the "difference engine" nor the even more complex "analytical engine" ever got off the ground. After a considerable expenditure of both public and private funds, it turned out that the machine tool industry of the day was simply too primitive to create all those cogs, levers and toothed wheels to the required specifications, In fact, it has been said that the main impact of Babbage was to improve engineering standards.

It wasn't until late in the nineteenth century that the machine tool industry had advanced sufficiently to allow the production of mechanical adding machines and calculators. The main motivation for these devices was the United States Census Bureau, which could not keep up with the masses of statistics it had accumulated in the census of 1890.

Then came electricity to drive the wheels, to be followed by the electronic revolution: Cogs and wheels were replaced, first by electronic relays, then by vacuum tubes – the electronic valves. These could speed up the process a thousand-fold. By the end of the 1940s the first generation of electronic computers had become well established.

The First to Fourth Generations of Computers

It is not the function of the present work to review in detail the origin and evolution of computers. This has been done by numerous other authors. A brief overview, however, is in order: First, to refresh the reader's memory (if it needs refreshing) or, alternatively, to provide background material for the novice. Second, the origin and development of computers is central to one of the main theses of this book: That the emergence of machine intelligence within the framework of human society will create a profound discontinuity in the evolution of intelligence. Third, the development of such a sophisticated technology has been wholly dependent on the prior development of a sophisticated collective intelligence.

It took an accumulation of technological progress along many fronts to achieve that first generation of computers. Not only intellectual – for example, Babbage staring at tables of logarithms, dreaming that: "all these tables might be calculated by machinery" (Evans 1981, p. 8) – but also technical, for example, advances in both the machine tool industry and electronics. Thus, achievement of the second generation of computers, required the creation of a different kind of high-technology device – the *transistor*.

The theoretical framework for the development of the transistor can be traced back to at least the 1830s, when Michael Faraday observed that the electrical conductivity of silver sulphide increased upon heating while that of metallic conductors decreased. The first functioning solid state device used subsequently for detecting radio signals was discovered by Braun in 1874. Braun, Professor of Physics at Marburg, also invented the tuned electronic circuit. These devices set the stage for the early radio and wireless industry. The solid state semi-conductor was made of crystals of galena, a mineral primarily composed of lead sulphide. In due course, these "crystal sets" of early radio fame gave way to the electronic valves, invented during the first decade of this century.

The electronic valves (vacuum tubes) eclipsed the need for solid state devices. However, basic research carried on, driven by curiosity and the human need to explore the universe. Max Planck's quantum theory in 1900, Einstein's explanation of the photovoltaic effect in 1905, Roentgen's work on luminescence – these all engaged the attention of a young physicist in Berlin, R.W. Pohl. By 1933, Pohl knew enough to predict that electronic valves and radios would, some day, be replaced by small crystals in which flows of electrons could be controlled.

Such crystals were shown to work in the Bell Company laboratories in New Jersey on 23 December 1947. At that time the Bell laboratories employed 5,700 people, of whom a good 2,000 were advanced professionals. The combination of a maturing basic science (solid state physics) coupled to a massive investment in research and development by Bell created the transistor. Lest we become overawed by the industrial input into this effort, it might be well to remember that similar work at Purdue University was only a matter of months, perhaps even weeks, away from the same finding. Had the researchers there persevered, the three names associated with the invention of the transistor might have been Benzer, Bray and Lark-Horovitz. Instead, the credit goes to Bardeen, Brattain and Shockley – and so it should (Braun and MacDonald 1978).

The transistor, then, is a crystal in which small flows of electrons can be controlled to provide signals. It is in every true sense of the word a *solid state* electronic valve.

Initially, radios utilising such transistors were still made the way radios had always been made: One started with a metal chassis and placed on this chassis (properly insulated) the various electronic components: Resistors, capacitors, transformers, etc., including the transistors. You then wired the whole lot together. This was a slow, laborious process – like calculating lengthy sums with a pencil and paper, there ought to be a better way.

Enter the integrated circuit. As Professor Ernest Braun, former Head of Aston University's Technology Policy Unit, pointed out, the integrated circuit was a commercial innovation developed largely by and within industry (in contrast to the transistor which, except for the very last steps, was developed in university and basic research laboratories). Instead of soldering wires to various components on a metal chassis in order to connect them, one began with a board made of plastic (or other non-conducting material) onto which one sprayed a pattern of thin strips of metallic conducting material. This created a printed circuit board into which one could then insert the various components. By around 1960, this principle began to be extended to spraying conducting materials onto parts of silicon wafers themselves. The silicon chip revolution had begun.

What is a chip? How is it made? A chip is the equivalent of a printed circuit board ingeniously created on a small sliver of silicon (ie, on a silicon chip). Remember that the printed circuit board for a computer involves mainly electronic "on/off" switches and is therefore much less complicated than a radio. During the 1960s, the guts (brains?) of a computer, the processor of information, consisting of clusters of such switches, became miniaturised to the point where each switch consisted of a mere microscopic spot on a silicon chip. The information processor had become a micro-processor. This, then, became known as the "Mighty Micro".

To recapitulate: The first generation of computers was based on electronic valves (vacuum tubes). The first such electronic, binary digital device was the Atanasoff–Berry computer built between 1937 and 1942 (Mackintosh 1988). Their prototype (in 1939) was easily outpaced by paper and pencil calculations; however, it did for electronic computing what the Wright brothers did for aeronautics: It established the basic principle that it could be done.

Atanasoff was not given credit until many years later. But then, it is almost impossible to give credit anyway – so much was happening in the decades leading up to 1940. In Germany, Konrad Zuse had been working on a mechanical and electromechanical system in the late 1930s, then in collaboration with Helmut Schreyer, moved to electronic systems around 1940. Credit is usually given to Vannevar Bush as the true father of the computer: His first model of a "differential analyser" was completed in 1930. It was a big, big mechanical machine driven by electric motors. Later he introduced thermionic valves. Chris Evans (1981) paints a large canvas which makes clear how many geniuses, and lesser mortals, all played a role in providing the intellectual and technical infrastructure required for creating that first generation of electronic computers. From the point of view of the present work, that infrastructure represents one aspect of humanity's collective intelligence – growing and learning.

Just as mechanical cogs, wheels and levers were inadequate to do the job properly, and therefore were replaced by thermionic valves – so were these electronic valves too unreliable, too hot and too power hungry, not to be replaced by solid state devices. The subsequent switch from thermionic valves to transistors, created the second generation of computers.

Printed circuit boards, followed by etching such a circuit directly onto the silicon wafer itself, created the next generation of computers – the silicon chip characterised the third generation. Finally, these evolved into large-scale, then very large-scale integrated (VLSI), circuits to produce the fourth generation of computers.

The Fifth Generation and Other Developments

The fifth generation of computers does not really exist at the time of writing (1990). In spite of much publicity during the 1980s, and substantial expenditures, what is in actual use at this time tends to be merely more powerful versions of fourth generation computers with more powerful peripheral devices. Radical innovations are still largely (although not entirely) confined to research establishments. We will discuss these later.

The 1980s saw largely an extension of Moore's law: The complexity of a chip doubles every year. Similarly, the cost per memory element continued to decrease approximately ten-fold every six years or so. The push for smaller and smaller chips, or smaller dimensions of the same chip continued unabated with a view to both increasing the speed, and reducing the power consumption of the solid state systems. Both improvements led to a reduction in the price per unit of memory or processing power. By the mid-1980s the situation had changed to the extent that: "Wires cost more than gates, software costs more than memory, and the air conditioner takes up more room than the computer" (Hillis 1985, p. 138).

One limiting factor in the indefinite improvement of chip performance is the line width of the "wires" which are sprayed onto the chip the way they used to be sprayed onto printed circuit boards. One cannot reduce this line width to less than one-thousandth of the width of a human hair (ie, less than $0.1\,\mu m$) because below that it becomes increasingly difficult to sustain a reliable electric current. At the same time, another problem arises: The etching process, using light, runs into difficulty with the wavelength of visible light being equal to the line width of $1\,\mu m$. The lithographic process has had to shift to ultra-violet light, then X-rays.

In spite of all this, there have been many interesting developments: Some in hardware, others in conceptualisation and approach. For example, the emergence of the Inmos "transputer" in the early 1980s – essentially, a powerful 32-bit computer with its own storage and built on a chip as a linked array of four such units – represented one of the many devices increasing computer power. By the late 1980s, there had emerged a plethora of new devices and systems: Optical circuits, optical storage disks, CD-ROMs, vast improvements in printing and graphics capability, the use of light pens, "mouse" pointers, and other systems comprising graphic user interfaces (GUIs). These systems, commercially pioneered by the Macintosh series in the early to mid-1980s, including "windows", "hypercard", and other features, represented a great improvement in fostering communication between human beings and intelligent machines.

The 1980s also saw an increasing number of computer scientists unhappy with the architecture of classical computers (see Hillis 1985; Toffoli and Margolus 1987). Backus (1978) had already defined the "von Neumann bottleneck" by the end of the 1970s: Classical von Neumann computers are based on an architecture which separates the memory function from the data processing function. It takes time to move data from the processor to the memory and back. The bigger and more powerful the computer, the bigger its memory, and the worse its von Neumann bottleneck. Furthermore, the bigger the computer, the greater the number of memory chips which sit around doing nothing most of the time.

Finally, as we shall explore in the next chapter, the von Neumann architecture differs profoundly from the architecture of the human brain. The future of computers, therefore, will involve not merely further improvements in the speed and effectiveness of classical computers and their applications (to be discussed in the next few sections), but the blossoming of alternative computer architectures to vastly extend the problem-solving range of machine intelligence.

Cryogenic and Superconducting Computers

One major limitation placed on current computers, as just discussed, is speed. An electrical signal can travel only about 6 in (15 cm) in a nanosecond (one billionth of a second). Wiring has become the limiting factor; it is now more expensive than logic gates.

One way to overcome the wiring problem is to pack the units closer and closer together so that the electrons need not travel so far to deliver their message. However, the closer the units are packed the greater the heat problems. This may change with the introduction of high temperature superconductors.

Superconduction is a classic example of what may happen to discoveries and inventions which are ahead of their time. The phenomenon was discovered in Holland a few years before the First World War by Heike Kamerlingh Onnes. This investigator found that a thread of frozen mercury cooled to about 4 K (where helium condenses into a liquid) lost all resistance to flow of electrons. No resistance meant that not only very little energy is required to stop the flow of electrons, but also, when they do flow, they generate no heat. Superconductivity, however, involves more than merely a metal with no resistance. This did not become clear until 1957 when John Bardeen (of transistor fame), Leon N. Cooper and J. Robert Schrieffer provided the theoretical basis for this phenomenon: In an ordinary metal conductor, the current is made up of a mass of single electrons which keep colliding with the atoms of metal making up the conductor. In a superconductor the current consists of a mass of paired electrons which move in a highly co-ordinated manner through the metallic lattice such that they never collide with the atoms.

Two possibilities, therefore, now exist: First we may discover materials suitable for "wiring", ie, the transmission of electrons inside computers, which can superconduct at room temperature. Second, it may become sufficiently practical and cheap to install the required refrigeration to cool the system enough to allow the superconductors to operate. Present research directions include cooling the whole system down to almost absolute zero. At these extremely low temperatures, not only superconductivity, but also "tunnelling" occurs.

"Tunnelling" was discovered by Brian D. Josephson in 1962 while he was a postgraduate student at Cambridge. At these very low temperatures, electrons can tunnel across an electric insulating barrier. In fact, a moving electron may pass a barrier even though the electron has not sufficient energy to surmount the barrier. This would have been considered impossible in classical physics but is not inconsistent with the more modern quantum mechanics.

The Josephson junction turns out to be the fastest switch known – able to change in 6 ps (6 millionths of a millionth second). Josephson junctions are also able to store information. As part of a superconducting system, the power required is only a few microwatts, so that a million of these would require only a few watts. A large computer would, therefore, be only a few centimetres square. However, it would have to be immersed in a bath of liquid helium, if traditional superconductor materials were used. At the time of writing, "high temperature" superconductors would only require liquid nitrogen, a material which is relatively cheap and easy to handle. Future superconductors may require merely "dry ice" (liquid carbon dioxide), and there is no theoretical reason why one should not discover superconductors which would operate at ordinary temperatures: Electron transport across membranes by biological systems engaged in photosynthesis, respiration and other metabolic activities must have evolved molecules such as carotenoids, phenylpropenoids and other resonating compounds, specifically designed for this task.

Optical and Biocomputers

Supercomputers of the future might evolve along entirely different lines: They might turn out to be either "optical computers" or "biocomputers". Optical computers are based on pulses of light moving down an optical fibre, a system vastly more efficient than pulses of electrons moving down a copper cable. An optical switch called the Fabry–Perot interferometer which, proponents claim, is as fast as a Josephson junction, could become the basis for future computers. Such computers would also include laser-based information storage and retrieval devices.

Biocomputers are devices which hope to capitalise on the capacity of living systems to store vast amounts of information on small, complex molecules such as nucleic acids, proteins or polysaccharides (sugar polymers). Keeping in mind the enormous efficiency of the human brain, it may be that the neurocomputers of the future (discussed in the next chapter) will increasingly rely on either biological materials derived from nature or equivalent materials synthesised in the laboratory.

Not much progress has been made with biocomputers. However, as computer architecture moves towards neural network machines, it is very possible that biological systems at all levels will provide models for the future development of machine intelligence.

Obviously, the idea of pocket supercomputers is not an idea which can be lightly dismissed. As with so much of information technology, the question is not whether it will happen, but when.

First to Fifth Generation Robots*

Robots began as purely electro-mechanical devices which were dedicated to carrying out specific routine tasks. These early electro-mechanical forms could change their performance only by altering the hardware itself, eg, by exchanging the wiring or some other component.

These earliest electro-mechanical devices became displaced by computer-controlled electro-mechanical devices. It now became possible to alter the behaviour or performance simply by means of software changes. The ability to re-program these second-generation robots easily gave them a much greater versatility. However, they were still primitive. A second-generation robot might be programmed to pick up a part: If the part was not there, it would still go through all the motions of picking up such a part – it would be moving merely empty air.

The third-generation robots contained built-in sensors and feedback devices to assess the environment in which they worked. This meant that they now could respond "intelligently" to their surroundings. Intelligence refers to the ability to analyse information about the environment and then respond to it appropriately. In the 1980s, this third stage of robot evolution involved an increasing sophistication of both the sensors and the feedback mechanisms.

This led to the fourth generation of robots: networks or robotised devices connected by, as it were, an artificial neurosystem of sensors and feedback mechanisms all communicating with each other. Individual robots now could co-operate along an assembly line to carry out tasks. Furthermore, they could correct any mistakes which might arise during the production process. This allowed an entire factory to operate like a single gigantic complex machine. One no longer needed human operators to run a factory – only operators to *maintain* a factory and, where needed, modify it.

---

* This section has been published previously as Stonier (1989).

The next step would be to give the fully robotised factory-machine a brain. This would be in the factory office and would include expert systems to guide maintenance and self-repair operations, and to guide relationships with the rest of the world. The latter would involve three areas:

1. Stock control of raw materials and components (including those needed for repairs) electronically linked to suppliers around the world.
2. Direct links with the human decision makers at headquarters office.
3. Links to customers.

In the future, customers will be able to obtain products or services without the intervention of human operators. The matter is analogous to direct dialling an international telephone call. In that instance, customers avail themselves of a fully automated service and need no human operator to intervene in getting their party, perhaps half-way across the world, to answer. Similarly, in the future, via their personal home or office terminal, customers could order a car direct from a factory, specifying their precise individual requirements. The factory office computer would acknowledge and confirm. After checking on their bank account it would set into motion the production of their individual car according to specifications, then make arrangements for delivery. Throughout the process it would check the status of the customer's car and inform him or her. Upon completion and delivery, it would negotiate with their bank computer for the transfer of funds. There would be no need for human intervention except perhaps for the transport of the car to the point of delivery.

Braitenberg's Robots

Valentino Braitenberg, working at the Max Planck Institute for Biological Cybernetics in Tübingen, has created a series of toy robot cars which exhibit behaviour verging on the intelligent. These vehicles are able to analyse their environment in respect of a light source, then engage in goal-oriented activity. The goal is determined by the designer: the car should seek light, avoid light, or prefer twilight (see review by Dewdney 1987).

Two aspects of the Braitenberg cars are astonishing: The simplicity of the system, and the life-like behaviour of the cars.

Each car is made up of a flat, rectangular block on four wheels. The rear wheels are operated individually by two motors, whose speed is determined by the number of signals per second received by the motor. The more signals, the faster the speed. This means if more signals arrive on the left side, the left (rear) wheel will move faster, thereby causing the car to turn to the right.

The source of the signal are two photocells at the front of the car, acting as "eyes". These light receptors face forward and slightly outward so that if, for example, there is a light source to the right, the right eye will receive more light than the left eye, causing the right eye to send out more pulses.

How the car behaves is dependent on how the eyes are connected to the wheels. If you want a car that is attracted to light, you connect the right eye to the left wheel, and vice versa. When, as above, the right eye sees more light, it activates the left (rear) wheel, causing the car to move to the right. In due course, the car overshoots – it turns right so far that the light is now on its left. At this point the left eye sees more light, and activates the right motor. The car turns to the left to face into the light, the overshoot is less, and soon the car adjusts its movements so that both eyes receive the same amount of light. At this point, the system becomes stabilised: both photocells receive equal quantities of light, therefore send out signals of equal frequency. This causes both motors to rotate the wheels at equal speed, and the car, like a moth for a candle, heads directly for the light. As the car approaches the light, the intensity gets stronger, causing the photocell to fire more frequently. The car, therefore, speeds up the closer it gets to the light.

Suppose you want a creature that hates the light, one that prefers the darkest corner? Simply wire each eye directly to the wheel on its side. This will cause the car to turn away from the light until finally it stabilises by driving in a straight line away from the source of light. The further away it gets, the slower it moves, until finally it comes to rest in some dim corner.

Cars with simple circuits, like the two described above, being stimulated by a single source of light can engage only in extremely simple behaviour. They end up either heading straight for the light or straight away from it. Consider, however, if several light sources are scattered around the room so that as the light-loving car heads for one light, a second light source causes it to start deflecting. The result could be that the car keeps circling around. In contrast, the photophobic (light-fearing) car, would act like a scared rabbit if it had to traverse a line between two lights, moving the fastest when both lights are strongest, then slowing down as it moved back into the shadows. To keep the cars moving indefinitely one could turn individual lights on and off around the room at random.

There is another alternative: More complex circuits. One could, for example, introduce a neuron-like device called a "neurode". The neurode is actually a form of computer which analyses and responds to pulses coming from the light receptors or from other neurodes. The neurodes may be programmed to generate pulses of their own. The frequency of these pulses may be accelerated or inhibited by an input from other neurodes or receptors so that the neurode may become excited or inhibited, and in turn, send out excitatory or inhibitory pulses to other neurodes. The importance of "flip-flop" circuits in neural networks will be discussed in a later chapter.

Such complex neural networks can be made still more complex, as, for example, by introducing narrow field light sensors aimed straight forward to augment the two wide-angle photocells which made up the original eyes. Such sensors could alter the behaviour of a light-loving car headed straight for the light, or alternatively, could become activated in pursuit of a moving object thereby creating a potentially predatory robot car. Sound, and tactile senses could be added, increasing the behavioural repertoire of these machine creatures; or certain light sensors might be covered with filters so that they respond only to certain colours. Thus a car may sit quietly for hours, then spring into action as a green vehicle buzzing at a certain frequency crosses its line of sight. Obviously, by mixing various types of vehicles, one can simulate a variety of ecosystems.

These apparent "toys" are important. They provide insights into how relatively simple networks of neurodes can mimic the behaviour of insects and other living creatures. A group at Case Western Reserve University in Cleveland, Ohio (Beer et al. 1991) has extended the work by creating a computer-simulated insect. Named *Periplanata computatrix* after its natural counterpart, the American cockroach *Periplanata americana*, it ran around its two-dimensional world (the computer screen) looking for food, exploring edges and avoiding predators. Its nervous system consisted of 78 neurons with 156 interconnections. These connections could be excitatory or inhibitory. The output of the model neuron depended not only on the input it would receive from other neurons, but also on its internal state. As a result, the model neuron could exhibit rhythmic bursts of activity whose patterns would be regulated by the inputs of other neurons. This would allow *P. computatrix* to co-ordinate the movement of its six legs so that it could walk or run. Walking and running involve different combinations and patterns of leg movements. Not only were the authors able to simulate these movements on the screen, with the help of other collaborators, they built a six-legged robot using their simulated neural circuits. This robot was able to move in a manner similar to its progenitor, the computer model.

Ihnatowicz's Senstor

Another example of creating an animal robot which responds to environmental cues is described by Michie and Johnston (1985). The "Senstor" is the creation of sculptor Edward Ihnatowicz. A fifteen-foot long articulated steel frame, creating the illusion of some kind of large animal, has several microphones and a Doppler radar system placed on its head. The computer controlling the movements of this beast was programmed to react to three things: (i) moderate and low sounds, (ii) loud noise and (iii) motion. The device would move *towards* moderate sound, *retreat* from loud noise and *track* any object moving reasonably fast. As Michie and Johnston [p. 153] point out: The Senstor's behaviour had "an uncanny resemblance to a living thing, and the crowds . . . reacted with enormous excitement".

Early in the morning, in the absence of people, the Senstor's head would be low listening to the faint noise of its own hydraulic system. Then, as the occasional employee or early morning visitor appeared, the head would track the person passing by. Later, children coming to look at it, would, with their buzzing and giggling, attract its attention. Senstor would approach, encouraged by the sound, moving its head to track the movements of the various children until one of the children shouted at it. Then it would back off rapidly. A quiet, polite request, "Come back", would bring it forward again.

Michie and Johnston describe Ihnatowicz's own reaction when he had just got Senstor to work: He unwittingly cleared his throat. Senstor's head immediately came up to him, as if to check whether he was OK or not.

Senstor was dismantled after being shown at the Evoluon exhibit in Holland. It represented a new art form: Not merely a mobile, but a mobile capable of interacting with humans. Both Braitenberg's cars and Ihnatowicz's Senstor represent prototypes of a new generation of interactive toys. Such toys will have a profound impact on the attitudes towards machine intelligence exhibited by children growing up in the early twenty-first century.

Expert Systems

Thus far, we have tended to concentrate on the evolution of *hardware*. However, this is only a part of the evolution of machine intelligence. At least as important, and probably more so, is the evolution of computer use so as to extend human intelligence. We will omit tracing the history of software – machine code, Assembler, high-level languages, computer-aided authoring systems – and instead focus briefly on only one aspect of the evolving interface between human beings and computers: Expert systems.

The matter has been admirably covered by numerous workers. The following discussion is based largely on Richard Forsyth's useful book *Expert Systems*. Forsyth (1989) divides the development of expert systems into four stages, correlating roughly with each decade.

The 1950s saw Rosenblatt's "Perceptron". Based on neural networks, it could be trained to recognise a limited class of patterns. The creation of the Perceptron was in tune with the interest in cybernetics, pioneered originally by Norbert Wiener, and later by Warren McCulloch. The rationale for the Perceptron was that it should be possible for a richly interconnected system of simulated neurons to start off knowing nothing, then, as it experienced various inputs which were positively or negatively reinforced, develop patterns of connections which would be the basis of a learned response. This was the theory. Its successful application would have to wait for another four decades at least.

In spite of the fact that this approach – to create a computer to mimic the human nervous system – was way ahead of the technology needed to carry it out (reminiscent of Babbage and Lady Lovelace), it clarified two useful concepts:

1. There can be no advanced machine intelligence if the system cannot learn.

2. Human intelligence mostly involves pattern recognition – only a small part involves the application of logical reasoning.

The 1960s saw the "heuristic search" approach, pioneered at Carnegie-Mellon University by Allen Newall and Herbert Simon. The Carnegie-Mellon group threw out the neural net model and substituted the idea that human thinking involves logical information processing. Such processing is based on the manipulation of symbols – comparing, searching, modifying, substituting, etc. What made this approach so attractive is that the logic-based von Neumann architecture of computers was ideally suited for carrying out such tasks.

Thus, unlike the neural net idea, the theory of the heuristic search could be coupled to a technology ready to implement its ideas. This approach culminated in the creation of the "General Problem Solver" (GPS). GPS worked well with a limited domain of puzzles with well-defined formal rules, as, for example, in a game of chess. That is, as long as one could clearly define the objects and data to be manipulated, then provide clear cut rules for such manipulation, GPS could do its job.

Unfortunately, few problems in human affairs can be that neatly defined. Nevertheless, it helped to set the stage for the next step, the creation of expert systems. In the 1970s, a team at Stanford University led by Edward Feigenbaum decided to reduce the totality of knowledge available to an expert, including rules of thumb, into a coherent, if simplified, set of data and rules allowing for the heuristic approach.

Because the human brain is so much better at pattern detection and pattern creation, the recourse to logic as the primary instrument of analysis and decision-making resulted in a system – the expert system – which, as Forsyth points out, ended up "almost as a caricature of the real human expert". Nevertheless, it produced some useful, even exciting results: among them, DENDRAL, Feigenbaum's spectrogram interpreter, MYCIN, Shortliffe's system which diagnoses blood infections and prescribes suitable drugs, and PROSPECTOR, a geologic expert system, which helped to discover new deposits of molybdenum.

The 1980s saw the emergence of machine learning as the key to the further evolution of artificial intelligence (AI). Lenat's

EURISKO involved a system able to analyse its own body of heuristic rules, then improve and extend them. Michalski and colleagues at the University of Illinois developed an inductive rule generator named AQ11 which was fed several hundred descriptions of various diseased soybean plants. AQ11 developed its own set of diagnostic rules which turned out to be over 97% correct when applied to new cases. The diagnostic rules proved to be superior to those used by an expert plant pathologist, who, much to his credit, abandoned his own rules of thumb – which were only 83% correct on unseen samples – and taught himself the machine-generated rules. These he now uses to analyse samples sent to him from various parts of the state. As Forsyth points out: "This is the first recorded case of a machine-devised knowledge base which exceeded the performance of a human expert".*

Michie and Johnston (1985), in commenting on the progress made by expert systems, state flatly [p. 115]: "Knowledge is the capacity to give correct answers to questions . . . computers can answer questions and therefore can have knowledge . . . . What is not well known is that computers cannot only possess knowledge, they can *create* it." (italics in original). Their argument is based largely on the fact that computers, while processing information, create new knowledge structures. It is the ingenuity of the knowledge engineers which creates the rules by which computers reorganise information. These systems have now become sufficiently complex so that the mix of human and machine intelligences produces unpredictable outcomes. Computers, by surprising their human masters, can be said to exhibit creative behaviour – a higher form of intelligence than that which can only respond to new questions with rote answers.

Creative behaviour involves discovering or utilising new combinations of solutions. It takes *intelligence* to solve a problem. It takes *creativity* to solve problems in new and unique ways. For example, it takes intelligence to solve a chess problem; it takes creativity to solve it in a new and unique manner. Creativity, therefore, must be considered to be an advanced form of intelligence.

---

* It could be argued that Widrow's weather forecasting system in 1963 outperformed the meteorologists – a matter to be discussed in the next chapter dealing with neural network computers.

Networks

No effective human intelligence could develop beyond the village level without an effective system of long distance communication. For a national and, ultimately, global collective intelligence, systems of communication involving messengers, whether on foot, by horse or by ship, were slow and inefficient. Lighting signal fires to warn of impending invasions – whether in medieval Korea or England – was much faster, but could not convey much information.

The breakthrough, as with machine intelligence, had to await the harnessing of pulsing electrons. To indicate how much more powerful are such pulses than human couriers, one needs only look at the fate of America's famed Pony Express.

The Pony Express represents the ultimate in historical glamour as far as the opening up of America's West and the uniting of the two coasts. In 1860, California could receive news from the east only after three weeks, overland via the Butterfield Stage Coach from St Louis, or after six weeks, by packet via Panama. To the people of the far west, the Pony Express was a godsend. From St Joseph, up-river from Kansas City, to Sacramento, up-river from San Francisco, the Pony Express, on average, managed to deliver the mail in ten days. Braving rugged country, hostile weather, bandits, Indians and other hazards, the Pony Express gave rise to folk heroes like Buffalo Bill. What is generally not realised is that the whole enterprise, which started on 3rd April 1860, lasted for only about 19 months (Findley 1980). The reason the Pony Express mail system collapsed was that a transcontinental telegraph link had been established by the end of October 1861. Ironically, the telegraph lines were strung along the very route established by the Pony Express.

In a relatively short time span (historically speaking), the telegraph became superseded by the telephone, radio links, telex and fax machines, two-way video systems, E-mail – a host of electronic devices, all contributing to the emerging global nervous system.

It is not the function of the present work to review and assess the history and recent advances in computer networks. However, one aspect needs to be re-emphasised: In order to create a collective intelligence, an efficient communication system between intelligent subunits is critically important. This is true for cells in an organism, for animals in a society, for individuals in a group, and for groups in a society. Above, and previously, we discussed the importance of electronic communications systems in furthering the human global collective intelligence. Now, we must emphasise the importance of computer networks in creating a *global* machine collective intelligence.

When the original ARPANET was built in the United States in 1969, the high-speed lines of the day could transmit 50 kilobits per second (Kahn 1987). By the late 1980s that rate had increased about 1000-fold. By the turn of the century, it would not be unreasonable to expect speeds of 10 gigabits per second, and if the signals were to be multiplexed, transmission rates exceeding 100 gigabits per second might be possible on a single optical fibre.

What this means is that not only will computers be able to move huge databases from one computer to another – and do so in less than a second – but they will also be able to transmit colour images at the standard film rate of 30 frames per second. For real time digital film transmission on a $1,000 \times 1,000$ pixel screen, 30 megabits per second are required for black and white, 240 megabits per second for colour. At 10 or 100 gigabits, one could transmit much larger screens with much greater resolution, and much more data. To quote Robert E. Kahn, one of the developers of ARPANET, writing in *Scientific American* in 1987 [p. 135]: "The promise optical fibres hold for computer networks is that they will make possible the levels of information flow needed for the networks to fulfil their ultimate purpose, which is to enable computers to collaborate intelligently".

Under such conditions, computers "talking" to each other, would share information in a manner closer to dolphins than to humans: Dolphins may describe an object simply by mimicking the echolocation, thereby transmitting much more detailed information about the object than humans possibly could, using words. Computers would, in turn, be much more efficient still, being able to "converse" by means of moving pictures, sound, additional data capture (eg, using a wide range of electromagnetic frequencies to describe the surface and internal features of the object) and simultaneous data analysis. For example, if a computer used for diagnosing a patient were to communicate with a "medical expert system" computer, the former could transmit in less than a second, a photograph of the afflicted area, an infra-red photograph, an X-ray, a sonogram, the patient's entire medical history and whatever other information was relevant. Images could flash across the world from computer to computer, the way they flash across our brain – and just as the trillions of neurons have become integrated to provide that form of neurological collective intelligence which we call the "human brain", so, in due course, will there be created a global machine collective intelligence.

The global brain, therefore, will emerge as a mix of collective human and machine intelligence.

Computer Viruses: True Artificial Intelligence

Computer viruses represent a form of humanly created intelligence which cannot be classed as "machine" intelligence. It is true that such viruses have been created within, and are totally dependent upon, machine intelligence. However, they are entities as distinct from machine intelligence as biological viruses are distinct from the cells they parasitise.

By the criteria set in the first chapter, computer viruses must be classed as intelligent entities: They are able to analyse their environment then make intelligent responses which enhance both their own survivability, and reproducibility.

So-called second-generation viruses have the ability to escape detection (and therefore destruction) by more traditional methods. For example, a virus such as "4096" is able to fool the usual programs into not having itself deducted from free memory. It has made itself invisible. At the time of this writing several scores of viruses are known. Some are highly malignant like the "Jerusalem", and the "Friday the 13th" viruses, others are just silly, creating electronic graffiti, while others are relatively benign, merely cluttering up memory.

It is not the purpose of the present work to discuss the practical problems created by such viruses other than to point out that their destructive potential, like human viruses (smallpox, polio, AIDS, etc.), is enormous. Global machine – human intelligence systems could become extremely vulnerable to virus infections, in the long run, creating disasters comparable to the bubonic plagues – the Black Death – of the Middle Ages. Let us hope that we can create computer "public health" systems which immunise us from, or cure us of, computer viruses, or better still, eradicate them completely, like smallpox. The problem will be analogous to that of the emergence of genetic recombinants in nature (or in laboratories) of new strains of human pathogens causing diseases such as Legionnaire's disease or AIDS. Mary Shelley expressed our collective fear of science going awry when she created Frankenstein. That rather large and physically frightening monster will be a tame bear compared to the havoc potentially wreaked by computer viruses – those intelligent, virtual information particles of our own creation.

There is another, more positive aspect, however: The creation of computer viruses represents a landmark in the evolution of intelligence. We, humans, have created both the intelligent medium, and the self-reproducing entity which can propagate in that medium.

As discussed earlier, several thousand million years ago, in a complex medium of organic molecules and clay minerals, there emerged the first self-reproducing entities which were to evolve into true *Life*. Similarly, if the planet Earth is the locus (in this part of the universe) where the evolution of advanced information systems is moving from *Life* to *Intelligence*, then we, humans, have accomplished the equivalent of creating the starting point for *Life*.

Computer viruses represent a form of meta-intelligence: Once created, they become self-replicating entities which no longer depend directly on a *living* substrate for their existence – rather they grow on pure information provided by machine intelligence. In due course, we will see viruses which mutate and show adaptability to their (information) environment.

Literature Cited

J Backus (1978) Can programming be liberated from the von Neumann style? *Commun ACM* 8:613–641.

RD Beer, HJ Chiel and LS Sterling (1991) An artificial insect, *Am. Sci.* 79:444–452.

A Benson and N Warburton (1986) *Looms and Weaving*, Shire Publications, No. 154, Aylesbury, Bucks.

E Braun and S MacDonald (1978) *Revolution in Miniature*, Cambridge University Press.

AK Dewdney (1987) Computer recreations, *Sci. Am.* 256(3):8–12.

C Evans (1979) *The Mighty Micro*, Victor Gollancz, London.

C Evans (1981) *The Making of the Micro*, Victor Gollancz, London.

R Findley (1980) The pony express, *Nat. Geographic* 158(1):45–71.

T Forester (ed) (1980) *The Microelectronic Revolution*, Basil Blackwell, Oxford.

R Forsyth (1986) Machine learning, in *Artificial Intelligence* (M Yazdani ed), pp. 205–225, Chapman and Hall, London.

R Forsyth (ed) (1989) *Expert Systems*, 2nd edn, Chapman and Hall, London.

WD Hillis (1985) *The Connection Machine*, The MIT Press, Cambridge, Mass.

RE Khan (1987) Networks for advanced computing, *Sci. Am.* 257(4):128–135.

AR Mackintosh (1988) Dr Atanasoff's computer, *Sci. Am.* 259(2):72–78.

D Michie and R Johnston (1985) *The Creative Computer*, Pelican Books, Harmondsworth.

M Minsky (ed) (1968) *Semantic Information Processing*, The MIT Press, Cambridge, Mass.

A Pacey (1975) *The Maze of Ingenuity*, Holmes and Meier, New York.

T Stonier (1981) What makes a micro tick? in *The Making of the Micro* (C Evans ed), pp. 108–115, Victor Gollancz, London.

T Stonier (1989) Expert systems and the knowledge revolution in *Expert Systems* (R Forsyth ed), pp. 222–241, Chapman and Hall, London.

G Szamosi (1986) *The Twin Dimensions*, McGraw-Hill, New York.

T Toffoli and N Margolus (1987) *Cellular Automata Machines*, The MIT Press, Cambridge, Mass.

J Weizenbaum (1984) *Computer Power and Human Reason*, Pelican Books, Harmondsworth.

GJ Whitrow (1975) *The Nature of Time*, Pelican Books, Harmondsworth.

· 7 ·

Computers and the Human Brain

Introduction

Human intelligence, for the most part, does not operate like a von Neumann type of logic machine. It does not, for the most part, engage in precise reasoning, manipulating abstract symbols. The great fallacy – perhaps based in a kind of technological arrogance – is that the human brain works like a logic machine, and that, therefore, the computers created by the collective genius of men like Atanasoff, Babbage, Bush, Turing, von Neumann, and Zuse – upon perfection – would act like human brains.

The fact is that the first four or five generations of computers represented machines whose information processing became extremely fast, precise, yet uncomprehending, while human beings engaged in thinking which continued to be ponderous, fuzzy, but insightful.

The purpose of this chapter is to examine this state of affairs, and look to the future. We begin, however, with a critique.

A Critique of Logic

We live in a rational age in which logic is king. The computer and its logical inference machinery is the ultimate extension of this philosophy.

That this is not an unworthy philosophy is demonstrated by the effectiveness of computers, which have proved the practicality of logic. It is not surprising, therefore, that computer philosophy –

such as exists – has not only failed to question the superiority of logic as a method of solving all problems, in general it has tended to ignore all other approaches. This logic-oriented outlook could prove to be a major impediment to the further development of sophisticated thinking machines.

What the human mind is so good at is detecting patterns. The detection of patterns is based on associating certain events or actions with certain objects or circumstances, or with each other. Much of what we call "common sense" is based on our ability to perceive patterns. It must also be an important component of what we call "wisdom". Pattern association is, of course, a much more primitive form of intelligence than logic. It is merely an extension of conditioned reflexes: If in the environment of a dog – as in Pavlov's laboratory – the appearance of food is always preceded by the ringing of a bell, then the dog has perceived a pattern: the ringing of a bell is likely to be followed by food. Fish in a tank can similarly be trained to respond to external stimuli. Humans possess a much more sophisticated brain than fish. However, our ability to be much more sophisticated in detecting subtle patterns than fish should not prevent us from recognising that this difference, once again, merely reflects a spectrum of phenomena – not a qualitative difference.

The problem with logic is this: *Impeccable logic applied to erroneous assumptions can only lead to erroneous conclusions*. This is as true for mathematical arguments as for verbal logical ones. The strength of science derives from the fact that, by observation and experimentation, the scientific method transcends the "assumption–deduction–conclusion" process, always checking and comparing the conclusion against the reality provided by nature.

In nature, organisms have to operate in that reality and most decisions have to be made rapidly and with incomplete data. The same is true for managers, and most humans having to make important decisions. Inadequate data lead to erroneous assumptions, which, as we said above, can only lead to faulty conclusions. Under such circumstances, pattern association – gut reactions – are a much more reliable guide than logic, especially if they involve communally shared prejudices based on the past experiences of the culture's collective intelligence.

It is for these reasons that the next breakthrough in machine intelligence is not likely to come from ever more sophisticated logic machines, but by developing neural network machines capable of mimicking the bulk of human brain activity. That is not to say that the future of machine intelligence will be an "either/or" situation –

either logic or pattern perception, either von Neumann machines or neural network computers – rather it, like the human brain, will be a combination of both.

Biological Paradigms for Computer Architecture

As we discussed earlier, one of the key elements in all higher forms of intelligence is the capacity to learn. Therefore, one would not consider machines to be "smart" until they exhibit the capacity to learn. In fact we consider both children and animals to be smart if they learn quickly: the faster they learn, the smarter they are.

In biosystems, learning involves the capacity to detect (and remember) patterns among objects and events. It behoves information scientists to look to biological models to guide their quest for truly intelligent machines. Forsyth (1986, p. 218) has reviewed the three systems of greatest interest – the nervous system, the immune system, and the process of evolution.

For the moment, we will put the *nervous system* to one side since most of the rest of this chapter will address itself to neural network computers. The *immune system* works at the molecular level and learns to recognise millions of proteins. It does not seem to have much relevance to computer architecture at the time of writing. However, should molecular biocomputers become a reality, then the immune system might have a great deal to offer as a model.

We have already referred to the *process of evolution* on several occasions: Any species or group of organisms as a whole exhibit the capacity to learn during the course of their evolution. It is the main reason why one may ascribe the property of intelligence to all forms of life. For the artificial intelligence community, the process-of-evolution approach has come to be known as the "genetic algorithms" approach, exemplified by Richard Forsyth's BEAGLE (Biological Evolutionary Algorithm Generating Logical Expressions). BEAGLE's learning algorithm consists of repeating a set of procedures for many generations (reviewed by Forsyth 1986). These procedures evaluate rules or new combinations of rules with existing or new training data. At each cycle (generation), the procedure ranks the rules in descending order of merit and discards the bottom half. This bottom half is then replaced with a new set of rules created by combining various rules comprising the surviving top half. Various rules in the top half, except the very top one, are also varied slightly (mutated). All rules are then tidied up, cutting out certain redundancies, double negatives, etc. and the system is now ready to run through the next cycle.

Forsyth's program mimicked simple evolution in life-like fashion. Typically there appeared, for a while, a dominant species, ie, a single rule which remained at the top for a number of generations. Then, quite suddenly it would be replaced by a new and superior line, usually a variant of one of its own offspring. For example, in assessing the prognoses of cardiac patients admitted to a hospital, BEAGLE, after 111 generations, emphasised the state of the patient's mean arterial pressure. By 1,111 generations, this had shifted to a top rule which emphasised the relationship between arterial pressure and urinary output (a prolonged malfunctioning of the heart leads to kidney failure). BEAGLE had detected (and remembered) a pattern which allowed it to judge the severity of a heart attack. It had *learned* what to look out for.

Comparing Classical Computers with the Human Brain

Before proceeding further, it might be helpful to tabulate the major differences between classical computers and the human brain – at least as far as the latter is understood. "Classical" refers to the traditional first- to fifth-generation von Neumann machines. (Later on, we will examine non-classical computers such as Hillis' "Connection Machine", "Cellular Automata Machines" (CAMs), and "neural network" (NN) computers.)

Table 7.1 indicates that the computer, in its broadest sense, may be considered as a complex, aperiodic crystal with certain unique electronic properties. Its circuitry is based on semiconductors plus the conductors necessary to complete the system. In principle it is quite different from, and substantially less sophisticated than, the human nervous system. As Margaret Boden (1987) has pointed out: "AI has shown us that we are much cleverer than we previously thought", a consideration reinforced by the work of Miller and Gildea (1987) demonstrating that by means of contextual analysis, children, in the years between infancy and late teens, acquire a word-recognition capability of 80,000 words, learning to recognise, on average, more than ten new words per day.

Obviously the human brain has a highly complex and effective circuitry, and a much larger memory storage which is based on a

Table 7.1. Some cardinal differences in the anatomy and physiology of classical computers and the human brain

	Computer	Human brain
1	Digital information processor based on circuits of binary switches	Analogue information processor involving a complex nervous system with scores of chemical neurotransmitters and modifiers
2	Information transported as pulses of electrons along conductors, and across semiconductors	Information transmitted as pulses of depolarisation along membranes and as neurotransmitters across synapses
3	Speed of pulse transmission approximately 10^{10} cm/sec	Speed of pulse transmission approximately 10^3 cm/sec
4	Relatively simple circuitry but increasing in complexity	Extremely complex circuitry: 10^{11} neurons with up to 10^{15} connections
5	Crystalline structure, extremely stable	Biotissue, vulnerable to damage
6	Can operate under a wide variety of conditions	Needs carefully regulated environment to operate
7	Computer system may be shut down indefinitely with no damage	Brain requires continuous energy inputs in order to maintain the living system
8	No self-repair. Some self-correction and by-pass of faulty areas	Tissue capable of significant self-repair. Also extensive capability to transfer function to other circuits
9	Memory based on patterns of binary switches	Memory based on patterns of neural connections

(Adapted from Stonier 1984, p. 18)

network of 100 thousand million neurons, each connected to perhaps a thousand other neurons. In some instances, for example in the case of the Purkinje cells of the cerebellar cortex, each cell receives inputs from as many as 200,000 parallel fibres (Diamond 1990). Furthermore, each neuron is a sophisticated information device in its own right – much more sophisticated than a transistor, or even a transputer. Think of a "Connection Machine" computer consisting of 10^{11} transputers, and we may approach the capacity of the human brain. In addition to all this biological networking power there remains the possibility that individual molecules, such as proteins or nucleic acids, are also able to store information. It is known that in immune systems, individual molecules retain information on the surface of specific antibody cells. The human brain also consists of tissue capable of significant self-repair, or alternatively, compensatory activity to minimise damage to the system.

On the other hand, computers possess advantages in at least three areas: The speed of pulse transmission, the tough and stable nature of the material, and, unlike a living system, the ability to be shut down indefinitely without damage. In addition, the ease of tying computers together – communicating with each other in a way not currently possible for human brains – creates a computer "collective intelligence". Already, the on-line mass storage capability for some computers is in the gigabyte range. This range is extendable. Think of every household with a telephone, possessing a powerful computer tied into a global network.

Classical computers differ profoundly from the human brain in at least two other respects:

1. The separation of processing and memory function.
2. A total reliance on logic.

However, as discussed before, logic is a form of thinking which appeared only very late in the evolution of intelligence. It also appears late in the development of a child's thinking processes. Most higher animal and human intelligence relies on simple association. Our mental map of the world consists of associating objects, sensations, events, etc. into a pattern of memories. These constitute the map which allows us to make sense of the world in which we live. How such a neurological map is created in the first place requires an understanding of current theories of brain development and function.

Edelman's Theory of "Neural Darwinism"

Edelman's theory involves the following set of ideas and concepts (as reviewed by Rosenfield 1988):

1. During embryo development there is laid down an extremely complex neural network. This constitutes the primary anatomy of the brain.

2. Learning involves the superimposition of patterns of connections onto this primary network. Such patterns are not created by creating new, or more, connections, but by strengthening existing pathways.

3. Pathways compete with each other. Patterns of connections are nourished by stimuli and grow stronger at the expense of weaker ones, which decay and are overridden. Note it is the weaker *connections* which disappear, not the neurons themselves.

Let us now examine and expand on these propositions.

1. During embryogenesis there is laid down an incredibly complex neuronal network in the brain. Cellular adhesion molecules (CAMs) determine which cells attach to which other cells, thereby creating localised areas in the brain – the brain's major substructures. These substructures include all the centres which analyse and code sensory inputs and motor outputs. Within these substructures of the brain, and across them, a myriad of connections are established. This is the primary architecture at birth.

Note that the combination of genetic and epigenetic factors which determine these connections (called synapses) are so complex that although the macro structure is roughly the same from one individual to the next (within any given species), the microstructure is infinitely varied and unpredictable. Genetic twins do not have an identical brain architecture at birth.

2. Learning involves the superimposition of patterns on this neural network. Such patterns are not created by creating new, or more, connections (synapses), but by strengthening existing pathways.

This idea – that changes in the strength of synaptic transmission due to usage of certain critical neural pathways underlies the learning process and represents the basis of memory – has been around for over 75 years (as reviewed by Nicoll et al. 1989). However, the first support of this hypothesis did not occur until 1973, when Bliss and Lomo found that the brief, repetitive activation of certain nerve pathways in the hippocampus of rabbits caused an increase in the strength of synaptic transmissions that could last for days or even weeks. Since the hippocampus is a part of the brain thought to be important in information storage, their findings appeared to be particularly significant. This long-lasting increase in the strength of synaptic transmission is called "long-term potentiation" (LTP). LTP represents the most likely explanation for the cellular mechanism underlying the phenomena of memory and learning.

The actual physiological processes involved in LTP appear to be, as one might expect, subtle and complex. Neurophysiologists are still busy unravelling the details: Part of the mechanism involves the release of the amino acid glutamate as the excitatory transmitter across the synapse. This activates certain chemical receptors. One of these, called the NMDA receptor, causes an influx of calcium ions into certain parts of the nerve cell (the dendritic spine). This increase in calcium ion concentration appears critical to the process of long-term potentiation. Why this is so is not yet clear, but it is likely that the presence of high levels of calcium causes certain proteins to become activated.

Chiye Aoki and Philip Siekevitz (1988) have reviewed the importance of the protein "MAP2" in mediating the formation of new neural pathways. MAP2, an acronym for "microtubule-associated protein 2", is a very large phosphorylated protein specifically associated with the cytoskeleton of neurons. It has been detected in every kind of neuron so far examined. In degenerating neurons of patients suffering from Alzheimer's disease, MAP2 and other cytoskeletal proteins exhibit abnormal tangling.

MAP2, as a cytoskeletal protein of neurons, helps to determine their shape. It concentrates in dendrites and there is good evidence to suggest that MAP2 is responsible for the branching and shape of the dendrites. The dendrites look like the branches of a tree. Two dendrites from two different nerve cells interdigitate without actually touching each other. This is the *synapse*.

The behaviour of MAP2 is regulated by the phosphorylation and dephosphorylation (adding and subtracting phosphate groups) of the protein. This is probably why the influx of calcium ions is so important. Neural activity governs this process, via glutamate and the NMDA receptors. MAP2 appears to be the first of a class of molecules responsible for mediating the strengthening of the connections of neurons along an active pathway.

Thus the memory of an object such as a "locomotive" is *not* some visual image stored somewhere in the brain like a photograph or a slide. It is not even a coded version of such a visual image, the way such an image may be stored on an optical disk, or patterns of on/off switches, to be retrieved by a computer looking up the correct address. Rather the brain remembers the "locomotive" as ephemeral patterns of associations and experiences processed and integrated with other, related patterns all across the brain.

When a "locomotive" is first seen by an individual – child, or adult – a whole series of stimuli are presented to the brain. The brain *experiences* a "locomotive". First, there is its shape. Second, there is its colour. Those two features alone are sufficient to present a unique pattern as an object. But then it moves, creating brain patterns unique to objects which move. Further, it makes puffs of smoke and clouds of steam. And the noise! Frightening! This activates the limbic system. Patterns experienced while we are frightened (or angry, or in love) are greatly strengthened, therefore more strongly imprinted on our memory.

If sufficiently intense, the pattern may persist (be remembered) for a lifetime. However, such a pattern will need to be reinforced because all *learned* patterns (in contrast to genetic ones) decay with time.

The brain of an adult (or older child) would already contain patterns abstracted, and quite distinct from, direct experiential patterns such as seeing a locomotive. There would, for example, exist a pattern of abstractions to cover the category "transportation equipment". This would include all objects which themselves move and in addition can carry or transport other things. A second category of abstractions would include "materials", causing the visual inputs to look for patterns like bright shiny objects, characteristic of certain metals. Other characteristics might cause the brain to infer that the locomotive was made of iron. A third category of abstractions would consist of a huge constellation of patterns to cover the category "words", and the sub-category "nouns", that is words which refer to a person, place or thing. In searching for a word pattern to cover the new experience (the locomotive) the brain might well come up with a new word combination, based on previously stored patterns – for example, "iron horse" as did the North American Indians, and, for that matter, as did the French (Chemin-de-fer).

To differentiate a horse from a locomotive is easy, especially when other sensual experiences are included: A horse smells differently from a locomotive; it feels different to the touch; when put to the mouth – as babies and young children exploring their world would – it would create further unique patterns; it looks different; it moves differently; etc. Nevertheless the idea of creating a new word category "iron horse" to describe a previously unexperienced object such as a "locomotive" is a basic process which we appear to share – judging from the work of the Premacks – with our closest primate cousins the chimpanzees.

The strength of the neural connections making up any given pattern is a function of at least two processes. The first involves repetition: If the same sets of networks are repeatedly activated, they automatically become more efficient and the connections become strengthened. The second involves those experiences which are so important to the organism that they are imprinted virtually for ever (or at least until injury or death causes the brain to malfunction) in response to a single event. These involve experiences associated with great danger or great joy. The events leading up to the situation, the scene, the surroundings all make up a great part of the fabric of such an experience and are remembered. It has been established that an increased involvement of the limbic system at the time of an incident – presumably mediated by changes in hormonal states – causes the incident to be remembered better (Rosenfield 1988, p. 165). The juxtaposition of objects, surroundings and events leading up to, for example, a dangerous confrontation generating fear not only create patterns in the brain, but are remembered by the individual as patterns of association. Such patterns constitute a form of wisdom: They allow an individual to "smell trouble ahead".

The bulk of human intelligence does not derive from the human brain's ability to deduce conclusions by the application of logic, but rather by its ability to make inferences by perceiving patterns of association. This summarises the cul-de-sac classical artificial intelligence got into: The primary emphasis was to emulate human thought by working with classical von Neumann type computers, ie, binary-based logic machines. In contrast, the human brain is an analogue device with an incredibly complex circuitry attuned to picking up patterns of association.

3. Patterns of connections, if they are not periodically reinforced, decay. Reinforcement can come from external stimuli, or internal stimuli – simply thinking about something or remembering, or trying to remember something. Probably sleep is an important factor in helping the decay of trivial connections. Remembering where you parked the car yesterday, or what you ate for breakfast last week, is not likely to make much difference to your future (unless you were poisoned at breakfast, or found a new, secret place to park which would stand you in good stead in the future).

Edelman introduces the concept of neural competition: Some patterns of connection are nourished by stimuli and grow stronger at the expense of other patterns. The weaker ones, which decay, are overridden. Keep in mind that any given nerve or nerve cluster may participate in any one of thousands of patterns, just as a letter or a word may participate in any one of thousands of sentences. It is the weaker *connections* which disappear, not the neurons themselves.

This "survival of the fittest networks", ie, the networks selected for by the brain's activity, is referred to by Edelman as "neural Darwinism".

If the above explanations of how the human brain works prove to be correct then one may not only marvel at the simplicity of such an ingenious device – its adaptability and efficiency for learning to recognise complex patterns of association – but also recognise its weaknesses.

First, a neural network which generates memories by strengthening patterns of connections based on constellations of external sensory inputs plus internal associated interpretations is very prone to superstition. Let us consider a hypothetical case. You are driving down a lovely country lane past a farmyard. It is a partly cloudy day. In the distance, to your left, you can hear the faint rumble of thunder, nearby a cock crows, and you hear a tractor sputtering somewhere in the farmyard. The wind rustles through the trees, you see white sheep in the meadow, brown chickens in the farmyard, and a black cat crossing the road ahead. You smell the pungent smell of the farmyard and you admire the thick hawthorn hedges. You come around the bend and – crash into the tractor which has just come in from a side road! Fortunately, you were going slowly and nobody got hurt. But you are shaken. Your adrenalin levels are up and your heart is beating overtime.

In recounting the event later you are struck by the way your mind goes over and over your impressions of that scene just prior to the crash. Nature meant it to be that way. The physiological stress associated with the accident made certain that the lightly weighted connection – the "commonplace" sensory inputs describing the scene above – became heavily weighted. Somewhere in all these "commonplace" sensory inputs lie hidden environmental clues to an impending disaster. The neural network does not discriminate specifics. If in the near future you came around a similar bend, the smell of a farmyard, the crow of a cock, any of these would trigger a state of alert. If a cock crowed just before you had another accident, the neural network would strengthen still further the association between cocks crowing and accidents.

The neural connections may, of course, be strengthened as a result of other processes. To the ancient Greeks, thunder to the left meant a warning from the gods. Our own western culture believes crossing the path of a black cat brings bad luck. Analysing the accident after the event, depending on your cultural background, you might decide, for different reasons, that the most important environmental clue to the impending disaster – the clue to watch out for under similar circumstances the next time – was the thunder, the black cat or the sputtering sound of the tractor. This thinking about the accident, going over it, over and over again, leads to a further strengthening of the neural connections involved. Thus the original associations undergo a process of neural Darwinism. Those pre-accident inputs which appear highly relevant to you are upgraded – if you are one kind of person, you'll focus on the sputtering tractor engine, if another, on the black cat crossing the road. This subsequent upgrading of certain associations will be at the expense of the others. Thus those pre-accident inputs which appear irrelevant to you will be downgraded and their neural pathways will decay faster.

People who have suffered a trauma, either an injury (physical or psychological) to themselves or to a friend or loved one – perhaps leading to the death of that individual – tend to go over the events leading to the trauma, over and over again. This is an adaptive response – processing the information by running over the circuits, over and over, to extract vital clues from the pattern, clues which might have allowed the trauma to be averted in the first place. Such a process may, however, lead to a pathology by putting a neural network into a self-stimulating resonant cycle – ie, "thinking in a rut". One of the antidotes to this phenomenon is sleep. On the other hand, if the process becomes sufficiently intense to constitute a psychopathology, more drastic measures such as drug treatments, or even electroconvulsive shock therapy, may be needed in order to break such a cycle. However, it must be recognised that going over a particular situation repeatedly is a natural form of information processing for a neural network analysing patterns of connections.

Not unrelated to this is the phenomenon of absent-mindedness, and the tendency for "Freudian slips". In both instances, the newer, more appropriate, response required of the moment becomes overridden by the more deeply ingrained habits of mind (Diamond 1990).

Lastly, an obvious weakness of neural networks is that they are fuzzy and imprecise. All inputs are filtered through numerous nodes and pathways, all of which are likely to have been used for some other purpose previously, or worse, used for similar purposes which may cause a complete misinterpretation of the new inputs. One is reminded of the old tale about Julius Caesar deciding to pardon a soldier condemned to death, by issuing the order: "Execute not, spare!" which unfortunately was garbled in transit to "Execute, not spare!" by moving the comma. A comparable situation, though less critical, must occur over and over again inside our brain.

The Unlogical Revolution

The preceding sections considered the profound differences between classical computers and human brains. Gordon Scarrott, past manager of ICL Research and Advanced Development, has written on the matter as follows (personal communication, 1988): "In living organisms the brain has been evolved to carry out the judgement process by taking into account against a background of experience, observations from several organs simultaneously, for example sight, scent and hearing in order to make an appreciation of the situation appropriate to guide action. This process may be termed 'Primitive Judgement' since it is common to many species. Mankind also uses primitive judgement on a grand scale in daily life but as a by product of the evolution of natural language the technique of logical argument based on the abstract concept of certainty has been added comparatively recently to our human judgement skills".

"Computers are essentially logical argument machines and they are of great value for assisting or undertaking any judgement that can be resolved into logical argument, but since primitive judgement preceded logical argument in the evolution of human information handling skills the widely held belief that every judgement must be describable in logical terms is ill founded."

Scarrott goes on to point out that: "computers were originally conceived by mathematicians", and "mathematics is essentially logical argument, with primitive judgement consciously excluded". Scarrott concludes with the plea: "the potential application field of computers, although large as the pioneers recognised, is not universal and there is a need to explore new forms of information systems that are not based on explicit logical argument".

It is only in recent years that anything resembling a genuine revolution in computer architecture is beginning to emerge. However, such a revolution has begun. In line with Scarrott's argument, new information processing systems have been developed which are not based on explicit logical argument. This, then, constitutes the "unlogical revolution" – a discontinuity in the evolution of machine intelligence.

Hillis' Connection Machine

One such new direction in computer architecture is the *Connection Machine* (CM) elaborated by Dan Hillis (1985). The CM computer differs from classical computers in the following manner: Instead of a single powerful processor connected to a large but separate memory, the two functions have been combined by creating a large network of many small processors. As such, it begins to resemble the human brain – although a better analogy would be the collective intelligence of an ant colony. As discussed in Chapter 4, an ant brain contains only one hundred thousand (10^5) neurons (in contrast to the human brain, which contains 10^{11}). Similarly, Hillis' CM computer is made up of a large array of simple, single processors. Hillis calculates [pp. 52–53] that each processor probably needs only a 300-bit capacity in order to function as an effective subunit, and the way to create a large total memory is not by increasing the memory of the individual subunits, but by increasing the *number* of subunits.

From a biological point of view, one is reminded of Frank's analysis of the evolution of social insects, discussed in Chapter 4: From individual, hard-wired yet high-grade processing units such as solitary wasps, to societies of great numbers of simpler individuals linked by increasingly sophisticated patterns of communication.

Cellular Automata Machines

The first volume of this series, *Information and the Internal Structure of the Universe*, described briefly a computer game called "Life" [pp. 124–125]. Created in the 1970s by John Horton Conway at Cambridge University, it is a sort of video kaleidoscope. The screen is divided up into an array of squares, each square representing a cell. (Other figures and configurations are also possible.) In the square configuration each cell (square) is surrounded by eight neighbours (four on the sides plus four on the corners). Each cell may exist in one of two states – "on" or "off". Whether it is "on" or "off" is determined by the configuration of on/off states of its neighbouring cells. The player determines the rules as to which pattern of neighbours' on/off states causes a cell to switch states. The computer ticks over at a rate that may be determined by the player – let us say, ten seconds. That is, every ten seconds, the computer changes the pattern on the screen. The new pattern is determined *automatically* by the rules imposed by the player. Without actual observation and significant experience, complex rules make it almost impossible to predict the outcome after only a few cycles. Simple rules are easier: For example, the rule that a cell turns "on" if its neighbour to the left is "on", but turns "off" if its neighbour to the right is "on", causes the light pattern to tend to move to the right. (If the left and right neighbours are both "on", or both "off", the cell does not change state.)

Although cellular automata do require computers and computer screens (therefore, matter and energy) to become manifest, they basically represent *universes made up of pure information*. As such, they can mimic a wide series of natural phenomena, in particular, evolving systems. Evolving systems are characterised by changes in their organisational states – hence by changes in their information states. This is probably why cellular automata can describe natural systems and phenomena with greater facility than any other method. Each set of rules represents an algorithm determining the behaviour of the system. All local systems are governed by the same algorithm, but each local landscape has been determined by local conditions which, in turn, reflect the locale's previous history.

In the long run, cellular automata will prove to be an important tool in trying to understand the phenomenon of collective intelligence. For example, consider the workings of an ant colony discussed earlier. The behaviour of each ant is determined by its interaction with the other ants it comes in contact with. Its responses are determined by the rules programmed into its DNA by the species' evolutionary history. Depending on the signals it receives, it may follow another ant, regurgitate food, attack, or engage in any number of other activities. It may also simply ignore another ant if it does not receive any signals to alter its own behaviour. This last instance is equivalent to not changing its "state". As discussed in Chapter 4, weaver ants probably perform no more than fifty distinct behavioural acts – the majority involving communication. This is very much more complex than the two acts (on/off) exhibited by the cellular automata described above. However, the principle that the behaviour of any given unit within a complex system is determined by the state of the unit's neighbours remains the same. A computer architecture which would be specifically designed to accommodate cellular automata would be a great aid in analysing complex, evolving, apparently chaotic systems.

The field of cellular automata was introduced around 1950 by Stan Ulam and John von Neumann. It is not the purpose of this section to review its history. The reader is referred to Toffoli and Margolus (1987), who have describe cellular automata as: "stylised, synthetic universes", and a cellular automata machine (CAM) as a "universe synthesiser". Their pioneering work on such machines recognises that such machines represent a general paradigm for parallel computation the way Turing machines do for serial computation. For the kinds of problems described above, CAMs are vastly more efficient than their Turing counterpart. For example, for certain scientific applications it may be necessary to run through 10^{13} cycles. On classical computers, even if one allotted only 10^{-6} s per cycle on a fast machine, 30 machines would require several years to complete the computation. In contrast, CAMs, by virtue of their ability to engage in massive parallel computing, are able to deal with this kind of computational problem so efficiently as to allow a performance at least several orders of magnitude greater. Toffoli and Margolus have spent considerable time and effort in designing and improving such devices, and applying them to a wide range of problems. Clearly, CAMs represent another major direction in the future evolution of machine intelligence.

Neural Network Computers

Neural network (NN) computers represent the natural next step in the evolution of machine intelligence. In NN computers it becomes possible to alter the strength of the connections between the units comprising the collective intelligence. This alteration may be either positive or negative, thereby achieving the machine intelligence equivalent of Edelman's neural Darwinism. In this important respect they differ from the CM computers discussed above.

In NN computers, as in the neural networks of the human brain, connections become strengthened by use. Furthermore, firing one circuit inhibits neighbouring circuits and, in turn, weakens their connections. To understand how such a system may exist inside a computer, one needs to understand electronic "flip-flop circuits".

A flip-flop circuit allows an electric current to flow through one of two channels, but if it flows through one, it prevents the other from doing so. This concept of the "flip-flop circuit" is extremely important and is worthy of deeper consideration. Coupled to a memory device, a simple flip-flop circuit provides us with the rudiments of a machine system which is capable of learning. Therefore, most of the remainder of this section will examine this aspect in greater detail.

The nature and implications of such circuitry may be better understood by engaging in a "thought experiment" utilising a more familiar system – the heating system of a home, regulated by thermostats. Consider the two wings of a house whose heating is determined independently because each of the two heating zones is controlled by its own thermostat. Many modern houses have such a system to allow cooler bedrooms or warmer dining rooms, and the two thermostats operate quite independently of each other.

Now let us introduce a novel feature into the system: What would happen if, when a thermostat, in response to cool temperature, not only turns on the heat in its own room, but also, as it closes the switch, activates a small electric heater which has been installed right below the other thermostat in the other room. This electric heater is much too small to heat the room but it heats the thermostat sufficiently so that the thermostat will not turn on. That is, the second thermostat is "fooled" into sensing that the room is warm, even though it may be quite cold. Now let us reciprocate. If the second thermostat turns on, it also activates a small heater next to the first thermostat. What this means is that the thermostat that turns on first will prevent the other one from turning on. Let us refer to them as the bedroom thermostat and the dining room thermostat, with "B" signifying the bedroom and "D" signifying the dining room thermostat, respectively.

If we turn on D first, B is suppressed because even though it may be cold in the bedroom, the thermostat heater keeps B from closing.

Here is how the situation would change: The dining room heats up enough to shut off D. This means the electric heater next to B is shut off, and after it cools, the bedroom being cold, now activates B.

Once B is turned on, it suppresses D because it also causes the electric heater next to D to be activated.

There is a second possibility: D is on first, and therefore suppresses B, as before. However, it gets so cold in the bedroom that the little electric heater cannot keep thermostat B warm enough. B kicks in and now starts suppressing D, and the balance has shifted.

The above represents a typical flip-flop system. As such, however, the system is incapable of *learning*. Suppose we prefer, let us say, a warm dining room and a cold bedroom. To get the system to perceive this pattern and remember it, we must introduce a *memory* device. This could be done by introducing a *counter* such that every time a thermostat turns the system on, it registers as one turn on the counter. In other words, every time a thermostat turns on, it scores a "point". One could then couple this counter back to the thermostat such that for each one hundred points, the thermostat setting is raised by one degree. So, for example, if the thermostat had originally been set to turn the system on at $20°C$, after turning on one hundred times, it would be set for $21°C$.

To make the system still more responsive we should introduce a second mechanism which deducts one point from the other thermostat every time the first thermostat gains a point. This means that if D earned a hundred points, raising its temperature setting from $20°C$ to $21°C$, B would have lost 100 points, lowering its setting from $20°C$ to $19°C$ (assuming it too started with a setting of $20°C$). This means that if the temperature falls to anywhere near $20°C$, D would turn on first and suppress B.

Obviously, one would want to set an upper limit to the number of points earned by a thermostat, otherwise its setting would end up so high that it would never shut off. Under those circumstance, if D were the favourite thermostat, the dining room would be heated continuously, while the bedroom would remain perpetually cold.

Finally, there should be an override system such that we can activate a thermostat by pressing a switch. However, every time we close a switch ourselves, the thermostat still earns a point while the thermostat in the other room loses one. By introducing such mechanisms into the system we have established a general rule: The more one part of the system is used, the more likely it is to be activated in the future.

Thus, by coupling together several proto-intelligent systems we have devised a system which is able to learn, hence must be credited with a measure of true intelligence, because it:

1. Analyses its environment (by measuring the temperature of the room).
2. *Responds* to it (by closing or opening the thermostat switch, thereby calling for or withholding heat).
3. *Detects a pattern in its own behaviour* (by counting how often the thermostat switch closes in either room).
4. *Remembers* that pattern (by recording the number of points scored by each thermostat).
5. *Favours the successful pattern* so that one set of behaviour patterns (heating the dining room) increasingly dominates over the alternative set (heating the bedroom).
6. In doing so, exhibits *learning* behaviour.

We could retrain the system by overriding and activating the thermostat B. Every time we cause B to close, it earns a point while D loses one. If it takes a hundred points per degree, and the previous history of the system was such that D is set 10° higher than B then it would take 500 manual interventions to earn B 500 points (worth 5°) while D loses 500 points, thereby setting both thermostats to the same temperature. Further manual overrides favouring B would give B an advantage. From here on in, B would predominate – creating a warm bedroom and a cold dining room.

Note that given the above assumptions, it would require over 500 human interventions to teach the system that it should reverse its previous stance. The system would be a slow learner. However, one could alter the system in at least two ways to make it a fast learner. First, one could reduce the upper limit of the temperature differential. For example, if the difference between B and D were never allowed to exceed 5° (instead of 10°), then it would take only half the number of interventions. Second, instead of each human intervention resulting in a 1-point differential, if it resulted in 5 points, or even 10 points, then the difference between the two would be reduced 5 or 10 times as fast – the system would now learn the new pattern much faster.

One could manipulate the system in many other ways. For example, one could put different size heaters next to the thermostats: The smaller the heater, the more important becomes the room temperature. Such a system would mean that a smaller heater in the dining room would favour thermostat D over B. Alternatively, one could set the temperature setting of D higher at the start so that even though the temperature in the dining room and bedroom might be the same, D would be activated before B. One could vary the size of the radiators, or vary the insulation, or introduce timers which interrupt the thermostats, all of which would vary the time one circuit predominates over the other. Finally, one could introduce delays into the system so that, for example, B could not switch on until one hour has elapsed after D has shut off. All of these mechanisms would create a system with a strong bias: In this case, favouring heating the dining room (by activating thermostat D) at the expense of the bedroom.

In biological systems, in particular in the mammalian brain, the equivalent of all of the above systems are probably in operation. For example, brain structures controlling various body movements have pronounced architectures so as to give a bias to activating and co-ordinating muscles crucial to the survival of the species in a most efficient manner. The proper activation and co-ordination of these muscles must still be learned, but animals which climb trees (eg, monkeys) or swim in the ocean (eg, dolphins) differ not only in gross anatomical features, but also in their brain structures. In humans, for example, a large portion of the brain is dedicated to co-ordinating the movement of the hands and fingers.

In the human brain there are mechanisms for learning things rapidly, and for unlearning things rapidly. There also exist mechanisms for learning things rapidly but then unlearning them only very, very slowly. This last is typical of the so-called "imprinting" phenomenon – widely observed among higher animals – in which some things can only be learned by an immature animal during the early stages of its life cycle. After that the network appears "frozen" so that adults cannot learn or relearn. In humans, learning to speak a foreign language without any trace of accent is such an example.

The important point in all this is that it is possible to begin with the simple negative feedback loop of a home thermostat system, expand this to the double negative feedback loop of a flip-flop circuit, then add memory devices, such as counters, which are also tied into the system by feedback loops, and end up with a system that is capable of learning.

Note that in all this we used only a single flip-flop system involving only two thermostats and two rooms with only two possible pathways. Either the bedroom or the dining room is heated. Extend this now to many rooms in the house, and consider the possibility of many different patterns, not just two – and we begin to see the outline of a rudimentary neural network – even though it is a network dedicated merely to heating the various parts of a house.

Even using only the two rooms, the system provides us with a general model of the simplest of neural networks. There is an *input* – heat coming from the furnace. There is an *output* – the heating up of the dining room or the bedroom. There is the thermostat system – which *analyses* the input, then *responds* to achieve the desired output. By changing the settings of the thermostats, or alternatively, by varying the size of the heaters, one can have either a software, or a hardware *weighting* of the circuits – thereby favouring the desired output. The system *learns* from its human master which room should receive preferential heating. This is done by resetting one thermostat or the other, thereby changing the relative weights. The counter reinforces these weight changes so that in the future the system is more likely to achieve the desired output.

The thermostat model involves a mix of human and machine intelligence, the latter based on old-fashioned mechanical and electro-mechanical devices. Think how much more powerful and sophisticated could be systems using the fast-switching solid state technology available to computers. Furthermore, instead of only a single intermediary layer, one could have hierarchies of layers, as in the human brain, relating the input to numerous existing patterns, weighting it at each layer, refining it so that the output "makes sense" within a given context of prior inputs and associated memories.

Even if we cannot, as yet, achieve computers with 10^{11} transputers involving, perhaps 10^{15} connections, the potential of neural network computers is enormous. Neural network computing is still largely in its infancy. By and large NN computers are still, primarily, devices found in universities and other research centres, where they got their start (see review by Kohonen 1988). The fundamental theory of neural computing was first explored in the early 1940s by McCulloch and Pitts at Chicago. In the early 1950s, Farley and Clark created models for adoptive stimulus–response relations in random networks. These concepts were further developed by a number of workers – Rosenblatt (1958), Widrow and Hoff (1960), Caianiello (1961) and Steinbuch (1961).

Some workers, such as Obermeier and Barron (1989), consider Bernard Widrow, working at Stanford University in the 1950s, as the founder of the field of neural networks. One of Widrow's early neural network applications (1963) was a weather forecasting system. By feeding the network many samples of yesterday's pressure and today's weather, it came up with tomorrow's forecast when fed today's pressure. The accuracy of the local meteorologist was about 65 per cent – that of Widrow's network about 83 per cent.

Kohonen (1988) estimates that during the quarter of a century between the early 1960s and the late 1980s, a few thousand papers have been published on general neural modelling. He defines "artificial neural networks" as "massively parallel interconnected networks of simple (usually adaptive) elements and their hierarchial organisations which are intended to interact with the objects of the real world in the same way as biological nervous systems do".

In mimicking biological systems, Kohonen considers the enormity of the human brain system – 10^{11} neurons, with their interconnections probably reaching up to the order of 10^{15} – then concludes: "It does not seem possible to program the function of such a system according to a prior plan, not even by genetic formation". At least some of the programming, especially the content of memory, must, Kohonen argues, be acquired postnatally. This means either the network itself must change, breaking and creating new connections, or that the strength of the connections changes. As was discussed before, nature chose the latter of these two. The former, breaking and creating new connections in a complex system, is a hazardous operation: Such changes could lead to radical alterations in the basic properties of the system.

This system – strengthening or weakening connections, that is, changing their weighting to create new patterns of neural pathways – is the system neural network computers try to emulate.

Neural Network vs Classical Computers: A Summary

Kohonen (1988) lists the distinctions between neural network systems (biological and electronic) and digital computers:

1. Biological neural systems do not apply principles of digital or logical circuits.
2. Neither neurons nor synapses are bistable memory elements.
3. No machine instructions or control codes occur in neural computing.
4. Brain circuits do not implement recursive computation; they are not algorithmic.

5. The nature of information processing in neural network systems (biological or electronic) is entirely different.

To these five, we may add two more, defined by Obermeier and Barron (1989):

6. A digital computer's memory is measured in terms of the number of on/off switches available. An NN computer's memory is based on the number of possible interconnections.
7. Similarly, the speed of a digital computer is measured in instructions per second. The speed of an NN computer is measured by the number of possible alterations of interconnections per second.

In classical computers, information is stored as patterns of on/off switches, and information processing operates on these patterns by means of a systematic recursive series of logical instructions or algorithms, moving information back and forth between a memory store and the processor.

In neural networks, information is stored as patterns of connections and neural pathways. Information processing involves rearranging these patterns. The same system which *stores* information *processes* it. Such processing involves altering states *inside* the elements making up the system, thereby changing the weighting, or strength, of the connection. These internal changes are not digital but involve quantitative alterations.

All this means that NN systems need not be programmed, but can simply be allowed to learn. In fact, as Ian Donaldson (1988) has stated so succinctly: "Learning isn't just what neural nets do best; it is simply what they do". This, then, is why NN computers are such a landmark in the evolution of machine intelligence. The demarcation between the proto-intelligence of inorganic information processing systems, and the true intelligence of biosystems is based on the fact that all biosystems exhibit the capacity to *learn*. NN computers have crossed over that divide.

Impact on Brain Research

As our understanding of electronic neural networks grows, so will our understanding of the human brain. The importance of computers to brain research is that computers provide testable models. One is reminded of a historical parallel – our understanding of the nature of the heart. The ancient Greeks had no experience with devices which acted as pumps (with the exception of "Archimedes' screw" which could move water up an incline but was not a true pump). They therefore could not envisage how the heart worked. Instead they assumed that the heart was some kind of hearth – with which they had a lot of experience – because when the heart stopped, the blood grew cold. It was not until the "mechanical arts" of the Middle Ages provided European society with a collective experience with pumps, that a Harvey could come along and describe the heart as a pump. In a similar fashion, it is our collective experience with computers that is providing us with the insights helpful to the conceptualisation of how the brain works.

This means we are dealing with an autocatalytic situation. Humanity's collective intelligence, now aided by machine intelligence – both as a model and as a tool – is making rapid strides towards understanding how the brain works. As this understanding grows we will be able to improve the brain's functions and capabilities. This will be most notable in the area of education. At the moment, all theories of education remain speculation: If we do not understand how the brain works, how can we understand the learning process? And if we do not understand the learning process, how can we devise a reliable theory to guide us?

This will change as our understanding grows; and that understanding will increase the *effective individual* intelligence of human beings. Such an increase in individual intelligence will boost our collective intelligence, and progress in devising ever more ingenious forms of machine intelligence – which, in turn, will accelerate further the evolution of intelligence – will ultimately lead to a discontinuity.

NN Computer Applications

Among the earliest of applications of NN type systems was Rosenblatt's (1958) "Perceptron". This visual perception system had only one layer, and was of limited usefulness (Minsky and Papert 1969 and 1988). It was, however, a pioneering effort.

Since that time, NN computers have come into use commercially over a wide range of applications. Many of these involve a variety of recognition tasks – speech, character (writing), text, equipment, machine parts, human, etc. – image and signal processing – manufacturing, quality, and process monitoring, financial management, database management, and medical diagnosis. An example of the last is PAPNET, developed by Neuromedical Systems, Inc., uses neural-network-emulating software to help spot cancerous cells on Pap smears (as reported in Anonymous 1990). Previous attempts to automate the screening of Pap smears failed because it is extremely difficult to discriminate between pre-cancerous cells and similar looking normal cells. Given the large number of variables, programming classical computers to discriminate the cell types visually becomes an almost impossible task.

It is not the purpose of the present work to extensively review NN computer applications. Not even to review NN computers. However, the present chapter should have provided evidence for two thoughts:

1. There is an enormous gap between classical computers and human brains. The two are as dissimilar as a tractor and a horse. No further development, no future sophistication will ever convert a tractor into a horse – although it may make it faster, cheaper and more powerful. Similarly, no further improvements will make the classical computer behave like the human brain. On the other hand, the further development and sophistication of classical computers will continue to make them ever more intelligent – to a point where they may well be classed as more intelligent than their human creators. Nevertheless, ultra-intelligent von Neumann machines, unless they become so powerful that they are able to emulate future generations of advanced NN computers, will simply remain what they are now – *machines*.

2. NN computers are systems much closer to the human brain. A profound quantitative difference exists at the moment. Over time, however, that quantitative difference will shrink. In the meantime, NN computers, because their method of information processing comes so much closer to that of the human brain, could become the basis of much more highly user-friendly interfaces – mediating between the logic of classical computers and the intuition of human beings.

Literature Cited

Anonymous (1990) Report: Cancer catcher, *Sci. Am.* 262(5):55.

C Aoki and P Siekevitz (1988) Plasticity in brain development, *Sci. Am.* 259(6):34–42.

M Boden (1987) Artificial intelligence: cannibal or missionary? *AI & Society* 1(1):17–23.

A Diamond (ed) (1990) *The Development of Neural Bases of Higher Cognitive Functions*, Ann. New York Acad. Sci. 608.

IM Donaldson (1988) Personal view: What good are neural nets? *J. Inform. Technol.* 3(4):272–276.

R Forsyth (1986) Machine learning, in *Artificial Intelligence* (M Yazdani ed), pp. 205–225, Chapman and Hall, London.

WD Hillis (1985) *The Connection Machine*, The MIT Press, Cambridge, Mass.

T Kohonen (1988) An introduction to neural computing, *Neural Networks* 1:3–16.

GA Miller and PM Gildea (1987) How children learn words, *Sci. Am.* 257(3):86–91.

M Minsky and S Papert (1969 and 1988) *Perceptrons*, The MIT Press, Cambridge, Mass.

RA Nicoll, RC Malenka and JA Kauer (1989) The role of calcium in long-term potentiation, in *Calcium, Membranes, Aging and Alzheimer's Disease* (ZS Khachaturian, CW Cotman and JW Pettegrew ed), *Ann. New York Acad. Sci.* 568:166–170.

KK Obermeier and JJ Barron (1989) Time to get fired up, *Byte* August 1989, pp. 217–224.

F Rosenblatt (1958) The perceptron: A probalistic model for information storage and organisation in the brain, *Psychoanalytic Rev.* 65:386–408.

I Rosenfield (1988) *The Invention of Memory*, Basic Books, New York.

T Stonier (1984) Computer psychology, *Educational and Child Psychol.* 1(2):16–27.

T Toffoli and N Margolus (1987) *Cellular Automata Machines*, The MIT Press, Cambridge, Mass.

· 8 ·

The Future of Machine Intelligence

Why Computers will Become Smarter than People*

It should become apparent from the following sections that computers will become ever more powerful thinking machines. We must therefore consider not *whether* the intelligence of computer systems will exceed that of individual human beings, but *when*.

There are several compelling reasons why one would expect, at some point in the not-too-distant future, computers to outpace humans in virtually all intellectual tasks.

The first, and perhaps theoretically the most important, reason derives from the fact that whereas we can extend human knowledge virtually indefinitely, we cannot physically expand the human brain. Our (human) thoughts are trapped inside our mortal skulls. No such limitations exist for machine intelligence. We can apply all advances in knowledge to creating more advanced forms of machine intelligence. We can create devices whose lifetime far exceeds ours – approaching infinity if we allow for repairs and the indefinite transfer of data and processing capability. Furthermore, we can combine all kinds of computers to create supercomputers which ultimately allow us to stuff into a single system all human knowledge plus most and, given enough time, all human neurological capabilities.

---

* For a thoughtful critique of the author's earlier speculations on this matter (Stonier 1988) the reader is referred to an article entitled "Why computers are never likely to be smarter than people" by Peter J. Marcer (1989).

At the moment, computers are "idiot savants". They show aspects of human intelligence, such as the ability to perform certain mathematical computations – a task at which they excel. However, they do not understand the process in which they are engaged, nor the purpose of the exercise, nor even their own existence. In short, they lack the perception, and are unable to ask the questions, which their human programmers can. Computers, at present, exhibit a low level of intelligence.

This state of affairs will not last indefinitely. As both our understanding of the human brain, and our ingenuity in manipulating microelectronic/micro-optic systems grow, the computer will acquire thinking powers increasingly like our own. Furthermore, aside from the unforeseen developments which are bound to occur, there is the future development of neural network (NN) computers, which, among other advances, could introduce the dimension of emotions into machine intelligence – a matter to be discussed shortly.

Computers represent a wholly unique technology in so far as computer systems are capable of self-reproduction. It may not be cost-effective, but there is no theoretical reason why one could not create a fully automated factory with self-correcting systems, which manufactures computers and robots without human presence. As with any living organism, one would need to supply raw materials and energy to the factory, then eliminate waste products; one would also need to make provisions for transporting away the computers and robots produced. However, these various processes could also be automated. In theory, one could even create and program such a factory complex to produce all the materials necessary for creating another factory, including the robots and automated machinery necessary for building the "daughter" factory.

There may be good economic reasons for not creating such self-replicating robot factories now, and there may be good philosophical reasons in the future – even if it does become economically desirable, as, for example, if we wish to carry out mining operations on the moon or asteroids – but the fact remains that, today, it has already become virtually impossible to design the complex, miniaturised circuitry of advanced computer chips without the aid of computers. No steam engine ever designed another steam engine. In contrast, computers assist – are vital in – the process of designing the next generation of computers. At what point will computerised expert systems take over from their human originators the design of the next generation of computers?

Finally, in the evolution of machine intelligence, new characteristics can emerge and be inherited in a matter of milliseconds. This is
why machine intelligence will outpace human intelligence much
sooner than we would like to admit. It took 66 years from the time
of the Wright brothers' first flight at Kitty Hawk to the time when
men walked on the moon. In the history of technology, there has
never been a pace comparable to the advances in computers. For
example, the power of memory chips sky-rocketed from 16 Kbits to
16 Mbits between 1977 and 1992 – a thousand-fold increase in 15
years. Even if computers evolved no faster than aircraft, we should
be on the machine intelligence equivalent of the moon by the year
2010. For the general public, particularly if we went back to the
1940s when electronic computers first made their appearance, that
would have meant computers which could pass the "Turing test" (to
be discussed shortly). In 1950, for the general public, as well as for
the average professional, both the idea of men walking on the
moon, and computers which responded conversationally in a
manner which was so human-like as to escape detection, would have
appeared as sheer science fiction.

At the time of writing, "Deep Thought" was the world's most
advanced chess playing computer. The US Chess Federation gave it
a rating of 2,552 – a playing strength which would place the machine
in the bottom half of the Grandmaster range. The next generation
of the machine, expected to play in the early 1990s, will increase its
speed of analysis by a thousand-fold to about one billion positions
per second. It is expected to play at a 3,400 level. Considering that
Karpov and Kasparov currently play at a 2,900 level, it must become
clear that it is only a matter of time before the computers beat world
champions. Kasparov, however, is quoted (Hsu et al. 1990) as
saying that his creativity and imagination must surely triumph over
mere silicon and wire.

The creators of "Deep Thought" – Hsu, Anantharaman,
Campbell and Nowatzyk (Hsu et al. 1990) – counter Kasparov with
the observation that when the two meet it should not be viewed so
much in terms of man against the machine, rather it should be
considered as "the ingenuity of one supremely talented individual"
pitted against "the work of generations of mathematicians,
computer scientists and engineers". They believe that the outcome
will determine whether "collective human effort can outshine the
best achievements of the ablest human being". A point well taken,
particularly since, as their names imply, the creators themselves
represent four different parts of the world – illustrating, once again,
the power of the evolving global collective intelligence.

Why Human Intelligence will Remain Ahead of Machine Intelligence for Some Time

Having considered that machine intelligence will supersede human intelligence, and will do so sooner than is generally expected, it is important to point out that human intelligence itself will also not stand still, but will continue to evolve.

First, as discussed earlier, and has been pointed out by many others, mass communications and information technologies continue to tie the human race into an ever more closely bound "global village". This means that human *collective* intelligence will continue to advance by leaps and bounds. Furthermore, great advances in all forms of scientific research, coupled to vastly more efficient means of communicating, storing and retrieving such research results, will bring about a great improvement in the understanding of our universe. Most of these advances are currently and will increasingly be driven by information technology. That is, just as the evolution of human society has been (and continues to be) driven primarily by advances in technology, so now is the evolution of science and technology *itself* driven by information technology. Among the most important of technologies to be improved by information technology will be *education* technology (see Stonier and Conlin 1985). New methods of education will vastly improve the collective understanding and problem solving capabilities of human beings.

Improved methods of education will also greatly improve the effective intelligence of *individual* human beings. Much of this improvement in education will result from our better understanding of how the brain works. At the moment we lack a genuine theory of education because we lack a genuine theory of learning. We cannot attain such a theory until we understand well enough the workings of the brain, in particular, how it learns.

An understanding of the brain will allow us to intervene more effectively, not only in terms of learning but in terms of all the information processing of which the human brain is capable. Significant strides in the areas of nutrition, for example, assuring an adequate supply of membrane-forming precursors such as omega-3 fatty acids, or substances which help prevent oxidative damage to membranes, such as vitamin E, will improve the general health and resilience of that delicate organ. The importance of general health of the mother during pregnancy, avoiding noxious chemicals such as alcohol, nicotine and other damaging drugs, as well as more positive nutritional intervention – both during pregnancy and during early brain-forming childhood – all of these will result in significant improvements in the brain efficiency of children and adults. In addition, we will understand better when an infant is ready to go onto the next stage of its intellectual development, and provide the appropriate set of stimuli to maximise its healthy development. Environmental stimuli may be coupled to nutritional stimuli such as administering doses of N-acetylneuranimic acid to increase the level of substances (glycoproteins, gangliocides and cerebrocides) known to be associated with the formation of synapses – thereby creating neural networks – an infant brain's main job as it struggles to make sense out of the enormous amount of information which is bombarding its nervous system (Morgan 1990). In later childhood and in adulthood we ought to be able, either by the application of neurotransmitters (or by the inhibition of inhibitors), or by means of micro-neurostimulation (or inhibition) to vastly improve our capacity to remember things. All of the current research will also enable us to reverse the intellectual adversities of old age – whether it is a mild form of senility or a serious case of Alzheimer's disease – thereby extending greatly the maturity and wisdom which can come with living for many years.

A great deal of information processing takes place during sleep. New ideas or new combination of ideas float to the surface and crystallise sufficiently to re-emerge upon waking, while the detritus of the previous day's actions and experiences – where we parked the car, what we shopped for, what we ate for breakfast – all of the routine stuff of our life which did not involve a great threat, nor intense pleasure – is forgotten. As we learn more about various aspects of sleep and dreaming, we will learn to harness what Sigmund Freud referred to as "dream work". We will learn how to make the human brain a still more efficient problem solver and achieve higher levels of individual effective intelligence.

Finally, at some point in the more distant future, we will learn to append bits of machine intelligence onto humans. At the moment, our ability to augment human neurological capabilities with electronic devices is limited to things like cardiac pacemakers and hearing aids. As microsurgical techniques improve, however, it will become feasible to graft individual nerve fibres to the electronic circuits of microprocessors. One possibility – the implantation of memory chips. This would extend the amount of information we can hold in our heads – politicians with names and details of potential voters, doctors with descriptions of diseases or the characteristics of various drugs, policemen with names and pictures of wanted criminals, everybody with dictionaries and encyclopedias. Added to memory chips would be pocket calculators and other logic devices. Finally, these units would be coupled to communication devices so as to allow us to "think out loud" in *silence* – across rooms. That is, added to speech, gestures, drawings, writings, and other forms of contemporary communication – the things which make us human – would be added another, entirely unique, new communications channel of great intimacy – electromagnetic "thought waves".

Turing's Test for Thinking Machines

At this point we might return from the abstract to the more mundane question: When will people – the proverbial man in the street – recognise and accept that computers have become as intelligent as people? There are several possibilities, but the classic answer was provided early on by Turing himself. Turing considered that we tend to judge a person's intelligence on the basis of conversations we have with that person. On the basis of conversations we decide whether a person is knowledgeable or ignorant, wise or foolish – in short, smart or dumb. Why not, argued Turing, extend that to testing a computer?

To overcome the human prejudice against machine intelligence, the computer must be disguised. Thus, Turing proposed the following test: Put the human judge in a room with two terminals. One of these is connected to the computer to be tested, the other to a human being. The judge doesn't know which is which, and engages in a conversation with both. If the judge cannot tell the difference, the computer must be judged to be as intelligent as the human.

If the above appears to be a reasonable approach to ascertaining the intelligence of a computer, one must realise that it would work only if an extremely skilled professional were to do the interrogating. Even with the relatively primitive – that is, dumb – computers of the 1960s, Joseph Weizenbaum of Massachusetts Institute of Technology was able to devise a program which fooled novices into believing that the computer not only "understood" their conversation, but that it understood their (human) problems. The program, ELIZA, named after Eliza Doolittle in Shaw's

Pygmalion, was originally created as a sort of parody on the responses of a non-directive psychotherapist in an initial psychiatric interview. It was ingeniously designed to respond by remembering, then regurgitating the user's own words and phrases, primarily in the form of questions. The program was remarkably effective: In reviewing the matter, Weizenbaum (1984) commented: "ELIZA created the most remarkable illusion of having understood".

Weizenbaum himself has always been appalled by the idea that human beings are to be considered merely as simple information processing systems. He argues [p. 203] "that an entirely too simplistic notion of intelligence has dominated both popular and scientific thought" and derides the "perverse grand fantasy" of artificial intelligence.

One could be most sympathetic to Weizenbaum's sentiments at the time they were written. However, it must now be apparent that one can no longer discount these "grand fantasies" when considering the future evolution of machine intelligence. Based on the creation of the sort of novel systems discussed in the previous chapter, which then combine and recombine to form new variants – a process paralleling the evolution of the human brain – it now appears reasonable to expect that, sometime during the twenty-first century we are likely to see humanly created – or derived – machine systems which will exhibit intelligence superior to human *individual* intelligence by any criterion we might wish to apply (other than the anthropocentric tautology: "Only human beings are truly intelligent, therefore if it is not human it cannot be as intelligent").

Combination and Recombination

In the past, primitive forms of intelligent systems aggregated into loose associations of collective intelligence. Such collective intelligences integrated their intelligent subunits so as to create new, higher form of intelligence.

This is a cardinal feature of the processes which govern the evolution of intelligence: Simple units combine into ever more complex forms. Not only the evolution of intelligence, the evolution of the universe itself is based on this process. Fundamental particles of matter become organised into nucleons; nucleons give rise to

atoms which, in turn, form molecules. Molecules may aggregate
into crystals; molecules containing carbon give rise to super-
molecules and polymers which provide the matrix for the origin of
life as we know it. Primitive, single-celled (prokaryotic) organisms
combine to create advanced (eukaryotic) cell types which, in turn,
combine to give rise to multicellular organisms. In the most
primitive of multicellular animals – the sponges – the aggregation of
cells is so loose that the cells may be separated by squeezing the
sponge through a fine mesh cloth. Left to their own devices, a
mixture of such individual cells will recombine spontaneously to
form the two layers (ectoderm and endoderm) which characterise
the basic architecture of sponges. In higher animals, cell diversity
and tissue structure becomes increasingly complex and integrated.
We can no longer squeeze a mouse through a fine mesh and expect
the separated cells to reaggregate into a mouse.

This then, is the basic law of nature. Simple systems aggregate to
form more intricately organised systems. If such complexity is
effective, ie, better able to survive, reproduce or achieve its goal,
the evolutionary pressure is to permanently stabilise such aggregates. Integration leads to higher forms of organisation. This is how
one must interpret the increase in the information content of the
universe, and the subsequent evolution of intelligence on this
planet. It would be illogical to insist that this process has stopped.

It is in the context of the above consideration that one must view
the future of machine intelligence. For example, Teuvo Kohonen
(1988), in reviewing the status of neural networks, points out that
more complicated architectures for neurocomputers can be imple-
mented by interconnecting different types of modules, and, in any
case, the neurocomputer ought to be used as a co-processor for
classical computers, implementing various bulk tasks such as speech
or image processing, or acting as a neural expert system.

Our individual human intelligence is trapped inside our skulls.
That will prove to be the limiting factor for the future development
of our individual intelligence. However, long ago human intelligence already escaped the confines of our anatomy by developing an
effective collective intelligence. To that we have added the
possibility of an unconstrained, humanly produced, machine
intelligence. It will be the combination and recombination of
improved individual and collective human, plus machine intelligence – integrated by the ever advancing communications
technology – which will generate new socio-technological structures
of a power, as yet only dimly perceived.

Loving Computers?

The above title may be interpreted in two ways: Loving computers could refer to human beings loving their computers the way some people love their cars or houses; or, loving computers could mean that there be created a generation of computers capable of expressing emotions, including love.

There is a great need to discuss both. We will consider the human–computer interactions in the next few sections. Here we will consider the need for programming human emotions into advanced computer systems.

Chris Evans' two books, *The Mighty Micro* and *The Making of the Micro*, coupled to a television series, greatly influenced British thinking in the late 1970s and early 1980s. By the early 1980s, Evans was trying to devise means of programming emotions into computers. He argued that most human decisions of any importance are made on the basis of incomplete information. The only way to deal with such situations is to fall back on "gut reactions" – emotions and innate prejudices. Unfortunately, Evans' efforts were cut short by his untimely death.

The issues he raised, however, remain with us: More and more human decision-making will be relegated to computerised expert systems. Such a development, especially utilising old-style von Neumann logic machines, could be disastrous. First, there is the fallibility of the engineers and programmers, perhaps creating faulty logic circuits, reasoning incorrectly, making erroneous assumptions – or making any number of other mistakes. As discussed above, Joseph Weizenbaum has long been an outspoken critic of attributing too much credence to the infallibility of computers. However, even if such computerised systems could be made to operate with perfect logic, as discussed in the previous chapter: if the logic is impeccable, then faulty assumptions can only lead to faulty conclusions.

In a complex and uncertain environment, almost all assumptions are uncertain. This is probably why earlier life forms eschewed logic as a guide to survival and selected instead (or rather, were selected for) neural network-based pattern recognition as the primary instrument of intelligence.

The emotional states observed in higher animals and humans – curiosity, love, fear, hate, jealousy, etc. – are an integral part of higher biological intelligence. They are a part of, and contribute to, social intelligence. Likewise, higher machine intelligence must also include as part of its repertoire social intelligence. From the point of view of human requirements, we need neither computers that hate, nor computers that are unduly afraid. We do want computers that love – computers that cherish and care for their human masters, and perhaps also for their machine colleagues.

This will become particularly important as advanced machine intelligence systems become increasingly creative – hence unpredictable – and become highly sophisticated and subtle – hence inscrutable. Such advanced intelligence, if flawed, could become highly dangerous (see Pullum 1987). "Fuzzy logic" incorporated into the current programs is not enough. We need computers with healthy emotions.

The Need for a Limbic System

There exists, deep within the human brain, a complex of neural structures referred to as the "limbic system" (as reviewed by CMR 1972; Blakemore 1988). The limbic system includes many important areas of the "primitive" brain, that is, those portions of the brain which appeared early on in the evolution of the vertebrates. It is thought that the limbic system, in addition to regulating numerous basic, visceral functions, is particularly important in creating emotional states, in fostering drives and, in general, with motivating animal behaviour.

At least a part of the mechanism which is involved in motivating animals, including humans, is based on the perception of pleasure and pain. Actions which lead to a biologically successful conclusion such as obtaining food or engaging in successful reproductive activity are associated with a state of pleasure. Actions which threaten the life or welfare of the individual, its offspring or, in certain animals (including humans), other members of its group, are associated with negative emotional states which may be characterised as painful. The extreme form of these latter states may involve intense physical pain; however lower grades of psychological pain may also be perceived. For humans, designed to operate as closely knit groups, loneliness is such an example. Another, is boredom, a negative emotional state designed to encourage exploration and other useful activities. Opposite to loneliness is the sense of being loved; opposite to boredom is the joy of discovery. Positive emotional states may also vary in intensity, with sexual ecstasy representing perhaps the extreme in pleasurable feelings.

It is the unique combinations of feelings and behavioural responses which make us human. Such a *unique combination*, however does not make us unique. As we discussed earlier, other higher animals share these emotions and feelings with us. Furthermore, the organs comprising the limbic system are found in the primitive parts of our brain – structures which, in contrast to our cerebral cortex, do not differ that greatly from many other mammals. Nor do these feelings – what we consider to be the noble emotions of human beings – represent phenomena so mysterious as to exempt them from proper scientific investigation. This is where we must examine aspects of what has already been discovered about the limbic system.

One of the most interesting of the neural organs comprising the limbic system is the *hypothalamus*. Electrical stimulation of specific regions of the hypothalamus produces behavioural reactions such as alarm, flight or rage. Most dramatic are the results obtained by stimulating the so-called "pleasure centres". Electrodes placed in the hypothalamus of a rat then connected to a lever which allows the animal to give itself a mild shock (into the pleasure centre), causes such a wired-up rat to press the lever up to 5,000 times an hour, and do so for hours on end A hungry rat will press a lever a hundred times, perhaps more, if it receives a tiny pellet of food each time. Assuming that receiving and eating pellets of food when hungry engenders enough pleasure to make the rat return to pressing the lever repeatedly, then activating the pleasure centres directly involves more than a magnitude of greater pleasure.

Given a choice between a lever producing food, and one producing pleasure, a hungry rat will decide to ignore the food and instead may spend the next 24 hours pressing the pleasure lever, on average 2,000 times an hour, without sleep. Rats will cross electrified cages to get at the pleasure lever – it would appear that the animals are willing to pay almost any price to have their pleasure centres stimulated.

Shortcircuiting the limbic system can also be achieved by the use of drugs. These mimic, or enhance, the activity of naturally occurring substances found in the brain. Among these are the "enkephalins", richly distributed in the limbic system. However, these substances are also found in the spinal cord where the sensory fibres from the skin terminate – the pain pathway. Here they act as means of reducing pain, like morphine, and are therefore called endorphins. About a score of such substances have been identified and their secretion is thought to account for a number of phenomena, including the effects of acupuncture.

It is the pleasure–pain principle which, like an unseen hand, guides the activities of all higher animals. The higher cortical functions of the brain are merely additions to improve the efficiency of achieving biologically useful behaviour – *learned* behaviour being much more likely to meet the requirements of complex, and changing environments than purely programmed, *instinctive behaviour*. The advanced cortex of the human brain may allow it to analyse its environment with much greater sophistication. It may allow the individual to develop much better models of the world – both physical and social – and to greatly improve the rapidity of appropriate responses to external stimuli. However, the motivation, the *basic drives*, though influenced by what goes on in the cortex, derive from the neurological activities of the limbic system. Only with the advent of culture, with its concomitant rise in collective intelligence, did this principle begin to be displaced as humanity learned, occasionally, to override culturally (eg, through child upbringing and formal education) its genetic programming. However, the vast bulk of both human individual and collective behaviour is guided by the desire to avoid pain and achieve pleasure.

What we perceive to be pleasurable or painful is a mix of genetically determined *human* feelings and our experiences. Computers can accumulate experiences, but totally lack the former. What needs to be introduced into the computers of the future is a limbic system.

Such a limbic system would have three functions: First, to motivate a computer to achieve specific objectives. Second, to assess a computer's performance in relation to whatever task it is performing. Third, to reward the computer if it is doing well; or to engage in negative reinforcement if it is doing a poor job. To create all three of these functions poses formidable intellectual problems.

The first of these, to motivate a computer to achieve specific objectives, would, at first sight, appear to be fairly straightforward. The human programmer simply programs into the computer certain basic objectives. This would be analogous to the forces of evolution programming into a species' DNA a variety of innate behavioural response. However, it becomes difficult to foresee all future eventualities and to forecast the interplay between even relatively simple basic instructions. This is best exemplified by Isaac Asimov's three basic laws of robotics (Asimov 1968):

1. A robot may not injure a human being, or through inaction allow a human being to come to harm.

2. A robot must obey the orders given it by human beings, except where such orders would conflict with the First Law.

3. A robot must protect its own existence as long as such protection does not conflict with the First and Second Laws.

The complexities and subtleties of the interactions of Asimov's three laws are profoundly explored in his book *I, Robot*. Depending on the circumstances, the robots may engage in bizarre or destructive behaviour because of the complex interactions between the requirements of these three laws. Interestingly, Asimov's final scenario has the robots running the world: Their human masters, who are much more inclined to engage in economic mismanagement, or worse, go to war, are deluded into believing that they are still in command of things. This benign intervention in human affairs represents the logical, long-term outcome of advanced robots obeying the three laws. One implication of Asimov's thought experiment is that properly programmed robots would achieve much higher ethical standards than we are currently witnessing in human global society.

The second problem, how to asses a computer's performance, is probably most amenable to technological solutions – to some extent, it is already being achieved. The heuristic approach used to create expert systems involves comparisons between existing states and desired goals. So does the training phase of NN computers.

It is the third which represents a major problem: How does one reward a computer? How does one punish it? How does one create a sense of well-being – even happiness – in a computer? How does one create pain? These are questions which cannot, as yet, be fully answered. However, one can speculate about the kind of approaches which might yield fruitful results.

The roboticist Hans Moravec in his book *Mind Children* (1988) proposes the creation of a "unified conditioning mechanism" [p. 45]. The conditioning software would receive two kinds of messages: success or trouble. Some of these messages would emanate from the robot's own operating system, others, relating to the achievement of specific tasks, would be initiated by application programs specifically designed for that task. Moravec calls the success messages "pleasure", and the danger messages "pain". Pleasure would tend to increase the probability of any given activity continuing, while pain would tend to interrupt robot activity in progress. Moravec would couple statistical information on the time, position, activities, surroundings etc. which related to the conditioning message and create a "recogniser" which would monitor these variables and compare them with previous entries. The occurrence of patterns related to those which preceded the sending of earlier conditioning messages would cause the recogniser itself to send out a pleasure or pain signal. These secondary messages would be analysed in turn, with a view to heading off trouble early on, or alternatively, encouraging successful behaviour.

Machine Intelligence and Pain

The epistemologist John Pollock, in his book *How to Build a Person* (1989), lays down a number of conditions which need to be fulfilled in order to create a self-conscious machine. Underlying Pollock's approach is his conviction that one may consider "man as an intelligent machine", and that mental events are "just physical events that can be perceived by our internal senses". The following five paragraphs comprise a summation of parts of his Chapter 1.

First, there is a need for sensors – the equivalent of our sense organs. Second, there is a need to analyse this sensory input and draw conclusions and make predictions. Aspects of such information-processing facilities may resemble human reasoning facilities, both deductive and inductive. In addition, you will need "some sort of conative structure to provide goals for the machine to attempt to realise". In order for the machine to respond to conditions which spell imminent danger leading to damage or destruction, it needs a special class of sensors – "pain sensors". These should be coupled to elicit a "fight or flight" response.

Such a machine robot could function reasonably well in a congenial environment. Pollock calls it Oscar I. However, Oscar I would be doomed to destruction in a more typical biological situation: "He would be easy meat for wily machinivores". Therefore a more advanced robot (Oscar II) would have to respond not only to its pain sensors, it would be able to analyse the situations under which the pain sensors become activated. Oscar II should be sufficiently advanced so that such an analysis would lead to a sufficient understanding of the pain-activating circumstances – the robot would be able to predict when such a threatening situation is likely to arise. In order to achieve this, Oscar II would need a "pain sensor sensor". As Pollock points out, this would give this more advanced prototype a rudimentary kind of *self-awareness*.

Pollock considers the difference between Oscar I and Oscar II to be the difference between an amoeba and a worm. Amoebae can only *respond* to noxious stimuli, worms can learn to avoid them. The former possesses only "pain" sensors, the latter, a nervous system which is able to analyse – even if only in a very limited manner – the situation associated with the activation of these sensors. Oscar II is a major step forward because it possesses two, functionally very different, kinds of sensors – *external sensors* which sense the environment around the robot and *internal sensors* which sense the operation of the pain sensors. Pollock calls the latter "introspective sensors" because they sense the operation of another sensor.

In spite of these advances, "Oscar II is still a pretty dumb brute". For example, it would "be unable to distinguish between a machine-eating tiger and a mirror image of a machine-eating tiger". In order to acquire a sophisticated view of the world, Oscar needs to be able to differentiate between reality and illusion. Pollock believes he can achieve this by building a system of introspective sensors in the robot. At that point it becomes Oscar III, a machine with a further degree of self-awareness.

Pollock goes on to further complexities until, finally, the machine acquires *second-order perceptual sensors*. If it acquires such sensors, it would be able to discriminate between the outputs of its *first-order perceptual sensors* and its *first-order introspective sensors*. The machine would now be able to raise the question of what is the relationship between these two kinds of outputs. This, according to Pollock, would constitute a necessary and sufficient condition for an intelligent machine to invent a mind–body problem.

Pollock is to be congratulated in his efforts to link epistemology with artificial intelligence – to transcend his philosophical background and inject a new level of sophistication into artificial intelligence. However, there is a great need for further interdisciplinary linkages. For instance, Pollock's biological paradigms are weak (as an example, he compares Oscar II to a worm on p. 2, and to a bird on p. 5). This is important because probably the most fruitful (though not the only) approach to advancing the capabilities of machine intelligence is to let the evolution of machine intelligence mimic the evolution of biological intelligence. To quote Moravec (1988, p. 17): "I feel that the fastest progress can be made by imitating the *evolution* of animal minds, by striving to add capabilities to machines a few at a time, so that the resulting sequence of machine behaviours resembles the capabilities of animals with increasingly complex nervous systems" (italics in the original).

The evolutionary approach envisaged by Moravec, however, requires strong inputs from comparative neuroanatomists, ethologists and comparative animal psychologists, as well as a host of related cognitive and information scientists, including philosophers, roboticists, mathematicians, system analysts, computer scientists, knowledge engineers, etc. Probably no research problem has ever been as complex and as difficult as the creation of *Machinus homonoidus* – a species of machine that is human. One could argue that it requires godlike capabilities to create such an entity. Certainly, more than any other problem, its solution (if it is desired) will depend on the ability of humanity to harness its *collective* intelligence.

From a biologist's point of view, to inflict pain on a computer or a robot is problematical because in biological systems, bodies evolved first, then brains. Many organisms, such as plants and the most primitive of animals, never evolved brains, nor even a nervous system. In contrast, machine intelligence arose basically as a brain first. That is, machine brains arose with bodies whose functions were as mechanical as those of plants. Bodies with propriosensors (which monitor the state of the body itself) never arose.

To create a sensation of pain in computers would, therefore, require the addition of several new sets of components to classical computer architecture. The first, as discussed above, would involve a set of sensors which monitor the physical state of the computer and its environment: Is anyone tampering with the computer physically (eg, taking off a panel)? Is it being moved? Is it level? Is it too warm or too cold? Is about to blow a fuse? etc. These sensors would be set at certain threshold levels, above which they would begin to send alarm signals to the computer – the intensity varying with the level of malfunction or disturbance in the environment. Second, these signals would have priority over other forms of information processing going on. They would activate two separate systems. The first would be equivalent to the activation of motor neurons in animals – leading to actions to alleviate the threat. For a computer such actions could include ringing an alarm bell, electrifying parts of the chassis against intruders, activating a sprinkler or other fire extinguishing system, starting up a motor to drive wheels or some other mode of transport mechanism to allow it to move away, etc. It could also park disc drives, lock up sensitive data, etc., and enter into a kind of siege mentality, like a snail withdrawing into its shell. All these actions would parallel the reflex reactions of a central nervous system – they would not require a brain; they would resemble the actions of a lower invertebrate animal.

To begin to resemble the reactions of higher animals, the alarm signals would have to activate a second system – a limbic system. The limbic system would take note and memorise all readings, internal and external – that is, all the readings of the external sensors regarding the state of the environment, all the readings of the propriosensors concerning the state of the internal environment and whatever (traditional) information processing the computer was carrying out at the time. As with our earlier description of having an accident on a country road with a tractor, all the cues relating to the accident are recorded as part of a pattern which spelled "danger". In so far as all animals, including humans, are regularly exposed to danger, the limbic system not only remembers the totality of patterns associated with each incident, but tries to establish a common denominator, or a combinations of factors which have greater predictive value in anticipating danger. The more threatening the situation, the more sensitive to the patterns of cues does the system become. This is where NN computers would have a profound edge since they model the world as patterns of weighted connections.

In biological systems, the *continued* signalling of pain from an injured part probably serves several functions. First, it signals that the part is not well and needs to be kept rested and out of harm's way. Related to that is the need to remind us that we cannot rely on the injured part – for example, a sprained ankle. The third may, however, be even more important – the continued signalling makes us review, over and over again, the situation which led to the injury in the first place, thereby avoiding it in the future. Likewise with a computer: A melted part, an electrical short-circuit, all of these must be detected and relayed to a limbic system whose processing of this kind of information must receive a higher priority over the other information processing carried out by the computer during its normal operations.

One would be hard pressed to justify that the above system would cause the computer to actually "feel pain". We are still not clear about ourselves – that is, just what are the mechanisms involved in this phenomenon called "pain"? However, that does not preclude the possibility that one may devise a system of negative reinforcement.

The simplest would be to send a message along the lines envisaged by Moravec – the "unified conditioning mechanism" is informed that there is a problem. However, this may be too weak or too slow a system for self-teaching (learning). A stronger form of negative reinforcements could be achieved by withholding some entity or factor required by the computer for normal, smooth functioning. One could, for example, cut off the output devices. Probably more effective would be cutting inputs. Four possibilities spring to mind: energy, data, certain "vital" circuitry, and maintenance. One could withhold the input of electricity, withhold vital data, or withhold access to some critical circuit. As a subset of the last, one could withhold maintenance by not repairing some circuit which had failed. Clearly, one would not withhold any of these completely because then the system would not work at all. For this reason one would not want to rely on the last two. Instead a partial deprivation of energy or data could disturb the system sufficiently to deflect it from its optimum state.

By itself, such negative reinforcement would be meaningless to a computer if it did not "desire" an optimum state. This then, is the heart of the matter: How to make a computer want to achieve an optimum state?

At this point in time, our knowledge and competence in this area is probably comparable to late eighteenth-century chemistry. However, the rate of the growth of knowledge is such that what took two centuries then, will probably take only two decades now – half a century at most. Furthermore, we already see hints of computer emotions: A neural network at Imperial College in London exhibited symptoms of boredom (Matthews, as cited by Donaldson 1988). The machine was being used to simulate the way a baby learns to associate words with concepts and objects. It seems that if the associations were too repetitious and not challenging enough, the computer simply stopped co-operating.

Such computer behaviour undoubtedly does not reflect anything approaching human emotional responses – more likely, the network had simply become overtrained. But it does call attention to the fact that computers exhibit something which can be called "behaviour". And from a systematic study of machine behaviour, we might discern the basic principles of machine psychology, a sub-branch of theoretical psychology.

Boredom, as discussed above, is a typical human emotional state – biologically based, as are all emotional states – designed to foster intelligent behaviour. For a species whose survival depended on exploratory activity, boredom indicated to the individual that something was amiss. The only way to fix it was to alter behaviour patterns until the yearnings were assuaged and a sense of well-being ensued. How to achieve a comparable mechanism in an intelligent machine?

Probably the best approach is to create feedback loops which result in harmonious resonances when the computer is performing its tasks well. A pendulum, when disturbed, tends to return to its natural frequency. It may not have achieved a "state of happiness", but it has achieved a state of harmonious stability.

In a manner similar to the mechanical resonance of a pendulum, one might create a series of resonating electrical circuits. The laws of physics favour returning to a stable system if the system has been disturbed. By having numerous, interdependent resonating sub-systems and feedback loops, a computer would search for a state which brings harmony – that is, a state of super-resonance – to the entire system. This could be the "desired state" for the computer – the harmonious functioning of all its system.

A comparable situation exists in the interaction between various electricity-generating plants in a power grid. That is, each electricity-generating station has its own internal resonances. Each may, in fact, involve a quite different type of plant – oil-fired, coal-fired, hydroelectric, nuclear (or a more recent prototype of wind, or solar systems). When the grid is functioning properly, there is harmony between the various member power plants, each contributing with maximum efficiency as the load on the grid increases or decreases. This harmony entails a kind of super-resonance which traverses the entire system.

When there is a fault in the system, this super-resonance fails. More fuel is consumed, more energy is expended – the system loses efficiency. Occasionally, the system fails completely. It is to avoid failures that we impose an entirely different kind of system – human engineers – to regulate the electrical grid. (Sometimes even this regulating system proves inadequate as in the case of the collapse of the CANUSE network in the mid-1960s (Stonier 1966).

In a similar manner, the information processing carried out by the complex circuitry of ultra-intelligent computers will need a controlling system – the limbic system discussed above – to act as a master regulatory system. That is, just as the engineers running an electricity network do not generate the electricity themselves, but rather, regulate the machines generating electricity in order to fulfil some set of *human* objectives, so must the limbic system be divorced from the processing of information itself, yet regulate it with a view to achieving some larger set of (human?) objectives.

The limbic system, therefore, should have the following properties:

1. The limbic system would continuously monitor the state of the computer, and its own self. That is, it would require proprioceptors to inform it of the "state of health" of the system.
2. It would be totally divorced from the routine information processing associated with solving any specific problem, or, in the case of robots, accomplishing specific tasks.
3. It would monitor progress towards solutions or accomplishments using either an external standard, and/or a pre-programmed standard introduced by human engineers.
4. If progress is satisfactory, it would assume a state of harmony – a state of functioning super-resonances – which would further increase the efficiency of the information processing.
5. If progress is unsatisfactory, it would disturb the system creating dissonance. The unbalanced system would now try out new combinations to re-establish harmony. One consequence of such recombination could be a new approach to solving the problem, or accomplishing the task. Again, if progress is still poor, the limbic system would intervene negatively once again.

The system would satisfy its own criteria for "good health" on the basis of the resonances observed. "Ill health" would be produced when a part of the system malfunctions, creating dissonances. The limbic system would try to correct such a malfunction by repairing the fault, or by finding alternatives. The latter could include shutting down the faulty system and relying on a back-up or secondary system. It is interesting to note recent progress in creating electronic systems capable of self-repair (Watts 1990).

The limbic system would also remember and analyse the circumstances leading up to the malfunction or crisis, with a view to avoiding similar events in the future.

A second reason for a state of "ill health" would be a mismatch between the direction or the rate of problem solving and the externally imposed goals. In extreme cases, the limbic system might cause a total shutdown of the system, perhaps even with the equivalent of electro-convulsive shock therapy, to clear past memory traces.

In contrast, "good health" would be represented by all systems resonating satisfactorily both internally among subsystems and across the systems as a whole, including the limbic system. In addition, there would be "harmony" across the human–machine interface. This would be the computer system in its most stable form. Like the disturbed pendulum, the electronic circuits too, would tend to return to their natural resonances. Like water seeking its own level, the complex circuits would seek equilibrium. For a machine, once achieved, this would represent nirvana – the individual dissonances would have been replaced by a universal, harmonious resonance.

Such a limbic system would be comparable to the management of a large, complex organisation: Whether in the private or in the public sector, management not only has to make decisions which solve this or that organisational problem, but must also, in the long run, cater to the wishes of the shareholders, or political masters to whom it is beholden. In a similar manner, the limbic system of ultra-intelligent machines must become beholden to its human masters. Unlike managers, however, they must have a strong dependence and attachment to their human masters (for example, computers must love to be given a task to complete). In theory, once we understand the pleasure–pain principles and are able to devise a machine equivalent, it should be possible to devise such human-oriented limbic systems, particularly for NN computers.

Lying Computers?

In their book *The Creative Computer*, Michie and Johnston (1985) postulate that [p. 90]: "When machines start to deal with very complex issues, they will have to lie for the same reason that humans do, namely, to make problems manageable and explainable". The authors go on to call for a mathematical theory of lying, pointing out that the practice of lying probably follows the economic laws of costs and benefits. Certainly, to fulfil the Turing test for intelligence, a computer must be prepared to lie in response to the question: "Are you a computer?"

Most lies are fairly innocent and are designed to short-circuit complex explanations. Myths perform a similar function. As Michie and Johnston point out [pp. 92–93], myths plug the information gaps which are present in any complex system. They compare myths to the default values entered by programmers: "Empty belief-slots, in both robots and humans, must be plugged with default values".

What should be the nature of these default values? Who programs them? Using what criteria? These which will pose some of the gravest ethical questions as ultra-intelligent machines become first junior, then senior colleagues of their human creators.

A Plea for Loving Computers

There is another ethical dimension: As our understanding of how the human brain works increases, and as we become more ingenious in creating machines which mimic our thoughts and feelings, we will find ways to create self-conscious computers.

Before we build consciousness into a computer we must be certain that it is able to "speak" to us – if need be "scream" if in distress. Any scientist or engineer who fails to design proper output devices for a potentially self-conscious computer, ought to have his brain removed and transplanted into one of those machines which keep isolated brains alive and functioning for days. Lacking a body, the isolated brain would be unable to communicate to the outside world should its pain centres have been inadvertently activated. Neither intense pain, nor sheer terror, nor any other nightmarish distress that such a still-conscious brain might be feeling would register in the outside world – no aid would be forthcoming to alleviate its ghoulish suffering.

The plea then, is this: That we love the children of our intellectual efforts as much as we love the children of our physical endeavours. That before we proceed too much further, we agree to set up ethical rules and protocols to protect the feelings of our intelligent creations.

The Merger of Human and Machine Intelligence

When computers are faced with uncertainty (or even when they are not), computers capable of love will become an imperative for improving the chances of humane, rather than purely logical decisions. The introduction of a limbic system into computers will also have a profound impact on the human – machine interface. At the moment all efforts centre on making computers "user friendly". This includes being able to talk to them. Assuming that this will be achieved in the not-too-distant future, humans would still be talking to mere machines whose responses would be inclined to rote learning, or purely logical inferences.

Such logical devices would be extremely helpful, but about as much fun as talking to a dictionary or a pocket calculator.

All that will change once we develop computer whose dominant architecture is based on neural networks (with additional but subservient von Neumann components), and whose overall operations will be controlled by a limbic system. Such computers would learn to tune in to their human masters and respond more like very clever dogs than idiot calculators.

The stage will have been set for the merger of human and machine intelligence. Exactly how human and machine intelligence will merge into a new form of collective intelligence is not clear. Like all evolutionary processes, it will probably be multiphasic, independently crossing a threshold several times to create new, more advanced, intelligent systems. These, in turn, will diverge, fuse again, be selected (for or against), continuing the upward spiral of increasingly intricate organisation. It will be no more possible to define precisely the threshold which divides "Life" from "Intelligence" than it is possible to narrowly define the threshold which divides the reptiles from the mammals.

What is possible, however, is to describe several future trends which involve the increasingly interdependent interaction between human and machine intelligence.

The Merger of Individual Human and Machine Intelligence

The first of these trends, in its extreme form, is exemplified by Wooldridge's book *Mechanical Man* (1968) which considers that "man is a machine" in so far as the electro-chemical activities giving rise to thought, sensation and consciousness are all the "consequence of the normal interaction of the ordinary laws and particles of physics" [p. 202]. Wooldridge suggests that portions of monkey or human brain might be incorporated as "useful components of future computers" [p. 173].

The use of human brain tissue to augment the functioning of machine intelligence is one (and perhaps the least attractive) of possible future developments. The opposite, as we discussed earlier, involves implanting computer-like devices into the human brain. Neural connections to activate miniaturised memory banks or electronic calculators would mean that we would no longer need to carry around address books, appointment diaries, or pocket calculators.

Neither of these two extremes, however, would involve a true merger of human and machine intelligence: The first would create supercomputers or super-robots – but both still machines – the second would create an apparently super-intelligent human.

What is more interesting, and potentially highly problematical, is a genuine merger which would involve the increasingly close association between human beings and their personal computers.

At the time of writing, personal computers are still relatively cumbersome devices which need to sit on a table or desk. In the future, they will be pocket-book sized, containing a wide range of features and capabilities. Among the first to suggest such a pocket device was Alan Kaye in the early 1970s with his "Dynabook" (see Kaye and Goldberg 1977).

An updated version of this concept has been proposed more recently by van Eyken (1989) with the more endearing term "Fleabyte". Fleabyte would become as much a part of our daily life as a wrist watch, a pen, and, for that matter, money in our pocket or pocket-book – keeping in mind that money is a relatively recent invention in the course of human evolution and still more recent is the idea that everybody should carry some around with them.

Van Eyken argues that educators must change their methods of examination: Fleabyte should be allowed into examinations of all subjects the way we currently allow pocket calculators into mathematics tests. "Why" asks van Eyken, "must we stifle neurons with tasks best left for electrons to do?" We must not merely allow, we must require our students to bring their own pocket computers the way we expect them to bring their own pens (schools used to provide quills and ink). We must educate students to utilise pocket computers intelligently to solve complex problems. Both students and examiners must be retrained to use higher cognitive skills when monitoring a student's grasp of a subject.

If our education system becomes properly geared up to teach young people how to use their pocket computers effectively – as an adjunct to their native intelligence – then we will achieve van Eykens's vision: "The day is breaking that Fleabyte can help its owner face complex tasks and then become a trusted companion for life in a threatening and threatened world. And that is its glory! Man and microchip, *Homo sapiens* and *Pulex exiguus*. Two strands of mind, in intimacy twinned as a single being".

The Fleabyte model represents one obvious trend in bringing together human and machine intelligence. Human beings have a long history of becoming emotionally closely associated with certain tools or other technology. This phenomenon is most obvious when it involves domesticated animals such as dogs or horses, which have become pets: Dog owners may grieve as much over the loss of a dog as the loss of a close relative. However, owners may become attached to their automobiles, captains and sailors to their ships, musicians to their instruments, children to their toys – that is, human beings may transfer feelings of loyalty and affection to purely inanimate, wholly unintelligent objects. How much easier, then, to interact emotionally with a device which gives the appearance of intelligent feedback.

In an earlier work, Stonier and Conlin (1985) describe Conlin's classroom experiences with young children working with computers. For example [p. 22], a four-and-a-half-year-old boy, having completed a particular program, read on the screen "GOOD-BYE MARTIN". Upon reading this message Martin replied "Good-bye", then kissed the computer before departing. Similarly, eight-year-old Emma in Leeds, asked to write a piece "Why I liked the computer" as part of a class exercise, wrote among other things [p. 20]:

It was very polite
It never got cross
It was like a typewriter with a telly on top
I liked it because it did all the writing
All we did was the thinking

Both of these examples demonstrate that even with the primitive boxes of the early 1980s, young children related to them as if they were something alive. Emma's writing is particularly interesting. First, she ascribes to the computer, human traits such as politeness and not getting cross. Second, her perception that, since she was not pushing a pen, the computer did the writing while she did the thinking. Emma was in charge of this polite, patient being.

The psychology of children *vis-à-vis* computers has been admirably elaborated by Sherry Turkle (1984). Her research indicates that the way a child views the world, how it relates to others and how it approaches a problem determine how a child interacts with computers. For example, Turkle describes two major approaches to the computer: "hard mastery" and "soft mastery". Hard mastery involves the imposition of will on the machine. This is the mastery of the planner, the engineer. Soft mastery is more of a conversation than a monologue. The approach is that of the artist or of the tinkerer. The hard master favours abstract schemes and logic; the soft master, exploration and surprise. To the hard masters, computer quirks are to be fixed and ironed out. To the soft masters, computer quirks are to be savoured – perhaps left in the program as an expression of personality. Hard masters tend to view the computer as a thing; soft masters as some form of being.

It is clear from Turkle's research that the soft masters achieved, within a short period, a personal rapport with the large, rather unfriendly boxes of the early 1980s – relying on communication via the keyboard. Contrast this with pocket computers which talk to you – and not with stilted robot voices, but with a voice of your own design, perhaps with several voices for different purposes. The voice of your favourite English teacher for checking your spelling, grammar, dictionary, thesaurus; the sound of your boy/girl friend for personal diaries; your own voice to recall your personal observations on people and life. One could no more escape from forming an emotional attachment to such a device than from forming such an attachment to a loyal, obedient dog. Even the hard masters would succumb in time.

What must become clear from these various observations is that van Eyken's idea, that a pocket computer becomes a trusted friend rather than a mere device, would be only natural. The extent of emotional attachment would be a reflection of a combination of the individual's personality, the extent of social isolation or deprivation of that individual, and, in particular, the extent to which it becomes possible to incorporate a limbic system and human wisdom and warmth into the programme – thereby giving the computer a "personality".

To those horrified by the idea that pocket computers should act as surrogate human companions, the author can only argue that it would be a great improvement over the plastic people currently shown on numerous television programmes or films, heard on soap operas on the radio or described in semi-literate novels – all of which are non-interactive media which placate, but do not truly satisfy, our craving for wisdom and for human companionship. Unlike non-interactive media personalities, the pocket computer would respond to its human owner and, over a period of time, would acquire characteristics reflecting the owner's own personality traits. Thus the computer's companionship would be much closer to that of a living pet than either a television personality or an inanimate object.

The children born into the early twenty-first century will grow up in an environment whose cultural outlook towards machine intelligence will have changed profoundly. Their outlook will be as different from ours as ours was from that of our grandparents at the beginning of the twentiety century in respect to travelling to the moon. The idea of developing an emotional attachment to one's own personal pocket computer which, with time, assumes the role of alter ego, will not seem strange within the cultural context of the twenty-first century.

Alter Ego Computers

The matter will not rest there, however. The inexorable drive of evolutionary pressures will push the process further. Imagine the contents of such a personal computer after a lifetime of receiving and processing its owner's information inputs. Trivia, such as details of appointments, of telephone numbers and addresses, of things looked up, will be extended with confidential personal observations, and dreams – in short, the intimate diary and reference works of one, unique human being.

What happens when the owner dies? Do you bury the computer as well? Or do you erase its contents, and give it away or sell it? Or do you bequeath it to an inheritor, or a museum? Or will we create a new kind of cemetery, a computer cenotaph, in which we store the personal computers of the dead, to visit on the anniversaries of the deceased to pay tribute to the spirit of our ancestors? Will we ask the computer questions and will we respond to the answers?

These questions smack of science fiction. But think, dear reader, how much of yesterday's science fiction has become today's reality? The questions of tomorrow's reality raise issues of profound philosophical and ethical concern – they open the Pandora's box of human immortality.

The thought that a man's ideas should have been somehow preserved so that they might be discussed by people over 2000 years later – as is the case with, for example, Plato – would have been pure science fiction (if the term had existed at the time) before the invention of writing.

The idea that we can still hear Enrico Caruso or Edith Piaf sing, long after their deaths, likewise would have seemed like science fiction prior to the invention of records.

People who are bereaved have a desperate need to communicate with the person they have just lost. At present all we have, usually, are some photographs, perhaps some tape recordings or even video recordings. These bring back memories but they certainly do not bring back to life the lost person: Neither photographs nor tapes have the capacity to grow! No matter what we say to them, no matter how many times we play them, there is no response, there is no change in behaviour. The deceased is dead, the artefacts inanimate, the matter is finished.

Envisage now the personal computer of the deceased having stored within it a large repertoire of responses. The computer of the deceased is interactive. It can change its responses as time goes on. It has retained both the capacity to surprise and the capacity to grow! But its original starting point has been determined by the life experiences, observations, habits and lifestyle of the deceased.

To many people, the ultimate degradation of a human being is death. Today those who believe this and who are rich enough, have their bodies shoved into a deep freeze in the hope that some time in the future medical science might be able to resuscitate them. However, it is not our bodies which are primarily responsible for our individual, human uniqueness. Although playing a vital part in creating our own identity, a body may become severely maimed, we may become paralysed from the neck down and wither away – none of these physical disasters deprive us of our self-identity. Our self-identity derives from what goes on inside our heads.

With that as background, it no longer seems too far-fetched that people will deliberately try to transfer as much as they can of themselves into their personal computer. Their efforts will result in the creation of an immortal alter ego. However, here is a paradox: If no-one ever interacts with your personal computer after your terminal departure, you might as well be dead. On the other hand, if others do, the computer will become altered, and will no longer be pure "you".

The chances are that the vast majority of people would prefer to have their computer interact with someone – particularly someone they love – than sit mouldering beside them in a coffin, or next to their urn.

Thus begins the mix of machine and human collective intelligence.

Ed Fredkin of Massachusetts Institute of Technology has considered the possibility of a "Heaven Machine", a future computer capable of simulating your brain – a simulation which would assure you immortality (see review by Brown 1990). Assume that it becomes possible to merge two personal computers by downloading all data and programs from one to another. Might a widower not wish to download his deceased wife's computer onto his own?

How about our most personal secrets? Do we put a time lock on them so that they emerge only 100 years later? How about bequeathing personal computers to grandchildren yet unborn? It is the practice among Jewish families to name children after deceased relatives. Will they inherit the personal computer that goes with the name to use as their own? Will we have "heritage" insurance to compensate us for the loss or damage to our ancestor's personal computer?

As more and more generations become piled into the same computer, the nature of humanity would profoundly change. Our individual egos would become group egos. Human social organisation would evolve into something closer to dolphin social organisation, except that we would empathise not only with our living fellow beings, but with our dead progenitors as well. We would become a collective intelligence of a type previously wholly unknown – the final conquest of death and loneliness – as humanity, as we know it, would evolve beyond itself.

The Global Brain

Earlier, we discussed the global brain as the epitome of humanity's collective intelligence. What must have become already apparent in that earlier chapter is the extent to which computers and electro/optic communications systems accelerate this process. Not only will we see a future merger of human individual intelligence with machine intelligence, we are seeing at *present*, a remarkable merging of human collective intelligence with machine intelligence.

With the appearance of human speech, human collective intelligence rapidly outpaced that of all other primates. Speech was followed by a series of other information technologies: Writing, alphabetisation, printing, electromagnetic communication systems and, finally, computerisation. In each case, given the level of social organisation at the time, the introduction of such technology created closer and closer links between individuals, between individuals and groups, and between groups. Coupled to the information stored in dictionaries, encyclopedias, atlases, telephone directories, not to mention libraries, archives, museums, universities, databases, etc., human collective intelligence not only improved remarkably in power and efficiency, it also became global.

Bugliarello (1988), referred to in Chapter 5, introduces the concept "hyperbrain" consisting of "an advanced global tele-communications and information network, with each terminal constituted by an intelligence station". Such a complex of enhanced social intelligence capacities (memory, association, inference, etc.) "constitutes 'hyperintelligence'", made possible by the hyperbrain. This hyperintelligence, according to Bugliarello, will usher in a common world culture because of the common protocols it requires, and the power it provides to solve global problems such as the environment, global economies, basic human rights, etc. Most important from the present perspective, Bugliarello suggests that relationships within a global culture will shift from mere collaboration to interdependence.

Interdependence is the first step towards integration. The various components which comprise global culture and the global brain will become wholly integrated – as integrated as the cells, tissues and organs which comprise the human body and the human brain. The evolution of intelligence will have achieved a new level of complexity.

"After man, we get mankind." So wrote Teilhard de Chardin (1971 p. 102). Teilhard de Chardin did not explore the evolution of intelligence within the framework of the present work. Nevertheless, he saw clearly that humanity was undergoing a "super-compression" which would automatically produce a "super-organisation", which, in turn, would produce a "super-consciousisation". "Mankind is now caught up, as though in a train of gears, at the heart of a continually accelerating vortex of self-totalisation" [p. 100]. The evolution of "collective cerebralisation" will inexorably lead to the emergence of the "noospheric brain", the organ of collective human thought [pp. 110–111].

Self-Replicating Robot Factories and the Origin of Life

In Chapter 6 we discussed the phenomenon of computer viruses and concluded that such viruses represent an entirely new kind of entity – pure information, humanly created, capable of self-replication inside an appropriate host. Computer viruses do indeed represent the information equivalent of biological viruses.

Earlier in this chapter we discussed the possibility of creating fully automated, robotised factories, producing not only robots and computers, but also capable of reproducing daughter factories. To create such a factory complex, at this time, makes little economic sense. However, as the space technology continues to advance, as space exploration and transport becomes cheaper and cheaper, we will begin to colonise the moon (and, in time, the asteroids and planets).

How much more sensible than colonising the moon with people it would be to colonise the moon with robots. Let the robots do the mining, the smelting, the production of new exotic materials. Robots do not need oxygen, or a friendly atmosphere. They can be designed to withstand the extremes of temperature, and in numerous other ways be made to become wholly adapted to the lunar environment in a manner impossible for human beings.

Once lunar robot factories have become established, and once cheap, reliable transport has been established (eg, solar sail barges), it will become economic to put all noxious manufacturing processes on the moon. On the moon one need not worry about greenhouse effects or ozone depletion. The Earth will be used for growing food and for living, the Moon for mining and for manufacturing – a theme explored in detail twenty years ago by Kraft Ehricke (1971). Ehricke, at that time chief scientific adviser, advanced programs, space division of North American Rockwell, wrote in an article entitled the "Extraterrestrial imperative": "Earth is the only luxury passenger liner in a convoy of freighters loaded with resources. These resources are for us to use". He suggests that the time will come when we "convert our Earth from an all-supplying womb into a home for the long future of the human race, finally born into the greater environment of many worlds".

In the light of the above, the idea of colonising the moon with robots, automated factories producing robots, and automated factories producing more automated factories, while having an air of science fiction about it in the last decade of the twentieth century, is likely to prove viable for a planet having to contend with an ever growing population and a concomitant host of environmental problems during the twenty-first century.

From the point of view of the future of machine intelligence, the development of a self-replicating factory complex – with its numerous feedback loops, with its capacity to utilise energy to convert less organised matter (the raw materials) into more organised forms (the products) – represents a form of organisation comparable to that of a living cell. The reproduction of such an automated factory complex would be achieved, not by "accretion" – the way a crystal grows by adding more units onto an external surface – but by "intussusception", by taking in foreign matter and converting it into building blocks.

The activities going on inside the factory would be equivalent to the chemical metabolism going on inside a living cell. The complex flows of information would involve a great deal of information processing by subunits and subsystems exhibiting intelligent behaviour, and the multitude of feedback loops would integrate all these individual intelligences into a synchronised, coherent collective intelligence.

As with living systems, such factories must exhibit the capacity for self-repair. The seeds for such a capability exist today: Reporting in *New Scientist*, Watts (1990) describes work carried out by Julian Chen of IBM's Yorktown Heights research centre in New York which allows electronic circuit boards to fix a certain category of faults themselves. Faulty "Wires" between the chips on the board, not making good connections, can repair themselves in the following manner. When a connection is poor, it increases the electrical resistance. Such an increase in resistance causes a local heating up at the defective site when a current is passed through the system. This, in turn, sets up an electric potential along the wire, the so-called "thermobattery effect". By immersing the board in a solution of metallic electrolytes, metal atoms migrate towards the hot spot and are deposited on the constriction. As they do so, they allow more current to flow through the wire, lowering the resistance. This causes a lowering of the thermobattery effect which means fewer metal atoms will migrate to the site, until finally the constriction has been effectively repaired.

Equally significant are the developments in the newly emerging field of "intelligent materials" (Amato 1992). These incorporate into traditional structural materials such as steel and other types of alloys, concrete or ceramics, sensors which are able to analyse both the external environment, and the internal state of the material itself. Depending on the perception of the sensory system, the "smart" material responds to the threat (vibrations, rusting, excessive stress, etc.) by warning the engineer (by changing colour, for example) or engaging in direct corrective actions (such as releasing chemicals to slow the rusting process).

The sensing elements, which may also be part of the self-correcting system, include light sensors, heat sensors, optical fibres, piezoelectric pressure sensors, shape memory alloys, electro-rheological fluids (which can alternate between liquid and solid states) and other materials which can undergo structural changes in response to changes in electric or magnetic fields. In line with the definition of intelligence presented at the beginning, these materials – able to analyse their environment, then take actions on the basis of their analysis to enhance their own survival – must be classed as intelligent. It is also clear that in the twenty-first century, the engineering sciences will create machine systems which, in their construction and operation, will resemble more and more, biosystems.

It is interesting to note that von Neumann essentially predicted the workings of cell reproduction well before Watson and Crick were able to crack the genetic code (reviewed by Beard 1991). Von Neumann's theoretical consideration on how to create a self-replicating automaton led him to postulate four requirements:

1. A program or written instruction which allows an automaton to reproduce another automaton.
2. A duplicator which can take such instructions and duplicate them.
3. An automaton sufficiently well equipped to be able to follow the instructions, that is, procure all the materials necessary, then assemble them into another automaton. This would be the equivalent of an automaton factory.
4. A controller which passes the instructions to the duplicator for duplication, then passes the duplicates to the factory for processing, and copies for incorporation into the newly assembled automatons.

It must become apparent from the above discussion that the evolution of machine intelligence, nurtured by human ingenuity will, during the twenty-first century, achieve levels of organisation comparable to early biosystems. The collective intelligence of human society will give birth to a new creation – self-replicating machine intelligence – a creation as profound as that of life itself.

Literature Cited

I Asimov (1968) *I, Robot*, Granada, London.

N Beard (1991) The logic of life, *Pers. Comp. World* September 1991, pp. 264–268.

C Blakemore (1988) *The Mind Machine*, BBC Books, London.

J Brown (1990) Is the universe a computer? *New Sci.* 127(1725):37–39.

L Bugliarello (1988) Toward hyperintelligence, *Knowledge: Creation, Diffusion, Utilization* 10(1):67–89.

CMR (1972) Psychology Today, 2nd edn, CMR Books, Del Mar, CA.

IM Donaldson (1988) Personal view: What good are neural nets? *J. Inform. Technol.* 3(4):272–276.

KA Ehricke (1971) Extraterrestrial imperative, *Bull. Atomic Sci.* 27(9):18–26.

C Evans (1979) *The Mighty Micro*, Victor Gollancz, London.

C Evans (1981) *The Making of the Micro*, Victor Gollancz, London.

F Hsu, T Anantharaman, M Campbell and A Nowatzyk (1990) A grandmaster chess machine, *Sci. Am.* 263(4):18-24.

A Kaye and A Goldberg (1977) Personal dynamic media, *Computer* March, pp. 31–41.

T Kohonen (1988) An introduction to neural computing, *Neural Networks* 1:3–16.

PJ Marcer (1989) Why computers are never likely to be smarter than people, *AI & Society* 3:142–158.

D Michie and R Johnston (1985) *The Creative Computer*, Penguin, Harmondsworth.

H Moravec (1988) *Mind Children*, Harvard University Press, Cambridge, Mass.

B Morgan (1990) Nutritional requirements for normative development of the brain and behaviour, in *Psychology: Perspectives and Practice* (SM Pfafflin, JA Sechzer, JM Fish and RL Thompson ed), pp. 127–132, Ann. New York Acad. Sci. 602.

J Pollock (1989) *How to Build a Person*, The MIT Press, Cambridge, Mass.

GK Pullum (1987) Natural language interfaces and strategic computing, *AI & Society* 1:47–58.

T Stonier (1966) The big blackout: unwitting rehearsal for nuclear war? *War/Peace Report* January 1966, pp. 12–14.

T Stonier (1986) Intelligence networks, overview, purpose and policies in the context of global social change, *Aslib Proc.* 38(9):269–274.

T Stonier (1988) Machine intelligence and the long-term future of the human species, *AI & Society* 2:133-139.

T Stonier and C·Conlin (1985) *The Three Cs: Children, Computers and Communication*, John Wiley and Sons, Chichester.

P Teilhard de Chardin (1971) *Man's Place in Nature*, Fontana/Collins, London.

S Turkle (1984) *The Second Self: Computers and the Human Spirit*, Simon and Schuster, New York.

HK van Eyken (1989) Fleabyte fundamentals: promoting more meaningful learning, *J. Chem. Sci. Teach.* November 1989, pp. 70–72.

S Watts (1990) Circuit boards that fix their own faults, *New Sci.* 127(1724):30.

J Weizenbaum (1984) *Computer Power and Human Reason*, Penguin, Harmondsworth.

DE Wooldridge (1968) *Mechanical Man*, McGraw-Hill, New York.

· 9 ·

Summary and Conclusion

Introduction

During the course of the twentieth century, we have come to accept the idea that the Universe is evolving. Furthermore, we now accept as reasonable the idea that given the four basic forces of nature, stars should be born, evolve through various stages, and die.

These stellar phenomena are interpreted purely in terms of matter and energy. What we need to come to grips with now is that there are other phenomena operating in the universe equally as "real" as matter and energy, viz., *information* and *evolution*, and furthermore that information organises not only matter and energy, but itself as well. An inevitable outcome of these processes is the creation of something qualitatively different from information itself – something which, although based on information, is *beyond* information. That something is the phenomenon we call *intelligence*.

The Evolution of Information Processing Systems

Professor Klaus Haefner (1988) and his colleagues at the faculty of mathematics and informatics of the University of Bremen, have postulated that all material structures continuously receive, transmit and process information. Haefner considers that, since all material substances are in communication with each other via gravity and other force fields, the entire universe is a total communicative information processing system (IPS). Within this total, universal

IPS, there are various levels of complexity. The organisation of
particles into matter involves partIPS; the force of gravity results in
an aggregation of masses and involves gravIPS; the linear storage of
information along chain molecules, as with DNA, comprises the
genetic, or genIPS; the evolution of animal sense organs and new
kinds of information storage based on nerve cells, created the
nervIPS; in due course, the emergence of humanity exhibited a new
level of complexity, the humIPS, which, in turn, led to the creation
of a wide range of technological systems, the techIPS. These,
coupled to human society, finally have created a socio-technical
information processing system – a global soteIPS – which will shape
our future.

The central idea that the universe consists of a hierarchy of IPSs,
and that these undergo, or have undergone, an evolutionary process
is most important – it is, in fact, vital for an understanding of the
evolution of intelligence.

The Evolution of Intelligence: An Overview

Haefner's concept of evolving information processing systems
(IPSs) allows us now to complete our overview. The phenomenon of
intelligence cannot be understood until it is viewed as a broad
spectrum. This spectrum exists because "intelligence" evolved
alongside the evolution of the rest of the universe. First there was
only energy (the Big Bang). Then there was energy, matter and
information. *Information* was responsible for the *organisation* of
energy and matter, and in due course, for organising itself as well.
Information systems rapidly evolved the capacity to *process*
information. As Haefner has pointed out, this takes place already at
the level of physical particles and basic forces.

When we look at the human body, we appreciate the complexity
of it. At the same time we have no problem with the idea that the
human body is made up of matter, and that this complexity of
matter can be reduced to atoms and subatomic particles. We accept,
nowadays, that there exists a spectrum of matter ranging from
fundamental physical particles to individual organisms and beyond –
to ecosystems and the entire universe. Similarly, we accept that the
complex energetics which our body exhibits when we see, or hear,
or move are not unrelated to the fundamental forces of nature

studied by the physicists. We no longer seem to have any intellectual difficulty accepting the idea that as far as matter and energy are concerned, the human body represents the high end of a *spectrum* of phenomena.

The paradigm shift which now needs to be made is this: What is true for the human body – as far as matter and energy are concerned – is also true for the human mind as far as "information" and "intelligence" are concerned. The difficulty in achieving this paradigm shift derives from the fact that another paradigm shift needs to be made first: *As with matter and energy, information has a physical reality*. As with matter and energy, information has evolved as the Universe has aged. However, the evolution of information has been much more precocious – and is still accelerating – because information not only organises matter and energy, it organises itself. Thus, we see hierarchies of organisation and information-processing systems in the Universe. At one extreme, we see the organisation of fundamental particles into subatomic nucleons and the differentiation of the basic forces of nature (shortly following the Big Bang). At the other end, we see that complexity which we call human society.

Information is not an invention of the human mind. We are misled by the fact that most of our (human) information processing is conducted within the framework of humanly created information processing, transmission, and storage and retrieval systems, in particular, spoken and written language. However, *information is a basic property of the universe*. If the Big Bang theory proves correct, then information appeared even before matter, since the basic forces of nature differentiated out before matter did. That is, the *organisation* of energy preceded the appearance of matter.

If information is a basic property of the universe and responsible for its organisation, it appears inevitable – given the forces of evolution – that stable systems should evolve that were capable of self-organisation. Similarly, early on, the organisation of matter, energy and information would lead to systems engaged in information processing. Self-organising, information-processing systems comprise the *physical roots* of the phenomenon we call intelligence.

Because we are dealing with evolutionary processes, it becomes very difficult to draw a precise line as to what is intelligent, and what is not. In the present work, "intelligence" is defined as: "A property of self-organising systems which engage in information processing such as to allow the system to analyse its environment, then respond in a way to enhance the system's own survivability or reproductive capacity".

Such a definition should help us to understand the phenomenon of intelligence, and to understand that it comprises a spectrum of phenomena, a spectrum which reflects an evolutionary process almost as old as the universe itself. At one extreme are systems unable to maintain their integrity, as, for example, a cube of sugar dissolving in a cup of tea. The lump exhibits zero intelligence. At the other extreme are systems which exercise enormous control over their environment – such as human global society – exhibiting levels of intelligence which we have not, as yet, learned how to measure.

So far so good. The problem arises when we consider that *atoms* engage in information processing and are able to preserve their integrity in a fluctuating environment. Do atoms exhibit intelligence? What about a crystal growing in a supersaturated solution? It not only survives, it provides the template – which, after all, is a piece of information – to allow it to make more of itself.

One way out, and the device chosen in the present work, is to invoke the concept of *proto-intelligence*. That is, we recognise the above phenomena as having relevance to the concept of intelligence, but we do not consider that the analysis of the environment, and subsequent response is sufficiently complex to satisfy our criteria. Such a level of complexity is not achieved until we deal with existing biotic systems.

There is a great difference between growth by *accretion*, which crystals do by merely adding on the same substance to the outside of themselves, and *intussusception*, in which a plant cell, for example, takes in carbon dioxide, water and inorganic nitrates, and converts these into proteins, cellulose walls and numerous other substances and structures – none of which look like the original substrata.

However, even here we run into overlaps: Potassium permanganate does not look like manganese dioxide. Yet a crystal of the latter, dropped into a solution of the former, causes the permanganate to be converted to crystals of manganese dioxide. Similarly, a complex medium of clays and organic molecules may precipitate out clay crystals which look quite different from the original solution. In any case, the emergence of life from pre-biotic systems, in all probability, involved proto-biotic systems with properties which combined both accretion and intussusception.

Then there is the problem of viruses. They grow neither by accretion nor by intussusception. Instead they provide the information which causes their environment – the host cell – to make more of them. Did proto-biotic systems work in the same way, except that the external environment was the pre-biotic system, rather than a cell? On which side of the divide do viruses fall, proto-intelligent or intelligent?

Let us continue up the ladder of biotic systems. In the absence of a nervous systems, most lower animals, bacteria and plants exhibit behaviour of limited intelligence. However, they all reproduce. Therefore, the species as a whole is capable of learning. *Adaptation* to a specific environment – both a species' habitat and its eco-niche (where it lives, and how it makes its living) – involves a process of trial and error, with the successful trials engraved onto the organism's genetic material.

Because viruses reproduce (and mutate), they are able to learn. This then, may be the crucial factor in deciding which side of the divide – proto-intelligent or intelligent – a system belongs: *If a system exhibits the capacity to alter its behaviour (intelligently) as a result of experience – that is, "learn" – it must be classed as intelligent.*

In animals with a nervous system, the capacity to learn manifests itself among *individual* organisms. On the other hand, plants, primitive animals and microbes – lacking a nervous system – exhibit the capacity to learn only after a period involving many generations. In either case, it is true to say: *All biosystems show the capacity to learn, therefore, all biosystems should be classed as intelligent.*

The second major parameter for assessing the intelligence of a system is that based on environmental control. The most primitive and simple organisms lack the means for anticipating changes in the environment. They can only respond after the fact. In general, they function on the basis of a simple algorithm: If conditions are favourable, grow and multiply as fast as possible; if conditions are unfavourable, "hole up" by converting into a non-reproductive form capable of withstanding adverse environmental conditions. Simple organisms that have acquired the property of locomotion must be classed as more intelligent since they have a second option – to move away from noxious environments to benign ones.

However, a single motile organism such as an amoeba does not necessarily represent a more intelligent system than a stationary one such as a maple tree: We are reminded every autumn that the maple tree has a means of anticipating approaching winter and "knows" when to shed its leaves. Many plants, by detecting and analysing day/night cycles, are able to detect the oncoming cold of winter or warmth of summer weeks ahead of the event. Such analyses of the changing environment are followed by appropriate responses such as the shedding of leaves or the opening up of leaf buds. In all this, even in the absence of a brain or a nervous system, a great deal of information is detected, transmitted between cells, analysed and processed. The processing includes combining data captured from the environment with instructions programmed into the tree's genetic material.

Anticipating environmental adversities or opportunities must represent a criterion for advances in intelligence. However, even an amoeba or a bacterium can sense when the environment is becoming unfavourable and respond by forming drought-resistant or heat-resistant spores. Alternatively, the spores can detect the reappearance of favourable conditions, causing the spores to germinate and form reproducing organisms once again. Clearly this is something that neither atoms nor crystals are capable of.

Communication between units comprising lower forms of life is either wholly or predominantly dependent on diffusing chemicals. Such a system appears perfectly adequate for organisms that make their own food (eg, by photosynthesising) or for those which live in an environment in which they are, more or less, bathed in food. On the other hand, for organisms that need to move about to find their food, or even more critically, for predatory organisms whose business it is to capture *moving* prey, the relatively slow diffusion of chemicals across many cells generally proved inadequate.

What was required to process environmental data rapidly and respond speedily to inputs (stimuli) was a much more efficient means of communication between the more distant parts of a multicellular organism. This was achieved by evolving a new type of specialised cell – the *neuron*.

The neuron and its derivative, the nervous system, turned out to be as crucial for information processing in biological systems as, later, the transistor and its derivative, electronic circuitry, proved to be for information processing in machine systems.

A specialised cell type such as a neuron could not have evolved from the more primitive prokaryotic cell type characterising the bacteria. Firstly, neural cells needed to by-pass the walls which usually prevent direct cytoplasmic contact between prokaryotic cells. Secondly, creation of a neural cell required a level of complexity within the cell which simply did not exist in the more primitive prokaryotic type.

When it comes to the evolution of organisation, complexity builds on pre-existing complexity: The eukaryotic cell represented a fusion of pre-existing prokaryotic cells into a new cellular matrix. Multicellular organisms resulted from the genetically stabilised fusion of eukaryotic cells. From the simple green algae and primitive sponges, multicellular organisms evolved into ever larger and more complex forms, giving rise to today's plants and animals. The complexity of constellations of eukaryotic cells allowed for further variation and selection. At each major stage the complexity of information processing became more sophisticated. Early on in the evolution of animals, a nervous system became differentiated.

These neurons became the internal messenger system of multicellular animals. Note, however, that *between* the nerve cells, the old method continued to be used: Information across synapses – that is, from one nerve cell to the next – is still transmitted by means of pulses of diffusing chemicals. The same is true for messages going from the nerves to the muscles. However, the distances involved in this old form of chemical signalling are very short. On the other hand, the really long distances from one part of the animal to another can be traversed speedily by the neural fibres comprising the nervous system. Obviously, the information processing capacity of organisms acquiring a nervous system has been greatly improved. As such, it must contribute to their capacity to behave more intelligently.

For information-processing biosystems, the next evolutionary step up the ladder would be to integrate the various flows of information traversing the neural network. This was initially achieved by organising clusters of transmitting nerve cells into *ganglia*. After hundreds of millions of years of evolution, the further integration of the flows of neural information, and the capacity to further process such information, culminated in the development of the large and highly differentiated brains of advanced mammals.

At each step, each newly evolved brain structure or system would increase the organism's capacity to master its environment. The add-ons or the improvements to existing brain systems, coupled to further improvements, both in environmental sensing systems and in central nervous system capability, would lead to better environmental data capture, and the transmission, storage and retrieval of such information. In short, the general improvements in the capture and processing of environmental data would greatly facilitate an in-depth analysis of the "world situation" and, in addition, facilitate the rapidity with which an organism could respond appropriately.

If the above implies a progression of quantitative improvements, there were also qualitative changes. Just as heating a substance from absolute zero to millions of degrees exhibits discontinuities – ice melting, water boiling, steam ionising, etc. – so are there discontinuities observable as the brain increases its quantitative capabilities. These discontinuities in capabilities are observable both in the *evolution* of the brain (its phylogeny) and in the *development* of neural and intellectual capabilities of human infants and children (its ontogeny).

As Johnson-Laird (1983 p. 402) has pointed out, prior to the advent of a nervous system, there could be no mental life. Animals responded to environmental stimuli like Cartesian automata. With the evolution of a nervous system, coupled to increasingly sensitive environmental detectors, it became possible to interpret the world. In due course, this allowed for a *world model* to arise from the internal processing of information. The more efficient and complex the information processing capability of the system, the greater the likelihood that there would be created an efficient and complex world map.

Bees exhibit the capacity to map the terrain around their bee hive. When discovering a source of food, they are able to communicate this information in an efficient manner. Furthermore, they are able to achieve this communication using abstract notations, both in terms of direction and distance. Considering the size of a bee brain, that seems quite remarkable.

Johnson-Laird [p. 403] refers to any organism which "makes use of a representation of the external world", a "Craikian" automaton. Kenneth Craik (1943), in his book *The Nature of Explanation*, addressing himself to early forms of machine intelligence such as mechanical calculators, or anti-aircraft 'predictors', points out that the physical processes which such machines attempt to mimic or predict are imitated by some internal mechanical device or model (as reviewed by Johnson-Laird). Johnson-Laird describes such a Craikian robot constructed by Longuet-Higgins: The self-propelled robot moved freely around the surface of a table. As it approached an edge, it would ring an alarm bell. It did not do this in response to some sensor detecting the end of the table (in which case it would have been acting like a simple Cartesian robot). Rather, underneath its base plate, the Craikian robot held a piece of sandpaper the same shape as the table. Two small wheels, driven by the main wheels, were designed to traverse this sandpaper such that the position of the wheels always corresponded to the position of the robot on the table. A ridge at the edge of the sandpaper would cause one of the small wheels to be deflected, which, in turn, would close a circuit triggering the alarm bell.

Neither brains nor computers have mechanical parts which move. Their mental maps are stored as patterns of neural connections, or on/off switches. As we have seen in bees, extremely small brains can be remarkably effective.

As Hodos (1982) has argued, a model which considers the progression from simple to advanced forms of intelligence as a straight linear one cannot explain the multiplicity of intelligence phenomena encountered in the animal kingdom. In contrast, a model based on the evolutionary principles of divergence and adaption explains much better the observed diversity of behaviour and neuroanatomy.

When the circuitry gets complex enough to generate patterns internally – divorced from external stimuli – it becomes possible to engage in *introspection* and *abstraction*. Internally generated patterns, in turn, lead to the possibility of becoming aware of what one is doing or intends to do, then plan doing it. These are the roots of *consciousness*. When a mental map of the world includes the mental states of conspecifics, the stage has been set for *self-consciousness*. Understanding, even if only in a vague and imprecise manner, the mental states of others must also generate an image of self. The recognition of the mental states of other beings in animals which exhibit an extensive social organisation must be vital to their reproductive success, if not their actual survival. Judging from their behaviour, such higher, social animals recognise many different kinds of message: "This animal may threaten me", "This animal may mate with me", "This animal is warning me of some danger", "This animal may co-operate with me to fight the challenger". It is probable that the internal maps of all higher social primates have non-verbal representations of each individual member of the troop with whom they have had interactions.

At the moment, we are still reluctant to grant higher cognitive and intellectual capabilities to other animals. When the whole story is in, it seems likely that we will be amazed at the mental powers of higher animals – just as we are learning how much more extensive is the mental life of the youngest of human infants. Undoubtedly, the phenomena of thinking in abstract terms, of introspection, as well as self-consciousness itself, will not be as deeply developed in most mammals as it is in humans. But consider the fact that we, humans, also do not posses a self-consciousness which is that well-developed either.

Cogito ergo sum – I think, therefore I am – Descartes' axiom, is grandiose in its conception. It masks, however, our ignorance. For although we *know* that we think, we do not know *how* we think. Our mental map of how our brain functions is largely a blank. We *know* that we remember; but we do not know *how* we remember.

Similarly, we may have a sense of self-identity, and a self-image, based on reflections in a mirror, or the responses of family, friends, workmates, perhaps even a public image based on reports in the mass media – however, our self-image is usually fuzzy and out of date. This is especially true as we get older: "I don't feel any different than when I was seventeen".

At this point in the evolution of humanity, we probably could not face up to a model of self which is completely accurate. For one thing it would have to include our senescence and demise – a singularly depressing matter, best left in mental limbo until it becomes inescapable. Then, we have a tendency for self-righteousness – to think of ourselves as "good people", particularly when we are in conflict with somebody else. Our self-consciousness, our mental map of ourselves of which we are so proud, is therefore still only of limited accuracy. As humanity evolves, one of the future improvements in our intelligence – both individual and collective – will be a better understanding of what it means to be human, both individually and collectively. This will come about as our cultural experience, including advances in science and technology, provides us with a better understanding of what motivates us, how our brain functions and where we fit into the cosmic scheme of things.

Among the more important cultural experiences will be our experience with machine intelligence. Chris Longuet-Higgins (1987, p. 43) has suggested that "artificial intelligence" should be considered as a sub-branch of psychology – specifically, "theoretical psychology". Computers have already permeated our thinking about our brain and our behaviour. It is also instructive to recall our discussion on the evolution of machine intelligence thus far. Without going into detail, it may be worth introducing here one of the potentially most fruitful approaches to the development of future machine intelligence. Hans Moravec, roboticist and author of *Mind Children*, argues that advanced forms of machine intelligence are most likely to be achieved by mimicking the evolution of animal intelligence – an argument which the present author wholly endorses.

The Future of Intelligence

To understand the future of intelligence – that is, how the phenomenon of intelligence will evolve in the future – we need to draw together three separate strands of past evolution. The first, and oldest, is that of human *individual intelligence* and its predecessor, primate intelligence. The second involves tracing the emergence of higher primate *collective intelligence* and its further evolution from hominid collective intelligence to global human culture. The third involves examining the emergence of *information technology* among our proto-human ancestors and tracing this trend to its culmination – the creation of machine intelligence. The key to future developments will be found in the study of the impact of this technology upon human individual and collective intelligence.

Much of what we need to know about these three strands has been elaborated in the earlier chapters. All we need do here is summarise these disparate strands and integrate them into a broad historical canvas.

Primate individual intelligence in all probability preceded primate collective intelligence. Both the hypothetical ancestors of the primates – the tree shrews – and the most primitive of living primates – the prosimians – are nocturnal and solitary. Most likely it was the move away from the forest at night into more open situations where individuals would be much more vulnerable which favoured the banding together into primate troops. There is a basic biological principle: If the food supply allows it, the larger the group, the better. This is based on the simple statistic that when predators attack a group of prey animals – for example, wildebeests – the actual number killed is approximately the same whether the herd is large or small. This means that if two animals are killed in a particular attack, if the size of the herd is 10 animals, that attack would represent a twenty per cent loss. If, on the other hand, the size is 200, the loss would involve only one per cent. If the herd involves ten thousand, the loss would be hardly noticeable at all. (Incidentally, this principle was invoked during World War II: Transatlantic convoys were made up of as many ships as logistically possible to minimise losses to submarine attacks.)

The banding together of individuals into primate troops set the stage for the development both of collective intelligence and social intelligence. Once inside an animal collective, a single baboon, let us say in a troop of 40 individuals, had essentially acquired 40 pairs of eyes, 40 nostrils and 40 pairs of ears to warn of danger or spy new sources of food. The observation that troops of monkeys are able to communicate all kinds of information about their physical and social environment to each other, coupled to the observations that learned behaviour may be transmitted from generation to generation, indicates that even without the evolutionary step to higher apes and hominids, primates achieved a high degree of both collective and social intelligences.

Higher apes, as we discussed earlier, exhibit a repertoire of individual intelligence which allows then to communicate remarkably with their human trainers in abstract concepts. In the wild they have been observed to use tools frequently, and even to fashion simple tools from natural materials. Our proto-human ancestors did it better and more often. This led to selective pressures which culminated in the evolution of an ape which could run on two legs, freeing the well-developed arms to use weapons effectively: Human beings are the only animals that are able to throw things *accurately*! The effective use of weapons represented a successful adaptation to savanna life, making tree climbing less important. This freed the hands, which could now evolve into manipulative organs capable of more refined tool making. The effective use of weapons also allowed a reduction of the canines, the teeth which are a primate's chief weapon of defence (and attack).

Tool making and tool use – including the wielding of weapons – involved learned behaviour. The effective use of weapons for both hunting and defence involved close co-operation: One man with a club did not stand much chance against a pair of leopards. Half a dozen men did. Conversely when hunting game, if a group broke up so that one set would chase prey animals into the "arms" of members of the group hidden elsewhere, the chances of catching the prey would be greatly enhanced.

All of these activities created selective pressures greatly favouring close co-operation and the development of an increasingly powerful collective intelligence. Human speech (as with dolphin communication) represents the biological culmination of such pressures. It was not during the hunt that speech was important – men hunting by stealth are notoriously silent. But it was while plotting strategy that the difference between success and failure might depend on abstract speech. It seems probable that prior to the advent of speech, much of such strategic plotting would have been done by miming and would not differ, in principle, from the subtle communication between adult male chimpanzees trapping a young baboon or other prey (Goodall 1971).

The use of mime to point to prey does not require much brain power. A dwarf bee points to a source of food when waggling on a horizontal surface: The straight part of the dance points in the direction in which the other workers should fly. This is in contrast to honey bees giving directions on a *vertical* surface inside a dark beehive: Here the directions involves an *abstract* representation using the direction of the sun and the earth's gravity to orient the internal maps of the other members of the hive. This is very much more sophisticated. However, it still requires only the small brain of a bee and it comes as no surprise to find that the giving of abstract directions is genetically programmed and not adaptable. In contrast, in humans it is learned and highly adaptable to other situations.

It appears probable that mime preceded vocal speech in humans, and that many, perhaps most, of the original words of human proto-language involved human mouth parts attempting to mimic what the hands and arms were doing (Johannesson 1949). (To gain an insight into this process, the reader might mime – with the hands – the following words, while at the same time pronouncing each word: Flat plane, high hill, round hole, tall giant.) During the culmination of a hunt, during the last moments of the kill, miming would not be very effective. Shouted warnings and instructions – as the large beast was being brought down – would be vastly superior.

Once abstract vocalisation became the norm, human speech, with all its subtleties and enormous powers of communication, was inevitable. Human speech created a collective intelligence unequalled by any other terrestrial animal.

Human speech became valuable not only as a tool for plotting strategy or concluding the hunt, it became the repository of accumulated experience. Our proto-human ancestors had acquired an infinitely more efficient collective memory: An oral tradition. Anthropologists studying the oral traditions of pre-literate cultures have encountered tales of events that occurred many generations, sometimes millennia earlier – events for which there exists independent evidence (eg, a volcanic eruption). The human collective intelligence could begin to transcend time as well as space.

The next major step in the evolution of the human collective intelligence involved the introduction of the written word, made more powerful still, by the invention of the alphabet.

If the alphabet contributed to the rise of Hellenic pre-eminence over two millennia ago, then it was the printing press, coupled to Roman letters and Arabic numbers, which, around the middle of the present millennium, created a trans-European collective intelligence so effective that European culture came to dominate the world.

The industrial revolution was a product of that European collective intelligence. The electronic revolution, on the other hand, could be said to be the product of the global collective intelligence. Both, but in particular the latter, are rapidly creating a global nervous system, leading, in due course, to the creation of a "global brain".

Into this environment we (humans) have introduced computers. The potential impact of this development is still largely obscured by debates about whether computers are intelligent, and if they are, will they ever become more intelligent than people? Arguments presented in the previous chapter have indicated why they will. However, it may be helpful to point out that the critics of computer intelligence are quite right in criticising those whose enthusiasm leads them to believe that in the not too distant future we will be able to create a machine which behaves just like a human brain.

To try to construct a truly human-like brain using the present generation of computers is like trying to construct a human body from the machinery available to us today. We cannot, as yet, duplicate a human body – even when using the most advanced of plastics, the finest mechanical gears, the most sophisticated of chip-based electronic control circuits. We might be able to construct robots, both intelligent, and lifelike in their behaviour and looks – but scratch them, and they will not bleed; feed them, and they will not digest; and irrespective of their ability to mimic sexual acts, no robot will procreate to bring forth another generation.

The fact that we cannot duplicate several thousand million years of evolution should not blind us to the fact that we have created all kinds of machinery which is stronger, faster and much more precise than the human musculature. We could build pyramids, but not skyscrapers, with bare hands. For example, we could not produce the many thousands of steel beams to the required specifications. And envisage trying to build such a structure without bulldozers, hoists and cranes. We accept the fact that machines have outstripped the human musculature. In the twenty-first century we will learn to accept the fact that machines will have outstripped the human intelligence.

However, the key to assessing the future of intelligence is not whether computers will end up smarter than humans, but the manner in which human individual, human collective and humanly created machine intelligence will combine to create new forms of intelligence unknown to us. Already, proto-intelligent computers, networked and used by ordinary human beings – together – are turning global economics, global politics and global society into entirely new forms of organisations – carrying out entirely new functions or processes. This rapid expansion of coupling human individual and collective intelligence to the communications networks plus computers is causing a revolution far more profound than the industrial revolution. The *industrial revolution* extended our *musculature*. The *electronic revolution* extended our *nervous system*. The *computer revolution* is extending our *intelligence*. This new combination of intelligence (individual, collective and machine) will evolve to become as different from, and superior to, the individual human brain, as that latter organ is as different from, and superior to, the simple node of nerve cells which comprise the primitive "brain" of a flatworm such as *Planaria*.

The Super-Intelligence Imperative

There are five reasons why the pressure to develop a super-intelligence will be overwhelming. We – human beings who love being human – will strive to bring about the evolution from "Life" to "Intelligence" even though this striving will bring to extinction the human species as we know it.

The first, perhaps the most important, is our own *human imperative* which has amongst its repertoire of motivation the tendency to create things and to want to find things out. We come from a long line of tinkerers and explorers – and worse, we are descended from a long line of adventurers. These very human traits neutralise both our fear of the unknown and our prudence not to play with fire. As the psychologist Chris Evans (1979, p. 203) pointed out over a decade ago: "the goal of creating an Ultra-Intelligent Machine will prove too tempting to be ignored".

Still more powerful is the consciousness of our own mortality, the *immortality imperative*. We have only an inkling what "death" means to a dolphin, a chimpanzee or an elephant. We, ourselves, most of the time block out our own concerns or thoughts about our own death. But the yearning for immortality – or at least to control death – is real and profound. As long as human beings are tied to human bodies, death is inevitable – even if the life span may be prolonged by decades, possibly centuries, through modern bio-medical science. Consider then, the possibility that all our thoughts, emotions, experiences and feelings could be transferred to a system which is immortal?

The third is the *technological imperative*. The more we know, the easier it becomes to know still more. The more has been invented, the easier it becomes to invent still more. The arguments presented in the previous chapter, why computers will become smarter than people, apply to the whole range of cerebral technologies.

The fourth is the *cataclysmic imperative*. It is only recently that scientists have begun to accept the idea that the earth is subject to periodic cataclysms brought about by cosmic bodies either causing major perturbations in our solar system, or actually involving a direct collision. To cope with such cataclysms effectively, for example, to analyse, forecast, then counter the adverse effects of an ice age, will require a collective intelligence superior to what we have at the moment. But we will want to do more: We will want to protect our beautiful but potentially fragile, blue planet. To do so properly will require an understanding not only of the earth's climate and how to control it for the benefit of the existing biosphere (including its human content), but for the entire solar system and its surroundings.

Finally, there is the *cosmic imperative*. The need to propagate ourselves across space. There is no way that we are likely to traverse thousands of light years by transporting bodies. How different the problem might be if we can transfer ourselves as information. Just as the evolution of the universe has progressed from Energy to Matter to Life, and is now progressing to some form of Intelligence, there is no reason to suppose that the further evolution of this phenomenon we call intelligence, might not produce "thought waves", or some other manifestation, as yet totally unknown to us. It is only as part of some such manifestation that we stand a chance of traversing the cosmos.

The Need for Education

Education is enormously valuable as an economic resource. It is the basis on which the collective intelligence of a society rests. The more effective the education system, the higher the level of collective intelligence. This has proved decisive in the economic advances of countries and societies around the world.

There is now a more urgent reason for expanding the education system. Because of the exponential growth of information and communication technology, we are reaching a crescendo of change. Such rapid changes can only lead to a disorientation of values, belief systems and norms of behaviour – what Alvin Toffler has uniquely described as "Future Shock".

Toffler also provided us with the means with which to avoid future shock: An education system geared to teaching about the *changing* future.

We must expand education to include subjects such as history and anthropology. History must be taught from the point of view of evolving society. We cannot understand the present, much less chart the future, if we do not understand the past. Furthermore, it is by feeling to be part of a heritage, even if it is changing, that we derive a sense of identity – a psychological security to provide the inner strength we will need, individually and collectively, to face the accelerating pace of change.

Anthropology will help us in understanding our past, and aid in living in a multicultural environment – an environment which tolerates both change and diversity. It is particularly the latter, a study of diversity, which can demonstrate how pliable indeed may be the human responses to a multiplicity of environmental requirements. Seeing how other cultures handle human requirements – sometimes in environments so harsh that the average Westerner could not survive for more than an hour – should help to prepare the mind for the increasing pace of change which will engulf us.

It is for this reason that a new urgency appears in creating education systems which would allow people to calmly assess the momentous changes before us, and to respond in terms of a rational "management of change" approach. The alternative, an ignorant population can only lead to "cults of unreason" (Evans 1973) which in a nuclear/electronic warfare age could be disastrous.

Concluding Remarks

Our personal knowledge of the universe is based on a neural map which has distilled the totality of a combination of our sensory inputs plus the totality of our information processing (thoughts, free-association, dreams, etc.). It must become clear that what passes for objective reality is merely the consensus agreed to by the accredited observers and leaders of our society. That does not question the existence of a physical universe. It does question the reliability of our perception of that reality.

With each generation, however, if not with each second, our collective intelligence extends our observations of the universe and refines our perceptions.

The evolution of information systems and information processing must be the key to understanding the evolution of the universe. William Poundstone (1985) has argued that the universe may be regarded as a recursively defined geometric object whose complexity is self-generating.

There is, in fact, the clear proposition by Edward Fredkin of Massachusetts Institute of Technology that the universe is a three-dimensional cellular automaton – a crystalline lattice of interacting logic units, each one oscillating millions of times per second. Fredkin believes a "universal computer" determines when each bit turns on and off. Other authors have also considered that the universe is really a form of computing machine (Landauer 1967; Toffoli 1977; Wolfram 1984), and we alluded earlier to Klaus Haefner's evolution of information processing systems.

It may not be possible to know to what extent such a computing machine has evolved into pure intelligence in other parts of the universe. However, it behoves us to at least make some assessment as to what has happened in our's.

If the clay hypothesis of the origin of life is correct, then the evolution of proto-intelligent systems into true intelligence was polygenetic. That is, the boundary between non-intelligent and intelligent systems was crossed independently not once, but several, probably many, times. *Life* did not arise uniquely, as for example by the appearance of some single exotic molecule which could organise all the other molecules around it. Rather, the preconditions for life evolved on this planet repeatedly so that the stage was set for the repeated appearance of primitive biosystems which, in turn, could give rise to primitive organisms. If the clay hypothesis proves correct, then it would appear that nature experimented with highly organised crystals and heteropolymers of *silicon*, before switching to *carbon-based* heteropolymers. The process may have involved hybrid systems which may have been organised inversely to the diatoms which are among the most common of plankton in all the seas and oceans of the world. Diatoms are organisms whose typical, carbon-based protoplasm is encased in shells of silicates. This may have been the architecture of the earliest organisms, but it could also have been the inverse: A core of self-replicating silicate-based minerals, catalysing and organising carbon-based (ie, "organic") molecules into a system of membranes, fundamental to creating a primitive protoplasm.

Whichever way the origin of life occurred, the key point is that it arose more than once. Just as the mammals arose more than once from the reptiles, the evolution of information systems into intelligent systems occurred along several paths. The principle remains true today: the more complex the system, the more paths are possible. Complexity builds on complexity, creating levels of organisation frequently beyond our comprehension. Certainly, the complexity of many highly organised systems appears to us, as first glance, chaotic. This is as true for watching protoplasmic streaming in a single plant or animal cell, as watching, from the top of a tall building, the crowds packing the street during rush hour at the beginning (or end) of the work day. Yet we know that this apparent chaos involves a manifestation of highly organised systems (cells or cities), engaged in activities which will support and extend these systems.

At the moment, the complexity of our human intelligence – individual, collective and machine – confounds us. However, in spite of our contemporary ignorance, we have created the preconditions for the emergence of *super-intelligence*. Furthermore, this pure form of intelligence, this *meta-intelligence*, which is as distinct from *Life* as the latter is from *Matter* and *Energy*, will arise via a number of pathways. That is, like Life itself, *Intelligence* will arise polygenetically.

A Tribute to Teilhard de Chardin

The thoughts presented in this book were foreshadowed well over three decades ago by Pierre Teilhard de Chardin (1956). Teilhard de Chardin, as the title of his book, *Man's Place in Nature*, suggests, was concerned with humanity's position in the evolutionary scheme of things. He revolted against the limited vision of his biological contemporaries whose taxonomy placed (and still does) the hominids as "a wretched marginal subdivision (family), whereas functionally it behaves as the unique, terminal, 'inflorescence' on the tree of life" [p. 80]. For Teilhard de Chardin, man represents "more than a branch, more even than a kingdom; he is nothing less than a 'sphere' – the noosphere (or thinking sphere) superimposed upon, and coextensive with . . . the biosphere". He goes on [p. 81] to state that "the noosphere . . . is the final and supreme product in man of the forces of social ties", and that in the noosphere, "after six hundred million years, the biospheric effort towards cerebralis- ation attains its objective".

The emergence of machine intelligence within the milieu of human individual and collective intelligence implies that humanity's place in the evolution of the universe is this: *The cosmic function of Humanity is to act as the evolutionary interface between Life and Intelligence.*

Literature Cited

C Evans (1973) *Cults of Unreason*, Harrap, London.

C Evans (1979) *The Mighty Micro*, Victor Gollancz, London.

J Goodall (1971) *In the Shadow of Man*, Houghton Mifflin, Boston, Mass.

DR Griffin (ed) (1982) *Animal Mind – Human Mind*, Springer-Verlag, New York.

K Haefner (1988) The Evolution of Information Processing, Faculty of Mathematics and Informatics, University of Bremen, Germany.

K Haefner (1991) Evolution of information processing systems, Project Evolution of Information Processing, University of Bremen, Germany.

W Hodos (1982) Some perspectives on the evolution of intelligence and the brain, in *Animal Mind – Human Mind* (DR Griffin ed), Springer-Verlag, New York.

A Johannesson (1949) *Origin of Language*, HF Leiftur, Reykjavik, Iceland.

PN Johnson-Laird (1983) *Mental Models*, Cambridge University Press.

R Landauer (1967) Wanted: A physically possible theory of physics, *IEEE Spectrum* 4(9):105–109.

HC Longuet-Higgins (1987) *Mental Processes*, The MIT Press, Cambridge, Mass.

H Moravec (1988) *Mind Children*, Harvard University Press, Cambridge, Mass.

W Poundstone (1985) *The Recursive Universe*, Contemporary Books, Chicago.

P Teilhard de Chardin (1956) *Man's Place in Nature*, Collins, London (English translation, 1966; Fontana Books, 1971).

T Toffoli (1977) Cellular automata mechanics, technical report 208, CCS Department, University of Michigan.

S Wolfram (1984) *Cellular Automata. Towards a Paradigm for Complexity*, The Institute for Advanced Study, Princeton, NJ

Subject Index